# Thoughts on Creativity, Spirit, and the Ethical Life

George Lowell Tollefson

PALO FLECHADO PRESS

Copyright © 2024 George Lowell Tollefson
All rights reserved.

ISBN: 978-1-952026-09-6

Library of Congress Control Number: 2024904781

Palo Flechado Press, Santa Fe, New Mexico

# OTHER PHILOSOPHICAL WORKS BY GEORGE LOWELL TOLLEFSON

*The Immaterial Structure of Human Experience*
*The Limits of Reason*
*The Thinking Process*

*Unbridled Democracy*

*A Healer of Nations*


Extracts from ***Unbridled Democracy***
*Spirit as Universal Consciousness*
*The Thinking Arts*
*Ethical Considerations*
*Moral Democracy*


Extract from ***Thoughts on Creativity, Spirit, and the Ethical Life***
*Key to the Philosophy of Immaterialism*

# PREFACE

These are random notes on the topics indicated in the title. They are in the order in which they were originally produced, with the exception that twenty-three previously written analyses of literary works have been distributed among them. The notes are followed by a synopsis of the immaterialist philosophy.

# Thoughts on Creativity, Spirit, and the Ethical Life

George Lowell Tollefson

# Thoughts on Creativity, Spirit, and the Ethical Life

Who is the individual in pain, sweat, and sorrow? She is the spirit that broods and rejoices through all things. She is a pinpoint through whom every position, every part of the whole, can be located. They live because she lives. And she lives because they live.

Religions endure because of the truths within them which are represented by their false symbolism.

Humankind thinks in symbols, even in its most rational moments.

Creative intelligences should be admired. But they are few. What is within the reach of every person is the development and maintenance of a good moral character.

Envy is unproductive. Every life is unique, and, when rightly understood, exhibits its interesting elements.

Spirit is in beautiful, refined things. It brings out their harmony, which is its unity.

# Thoughts on Creativity, Spirit, and the Ethical Life

There are things which can be conveyed in art which cannot be understood conceptually. For art penetrates beyond the outer shell of thought.

The short duration of a human life facilitates spiritual and intellectual progress. A person can rarely transcend the structure of her own vision, which is continually being refined and rendered more limiting. This isolation of the individual mind is necessary. But it can only be transcended by a new and separate awareness. Hence the superseding of one life by another.

Reason is fallible. It cannot know everything. But it is the most important and reliable tool available to human awareness. Imagination and access to emotional transcendence are necessary for creativity and insight. But it is reason which exercises judgment and clarifies discernment.

If God created the universe as separate with its attributes of space and time, then where is God? And when was this done? Whatever may be called God must be that from which the universe emanates.

Why does the Pythagorean Theorem, $c^2 = a^2 + b^2$, work when similar theorems at higher powers are understood not to? If this theorem is simplified to the relationship between the sides of a square and its diagonal, $c^2 = 2a^2$, it can be seen that the entire equation is composed of pairs of equal quantities.

The square roots are, of course, pairs of equal quantities in both $c^2$ and $a^2$. And the two $a^2$'s are a pair of equal addends. So, reverting to the original formula, $c^2 = a^2 + b^2$, it can be seen that $a^2 + b^2$ equals $c^2$. The addends, $a^2$ and $b^2$, are unequal. But they are together equal to the paired and multiplied roots of $c^2$. Moreover, they are equal to the paired addends of $2a^2$. So every aspect of the equation can be understood in terms of equal pairs.

Yet this does not hold with the equation $c^3 = a^3 + b^3$ because the higher power of 3 does not exhibit a relation of pairs of equals. For example, $2^2$ is $2 \times 2$. But $2^3$ is $2 \times 2$ followed by $2 \times 4$, which latter operation does not express a relation of equal pairs. Neither is this the case with $c^4 = a^4 + b^4$.

Though it is true that the roots of $c^4$ are $c^2$ and $c^2$, which are an equal pair, and the same is true of $a^4$ and $b^4$, this involves a double operation in which c is squared. Then the result is squared again. This is because $c^4$ is $c \times c$ followed by $c(c^2)$ followed by $c(c^3)$. Thus inequality is introduced. This is true of any equation similar to $c^2 = a^2 + b^2$, but at a higher power.

A person who is devoted to the life of the mind should not exhibit a lack of control over the body. The physical appetites, though exercised, must be kept in reasonable subordinacy to the will.

As universal consciousness, spirit cannot be defined as a person. But, since all things emanate from spirit, including person, it can be related to as a person. For what is potential within spirit can be actual to an individual awareness.

## Thoughts on Creativity, Spirit, and the Ethical Life

To worship anything is to pay obeisance to the institution in which it is enshrined. Universal awareness and being can only be loved and celebrated. It is not worshiped.

Every individual person represents the dignity of universal consciousness and being. But few are those who express it.

It is sometimes necessary to commit an act which is cruel in its effect. But it is not permissible to do so for the sake of the cruelty. Such an emotion diminishes the person who harbors it. For he wrongfully seeks to have dominion over another.

The biosphere is an organism made up of individual but interconnected creatures, just as one of those creatures is an organism made up of individual but interconnected cells. To bring irremediable harm to the biosphere is to become a cancer within it.

There is a means to an increase in understanding which lies deeper than imagination or reason. For insights may arise as emotional impulses which are then fleshed out by imagination and reason. These emotional impulses exhibit no material precedent, though they may alter the course of material events.

To live in the material is human. To become mired in it is animal.

Genius may involve high intelligence, talent, and perseverance. But its origin is unknown to the mind. For all these advantages may exist without genius and often do.

Cézanne's greatness as a painter was hard won. For he not only had to labor to create it. It was necessary for him to discover where it lay. This neither he nor anyone else could imagine prior to the discovery. It was simply felt as a direction, an inclination of emotion.

There are only men and women of genius. There are no gods but universal awareness.

Good art presents the imagination with emotions and sensations which, with some pertinent direction given by the work, the admirer must further organize meaningfully. The freedom within prescribed bounds which the admirer's imagination has in doing this is the measure of its creative involvement. The breadth and subtlety of the artist's means in producing the work is its greatness as art.

Beware the beguiling nature of time. Materially it has a long train, before and after. For it is an expression of the limitations of the mind. Without it, the intellect could not find a purpose. But simple consciousness, and thus simple being, is without these limitations. They are the eternal now, the singularity from which time unfolds and into which it returns.

# Thoughts on Creativity, Spirit, and the Ethical Life

Great spirits, like Jesus, Moses, Muhammad, the Buddha, and the writers of the Upanishads have been given a transcending insight with which to guide human understanding. But they always come surrounded by a motley company of followers who cannot see as they do.

Michelangelo not only expressed the emotional torment of his age. He understood the struggle of the human spirit in material confinement.

Many are born athletes of the mind. Few bother to train.

Philosophers endure long bouts in the wastes of abstraction because, like artists with their messy paints, they can see the vision beyond.

The gift of writing is the true mother of civilization. But then musical notation was born. And the generations could sing.

Hemingway's genius lay in his sensual and emotional sensitivity brought under a careful rhetorical discipline. His weakness lay in the insecurity of an ungoverned ego. He was also traumatized by his severe wounding in war and sought ever after to repeat the intensity, or sensory acuteness, of that experience.

Pissarro's paintings are Impressionist masterpieces. They are spiritually liberating. But there is also a burden of heat, hard labor, and smell of sweat in them.

George Lowell Tollefson

Every great artist, knowingly or otherwise, seeks the spiritual essence of the material. It is as though she would turn herself inside out and expose the internal structure that gives form to her flesh.

Great art is quite literally timeless. For it exists not only prior to its expression. It exists prior to its conception. Like the life of a human being, it is brought out of the timeless into an unfolding succession. Here it lives for a time. But in the spirit it never dies.

A true scientist not only follows the well-worn path of procedure, where it is the method more than the investigator which creates. He deviates from the path and cuts through the tangle of unknown imaginings.

Philosophy is the art of conceptual serenity. Or at least it seeks to be.

Reason is the discipline of imagination. It renders imagination useful. For it is reason which ensures that the imagination should behave like a horse under harness. A carriage could not go anywhere without a horse. But it is the harness which determines where it goes and the pace at which it does so.

Everything in the universe changes. If this is to be doubted, then everything intimately familiar changes. Motion is change. Every action and thought is change. So how can there not be an evolution of living forms? How can there not be termination, or death? It is in the nature of material phenomena.

There can be no complete distinction between the human and God. Awareness *is* God, even when it is limited. The material emanates from the immaterial, matter from spirit, body from consciousness. Not the other way around. The desire to give priority to matter is an attempt to make permanent what can only be subject to change, to consider what is derivative independent, to render what is subordinate dominant. Consciousness simply is. It neither comes nor goes. But the phenomena subject to awareness arise and pass out of existence. That is why consciousness cannot be defined, or put into a box and assigned limits. For it is itself the box which prescribes limits to whatever it surveys.

All of civilization is a move toward the subjectivization of experience. It is an attempt to bring the world into a harmonious unity. But what of the abruptness of the genius of Newton, Darwin, or Rembrandt? Does such a person not draw upon a unity which is greater than that which he creates? Does not a Mozart or a Bach bring to the world something which was not known to exist there?

What is the mystery behind the incomprehensibility of the origin of their work? And what is the reason why the work is inevitably incomplete, however polished and unified it may seem? For it may always be paralleled or superseded. The mind's revolutions are a continual turning about in a great hall of spirit. This source can never be exhausted. Hence the continual reinterpretation of experience.

Philosophy is the final overarching art. Unfortunately, it is only attempted by a few. And it is rarely well finessed.

Universal consciousness, spirit, is the deepest self. In the material rush of life, it is little regarded. Yet to do so is an exercise in self-amnesia among meaningless things. Neither can it be worshiped. For that extreme is also untenable. It is alienation and a turning away from what is true, which is simply that spirit is the person. Though it is also much more than the person.

Among genuinely creative spirits there is something which is overlooked by others. It is indiscernible to the mind. For it is an inexplicable inclination to turn to the right where the left appears to be a clearer way. It arises from a source beyond knowledge. Abraham heard it: a directive from within him, which could not be ignored.

Monet drew upon it and formed it into paint, as did Cézanne. Galileo wrought its physical relations in mathematics. Yet from none of the things into which it is embodied does it come. Rather, it informs them. The Cold Mountain poet Han-shan knew what it was, though it eluded him in life.

Sad to say, human beings would not be the complex, emotionally sophisticated creatures that they are, were it not for the heaviness of heart, sickness, horror, physical pain, and death

## Thoughts on Creativity, Spirit, and the Ethical Life

encountered in material existence. In proof of this, and in contradistinction to a professed desire for peace of spirit and mind, it is just such a wrenching tangle of trials informing the arts, high and low, that people flock to experience.

Wisdom is an intelligent and comprehensive understanding of one's circumstances. Cunning is the dull but focused ability to take advantage of others. In any one person, these two faculties are in inverse proportion to one another.

The soldier who gives her life to save those of her fellows does so because she has come to identify her own person so closely with others that, in such a moment of unreflective action, she is attempting to protect herself.

Any material attempt to set forth the nature of spirit would fail were it not for the impulse behind the attempt. The impulse is spirit.

Each of Hemingway's four important novels involves a reversal in perspective. Robert Cohn is not the villain in *The Sun Also Rises*. He is a victim of the misbehavior of the others. In *A Farewell to Arms*, Frederick and Catherine's escape to neutral Switzerland does not end the chaotic condition which war has imposed upon them and the world. Catherine dies.

In *For Whom the Bell Tolls*, Pablo is not corrupted into becoming self-interested, as Robert Jordan and Pilar appear to believe. He is self-interested from the beginning, as revealed by the story of their early days Pilar relates to Jordan. And in

*The Old Man and the Sea*, Santiago is a symbol, not of defeat, but of triumph through his accommodation and acceptance of his human condition.

The long short story "The Short Happy Life of Francis Macomber" exhibits a similar turn about in emphasis. For the Macomber character is not the deeper study. It is the cynical professional hunter Robert Wilson, who is shocked at Margot's killing of her husband. His shock reveals the nature of his cynicism. It is a form of pessimistic idealism. For it is Wilson's underlying idealism which is shocked.

In matters of human motivation and character, what is obvious is almost always not the case.

Creative artists do not always recognize the full implications of their work. For example, painters think in terms of the images, color, lines, and forms they employ. The work is felt into being. And much of what is felt comes from they do not know where.

The greatest art has its being not in the material creation of the work, nor in the mind of the creator. For it is logically prior to these. It is neither before, concurrent, nor after. It simply is. And it comes to the artist through an impulse, or series of impulses, which are felt in terms of an inclination.

There is, of course, a material element in art: that which is generally referred to as worldly experience, which includes study and thought. But these are like so many bricks which cannot of themselves alone define a structure, nor the mortar

## Thoughts on Creativity, Spirit, and the Ethical Life

which holds them together. Hence art reflects an age and a particular culture. But it also lends spirit to the age and the culture. It is the life of these. For, though life must have a material structure, it is not the structure. That is its temporal dwelling place and no more.

Human beings reason when they think logically. Any other form of systematic thinking is imagery sequencing. People share this latter faculty in varying degrees with other forms of sentient life.

The principal mode of continuing human evolution is now by means of culture.

It is better to live a life disciplined to received principles little understood, than it is to live a life of cunning.

Cunning is the animal capacity to counter or make use of another person's anticipated move and to do it in one's own interest, where no personal harm from another is expected.

The more a person learns to recognize and follow impulses from her deeper self, the greater beauty of character she achieves. Others will not understand the change. And many may oppose it. But it is worth the effort and sacrifice, as any elevated awareness knows.

A spiritually transcendent development of character cannot be conferred by any institutional or conventional practice because it must come from within.

It is permissible to judge another in one's own defense. But it inappropriate to share that judgment with others, unless it is needed in their defense as well.

There is no such thing as a community of one. But there is a oneness of community, which is seldom achieved and even more rarely sustained.

What has been referred to as "a marriage made in heaven" begins in the mind, not the groin. Matters of the heart are subordinate to the mind as well, though they may indicate what has not been thought of. For intelligent recognition is superior to unclear emotion and blind impulse.

In human beings, a development of intellect has outgrown the animal nature. As a result, a tension has arisen, the resolution of which is essential to humanity, the planet, and any portion of the universe in which people may be present. The intellect can achieve control over itself, its subordinate physical impulses, and its material ego. For it must. Only when it does can the intellectually enhanced powers of destruction unleashed by animal desire and defensiveness be arrested.

## Thoughts on Creativity, Spirit, and the Ethical Life

Honesty is the hardest virtue to practice. No one can do so at one hundred percent. And few give it any thought or significant effort, other than to create a social facade of probity.

The only hope for the human race is spiritual transcendence. This involves a sincere and determined reliance upon the deepest inner self. Yet few are aware there is such a thing. They live their lives like marionettes, moved hither and thither by superficial social proddings.

Every young person learns to develop a mask, a suit of armor with which to engage the world. As a result, no one knows who the other person really is. And, as a general rule, neither of them knows himself.

The universal spirit is not only within. It is the only reality. The rest is mere superficiality and show, a temporal display, like fireworks that are soon returned to darkness.

Among Ernest Hemingway's short stories is a series of vignettes. Some of these are the purest form of word painting. One is called *Evacuation Along the Karagatch Road*. It begins, "Minarets stuck up in the rain out of Adrianople across the mud flats. The carts were jammed for thirty miles along the Karagatch road. Water buffalo and cattle were hauling carts through the mud. No end and no beginning. Just carts loaded with everything they owned."

In a few words a picture of confusion and misery emerges, of human beings caught in circumstances beyond their control.

Rain and mud. Carts and animals jammed together for miles, the carts loaded with everything the people own. What is the cause of such desperation? What would bring so many people together in such a deplorable way? Clearly, it is war.

The vignette states, "The old men and women, soaked through, walked along keeping the cattle moving. The Maritza was running yellow almost up to the bridge. Carts were jammed solid on the bridge with camels bobbing along through them. Greek cavalry herded along the procession. Women and kids were in the carts crouched with mattresses, mirrors, sewing machines, bundles."

There are no fighting age men in this procession. There are only old men, women, and children. The young men are somewhere else, their families left to uprooted and uncontrollable circumstances. It would seem that, with everything lost to these people—their homes, the routines and security of normal life—the weather must also be against them.

Hemingway individualizes the suffering: "There was a woman having a kid with a young girl holding a blanket over her and crying. Scared sick looking at it. It rained all through the evacuation." What a fragile possession civilization truly is. It is like a pane of glass—transparent, but easily shattered into slivers of pain.

A great writer often leaves behind a residue of second rate works. These tarnish the gleaming surface of her purest expressions or reflections. So a distinction should always be made between what is pure and what is not. Such a line of demarcation must be widely promulgated and known, so as not to confuse the general public.

In its purest form, unalloyed to mind, Kant's source of sensation can neither be derived nor explained. And, as he would have it, time and space are intuitions, as is the manifold of sensation. But this is not so. For the former are not simply received. They are products of the mind in accordance with its limitations.

First, time is developed from the necessary sequencing of the mind's focus in its independent apprehension of individual sensations and groupings of sensations. Then there is a mental construction of space out of groupings of sensations into objects. And there is a subsequent recognition of temporal sequence in accordance with changes in the relations of the objects.

Consequently, it can be held that there are two mental sources of time, but only one of space. Initially, there is the non-incremental sense of time born of the necessary sequencing of sensation. Following this, sensations are reorganized in terms of space. And time is recognized accordingly. For its incremental measure is determined by the ever-changing phenomena of spatial relations. Beyond these limitations wrought by the mind, there is neither time nor space. There is simply the whole of sensation in an unfragmented, timeless unity.

The mind sees with imagination. And it uses reason to organize what it sees. The former is fertile but weak in application. The latter, taken by itself, is strong. But it is utterly sterile.

The word "philosophy" does not express anything about the possession of wisdom. It merely indicates a love of it. A philosopher is anyone who loves wisdom and likes to think about it in order to untangle its relations.

Philosophy should continue to be a search for a better life, as the ancients originally conceived it. That is achieved by an acquisition of wisdom. And the quest for wisdom is an investigation into the relationship between humanity and its circumstances. It is not a metascience in the manner of logical positivism.

Since philosophy is concerned with the whole of mental life, the whole of experience encountered by the mind, it must include that which is not explained by a material perspective, such as consciousness and the power of art. Whereas, positivism represents an investigation into material circumstances alone: those circumstances which are either known through the senses or are considered to be derived from the mind's powers of phenomenal representation. For this reason, logical positivism's limited perspective is insufficient to address the whole of philosophical concern.

In addition to this, it purports to derive its authority from Immanuel Kant. But upon closer investigation, it can be seen that his methodology did not preclude metaphysics, as logical positivists believe. It simply indicated that metaphysics should

## Thoughts on Creativity, Spirit, and the Ethical Life

not become a confection of rational speculation. Rather, it should be limited to a fleshing out of phenomenal experience where that experience does not itself supply a direct means of doing so.

This is to say that, where the mental life of humankind does not exhibit a meaningful unity, such a unity should nonetheless be sought. In other words, as in the example of consciousness and art not being adequately explained in material terms, metaphysics should be employed to bring them into a satisfactory union with empirical experience.

In determining the quality of a person, only a sound mind and a good character matter. And the one cannot be had without the other. A sound mind will necessitate a good character. For a low character implies a deficiency of the mind, which either does not see what is lacking in behavior or why it should not be in such a state.

Behavior is the expression of character. Though a proper demeanor can be feigned, it cannot be sustained. True character will inevitably be revealed.

El Greco captured the otherworldliness of renaissance Spain. This can be seen in the poets, Luis de Leon and Lope de Vega as well. Now contrast it with the extreme worldliness portrayed in Bernal Diaz's *The Conquest of New Spain*.

There may well be no such thing as perfection. Perfection is a vague human term, difficult to define in terms of a concrete reference. Good, better, best. These are comparatives. The concept "better" applies to something which is more of what it is than something which is less so. But "best," in the sense of absolute best, would apply to something absolute, which is merely an idealization.

"Chance" is a concept which is applied to the two extremes of human knowledge. For it appears to occur where understanding falters. For example, at the very small and precise, one arrives where accustomed causal relations break down. They simply are not tailored to this kind of minute observation. At the very large, diffuse, and complex, the same problem occurs. There is either too much, the material is too divergent, or there are too many factors involved to be brought under a reasonable collation.

It is for these considerations that it becomes permissible to assert that there is no such thing as chance. Chance is simply incomplete understanding. But, since such a claim may alarm the wary observer who would insist that some things are inherently not causal, but nonetheless regular in appearance, it is equally acceptable to allow that causal relations are essentially approximations, however precise they may appear to be in quotidian circumstances.

Mathematics is an ideal science and does not submit to a scrutiny based on observation. Rather, it follows rules of logic, one principle following another according to reason alone. But what happens when it is applied to a science of observation, like physics? Is there not a danger that the ideal

# Thoughts on Creativity, Spirit, and the Ethical Life

nature of that which is being used to lend structure to this latter science will be overlooked in its ideality? In other words, however close they may be in appearance to what is observed, can it be maintained that geometrical figures truly represent physical relations? And are there such things as instantaneous velocities and mathematical limits?

"Take a dark, pathless way into the forest, and you will find what you are looking for." In such a manner has the heart been known to lead, and lead true. When this occurs, there is nothing more convincing in demonstrating that there is a power, whatever it may be, which lies beyond human awareness. It is from this that the man or woman of genius greedily borrows, with or without gratitude.

Creativity is like life. It must occur. For it is always becoming, even when leading toward failure or death.

How sweet it is to follow Plotinus' speculations concerning beauty and the good to the purest fount of being. But how can one know what lies beyond human awareness? Reason is not enough. There must be a starting point in experience—that which can be referenced for a sense of intellectual security when a train of thought grows ever so lean from a lack of material sustenance.

A general perusal of biographies of genius makes it clear that such creativity does not arise alone from a high intelligence quotient. Many are those of such a preeminent faculty who never achieve anything exceptional. So it is evident that other factors must play a role. Two of these are focus and determination.

Another (though this is not always the case) is thriving in an era of high national confidence. Goya is an exception to this rule. But perhaps most important is that ineffable quality of insight which comes from one does not know where. It is merely felt along the mind in a peculiar manner which says, "this is right, this is the way."

Einstein's concern was that scientific theory must be deterministic (causal), regardless of whether or not physical experience is completely deterministic. This seems valid. However, it does appear that any exceedingly minute examination of physical phenomena will uncover a breakdown in causal relations. So all that remains is Hume's observation that material experience "generally" falls into a pattern of sequences. It is a pattern which wobbles in definitiveness under close scrutiny.

A question arises: why do human beings love the literary and dramatic arts, when these are full of struggle, tragedy, and buffoonery? Is it because people are immersed in material limitation and cannot evade the conflict and pain which results from it? Consequently, they hope to discover from such arts a means of dealing with these.

If so, then why does youth also not uncommonly take on such hardships as war? Is it their newfound freshness of being which makes them feel momentarily immortal and immune?

## Thoughts on Creativity, Spirit, and the Ethical Life

Perhaps. It is true that their minds are often not fully formed and can therefore entertain projects of reckless adventure. And it is likely that the vanity of personal machismo and national identity may induce them to such acts. But no person enjoys suffering. The draw is in the reputation gained in becoming acquainted with it, but not, they hope, too severely or too long.

So, in general, what is it which drives humankind to embrace its own misery? It can be nothing but this: the soul is emotionally enriched in this way. It gains a knowledge and understanding which could not be obtained within the high walls of an enclosed garden, where soft scents and gentle fountains utterly shield the person from hurt and harm and where the emotions lie dormant and undeveloped in a slumbering soul.

The fact is that this preferred knowledge and its enlargement in understanding are ornaments of great value for which many human beings would even court death. They can be likened to a flock of barnyard fowl, each of which observes its fellows to fall under the axe and knows it too will die, but nevertheless would not consider forfeiting whatever limited but daily enriched span of life it might yet obtain.

The parables of Jesus are beautiful because, even when leveling a moral criticism, they are informed with the peace and loveliness of Galilean life.

The human need to find focus, to dedicate one's life to something worthwhile, is a reflection of the unity of spirit within. It ties the world, all of experience, together—experience which is multiple in the refraction of life, but singular in purpose and meaning.

Van Gogh's art reminds one that his passion and intensity of feeling are but an unfolding in space and time of the unextended, indivisible presence of spirit.

In painting, photo-representation is unnecessary. It is not even desirable. For it must reference that which is not on the canvas. And this demands selection and a special ordering not generally found in material experience. On the other hand, an art reduced to color and line alone deprives the mind of vocabulary. It does not allow it to reverberate through corridors of meaning, settling everywhere and nowhere at once in a cumulative imaginative response.

Moreover, to express such an aesthetic response, one must not only emote, but think. And a person forms thoughts from imaginative imagery, which is, in its turn, a product of the material experience of objects and physical events. Is a Kandinsky or a Mondrian painting as profound and meaningful as a Rembrandt, a Michelangelo, or a Velasquez? Granted these latter are among the very greatest. But is that not the goal of art?

As a middle approach, a work by Paul Klee seems largely abstract. It is a subtle blending of forms, controlled (often muted) color, and texture. But it is more than this. For there is always a suggestion of experience, however indistinct. Proceeding in a different direction, Matisse exhibits a purity of hues: blocks of often saturated color. But the rhythmic rendering of figures and objects he employs grounds them in a common recognition.

This reference to the physical beyond the tools of art is what has often been referred to as "returning to nature." To even begin to think, the mind must draw upon objects. It must seize upon the vibrant core of events. Only then can it pursue its way through the labyrinth of experience and emerge in an acquisition of meaning.

Music is different from painting because it takes possession of sound, which it unfurls in time by means of timbre, rhythm, melody, and variation of motif in an ongoing contra-play. These are like actors in a drama unfolding shadows of character within a context of one another. They are analogous to physical movement. But a painting only has movement in the mind. It is the vital activity of unleashed imagination. And imagination needs access to objects, however subtle in reference.

A great work of art will grow out of the depth of a person's spirit, her deepest consciousness. It will include her experiences as an influence. But it will not be the sum of them. For there is more to any person's inner life than material circumstances. There are the quiet proddings of universal consciousness, of which individual consciousness is but a fleeting expression.

Ernest Hemingway's novella *The Old Man and the Sea* expresses more than the tenor of its narrative. The story of old Santiago speaks of his fruitless efforts with the big fish and the sharks. And prior to that, it laments his bad luck for going eighty-four days without catching a fish. But the reader knows that in this simple story the author is presenting life in general, life with its hardships and disappointments, its struggle and, most importantly, the endurance of a strong and noble heart. It is clearly Hemingway's swan song. It says that it is the effort that matters, not the mistakes and shortcomings of an all too human protagonist.

As David Hume pointed out, there has never been a formal social contract in the manner of Hobbes and Locke. But, since it is Hobbes who originated the idea, the question as to its validity lies in the matter of what he intended. Was what he called a "state of nature" a state of human existence? And, arising out of this, was the social contract a formal agreement?

If the implications of his argument are examined with penetration, it can be reasonably discerned that he was referring to an elemental condition of human nature as constituting the "state of nature." He observed that people left strictly to their own devices will be inclined to behave defensively and without regard to the interests of others. So they must be "civilized." And this is accomplished within an orchestrated social context of give and take.

But it does not mean that a social contract is formally agreed to. Rather, it is generally imbibed from infancy. For this procedure can be traced back to pre-civilized tribal society. The modern community is simply an extension and elaboration of what has always been. In one form or another, human beings live in social conformity. It is as much the case with a tribe as it is with a modern nation or megacity.

The importance of the present elaboration upon what may be regarded as a self-evident topic is that it suggests a pervasive significance of unreflective emotional life. Much in human practice occurs by trial and error with little or no reflection. Religion, morals, political and social structures—these all grow and prosper like mushrooms in a dark forest. They are largely a matter of unreflective human interaction and emotional life.

At least, they are in their origins. But, when genius does arise in the midst of such events, it is generally to arrange them in a contemplative order. Yet, in the ascent of such creative persons, what can be overlooked is that few things are born naked in a void. Genius builds upon practice. Great seers and leaders of a more mundane variety tend to arrive at a comprehensive understanding of what already is.

What is remarkable is the insight of such an individual. For the issue is not one of determining the circumstances out of which the insight arose. It is a matter of determining what shed such a light. It may have come from a cumulative weight of experience which led to a natural insight.

Or it may have taken the form of a spiritual leap. In the latter case, the reflective mind is nudged toward its new outlook by an ineffable feeling which takes the form of a strong inclination to view matters in an unanticipated way. Nothing prior to the insight leads to it. It simply appears.

Beginning with Socrates, the four greatest philosophers in Western antiquity were Socrates, Plato, Aristotle, and Plotinus. They were complete systemists, taking the whole of reality into question. Following them were the Stoics and Epicureans. For the latter began with an ethical perspective, assuming a metaphysical setting for that view and regarding it with less attention to detail.

The same is true concerning twentieth century existentialism, ostensibly beginning with Heidegger. This modern philosophical position takes the form of a literary pose, evading broader philosophical questions by working within a non-metaphysical perspective. Such thinkers resemble the Stoics and Epicureans of antiquity. Logical positivists may also be added to this company. For they consume the pip within the fruit while ignoring its housing of flesh. Nor does it matter that Kant is their excuse for doing so. For he did not do it himself. Consequently, he is much the greater philosopher.

If a person should approach universal consciousness as God, and do so in a personal manner, how might this be done? Certainly it could not be held that universal consciousness is a person. It is indivisible and unlimited, while personhood is a limit. Limits cannot be placed upon the infinite. Yet it is nonetheless the case that all things emanate from universal consciousness. And personhood is one of those things. Consequently, it is on just such a basis that it becomes possible to approach universal consciousness in a personal way.

# Thoughts on Creativity, Spirit, and the Ethical Life

When the Old Testament prophets intoned the retribution of an angry God for the sins of the Northern Kingdom of Israel and again for those of the kingdom of Judah, they were very much in tune with the spirit. This gave them clarity of vision and insight into the manner in which the selfishness and hedonism of the people was weakening their respective societies, making them prey to rising kingdoms in the east. It was on this basis that the prophets gave their warnings and predictions.

However, egoism arises from the isolated awareness of individual persons. So the spirit, or universal consciousness, is not an egoist. It has no need of the satisfaction of revenge. Thus what is referred to as the "retribution of God" is in fact a falling back of the people's behavior upon themselves.

As they become increasingly divisive, they suffer the consequences of that divisiveness. So, when the results of their behavior overcome them, they are at last made to see the truth which they had blocked from their minds. Thus the spirit of truth within them, expressed by the earlier awakened consciousness of the prophets, convicts them within their hearts.

A person cannot know the will of spirit any more than she can know the will of another person. The complexities of any mind other than her own are too great. How much more the complexities of universal awareness! But this does not mean that the spirit cannot be approached on a personal basis. Rather, it indicates that the response to that approach is whatever it will be and must be accepted.

Faith is a corruptive concept if it means the suspension of reason. There is nothing more important than a mind in possession of itself. On the other hand, there is no act, however logical and conclusive, that is not tinged with an element of faith.

As consciousness is awareness, it is reasonable to assert that universal consciousness is cognizant of everything that emanates from it. But nothing more can be said of it. For any idea of its perfection, its absolute knowledge of itself, or its purposeful design in relation to what emanates from it, is utterly meaningless to human understanding, as having no reference to experience.

Death is a falling away, not only of the physical body and material experience, but of the outer self (the ego constructed shell within which people live). All that remains is the inner self, immobile, timeless, and without location. It is as though that person had lived her life inside a box camera, able to see only through a tiny aperture. When the box falls away, everything is revealed.

There is memory beyond death. But it is not a form of recall, as exercised by the material mind. It is the simple, immediate knowing of universal consciousness.

The loss of the outer, material self need not be feared. For it is a fiction. The inner self, which sits back and views the passing

## Thoughts on Creativity, Spirit, and the Ethical Life

panorama of life with calm disinterest, remains. At certain moments, this self is encountered in the course of life. It is who a person is.

No two things are exactly alike. It is true that an observation of the proportionality of causal relations leads to precise mathematical concepts of energy. But upon closer observation, it is discovered that these proportional relations break down into probabilities. This results in double vision when there is an attempt to apply the original macrophysical ideas to subsequent microphysical observations. So what must be accepted is the fact that human awareness is provided with a sufficient regularity in the input of mental impressions to form causal relations. Yet, if these are examined closely enough, it will be found that they are not as regular as they initially seemed.

F. Scott Fitzgerald's "Babylon Revisited" is a small masterpiece set in early 1930s Paris. The stock market has crashed and a young man, Charlie Wales, returns to the scene of his former revels. In the days before the crash, money had been fluid and was poured out like the quantities of alcohol that usually accompanied it.

But now Charlie has a purpose. He is sober and hopes to retrieve the child who was taken from him and placed under his sister-in-law's control when his wife died. The sister-in-law, Marion, is "a tall woman with worried eyes," who feels an "unalterable distrust" and "instinctive antipathy" toward him. She blames him for her sister's death. Nevertheless, Charlie is reformed and confident.

Paris in the 1930s, like any large American city, but with an old-world culture and charm, is a place of pleasant lounges, expensive restaurants, and plush hotels, where safely discarded memories can reemerge in a chance encounter with irresponsible, unreformed friends. Duncan Schaeffer and Lorraine Quarrles are such friends.

Lorraine is "a lovely, pale blond of thirty; one of a crowd who had helped them make months into days in the lavish times of three years ago." Fitzgerald says of Charlie, "As always, he felt Lorraine's passionate, provocative attraction, but his own rhythm was different now." Or so he thinks. Marion sees it differently when she meets these friends.

Duncan, Lorraine, and Charlie, are remnants of the "Roaring Twenties," which made Fitzgerald famous. He understood its exuberance and hope. And he had experienced the emotional collapse, the psychological strain of its aftermath. He could tell it richly and simply in stories and novels, opening the human heart on a page like a cactus flower when rains have come.

A work of art must both move and enlighten. If it does not affect the emotions and the intellect simultaneously, its intrinsic value will fall off precipitously in such a manner as to ensure that it will not endure.

Conceptual art fails to move the emotions at the moment of contact. At first view, totally abstract art lacks a means of initiating and sustaining thought. Consequently, neither is aesthetically complete.

Emily Dickinson is one of America's greatest poets, if not *the* greatest. But the superficial simplicity of her verse obscures its metaphysical (philosophical) nature. Observe the poem in which she compares the mind of God to the human brain and finds them equivalent. What profound depths this reveals concerning the relationship between humanity and God!

Gustave Flaubert's realism, as set forth in the novel *Madame Bovary*, is so stark—no positive characters—as to defy a willing acceptance of the importance of its truth. How can it be maintained that the work is completely objective and that the author is not present in it? It is he who has made the selection. Still, it cannot be denied that the book is great, however slanted in perspective.

This is the case with any production of the human mind. To refuse to acknowledge the power of a great work because it does not fully accomplish its purpose would be wrong. The mind is hedged in by limitations and cannot possibly exhibit a fully comprehensive vision. Like a horse with blinders, it must follow a straight course. And if this should detract somewhat from the fulfillment of its truth, it should be remembered that its narrowness of perspective also serves to render that truth in sharp definition.

Universal consciousness cannot be understood in terms of humanity. It would be like representing a tree by its fruit.

Rather, the reverse is necessary. Humanity must be recognized in universal consciousness.

Rather than individually castigating persons, peoples, or nations for what they have done, it is more in accord with reason to acknowledge that the human race in general is frequently prone to a nasty demeanor, whether overt or covert in presentation. For it is in consideration of the whole of humanity that a solution to its eternal behavioral problems may be found.

Nothing simpleminded, biased, or temporally limited will suffice as a means of categorization. Rather, a look into the transcendent and its capacity to transform is what is needed. And this cannot be brought about through the agency of beliefs held without critical analysis, nor as something revealed to a few. For what is needed involves an intelligent participation by the individual. Consequently, it can only be discovered within each person and managed by the same, once the necessity of doing so has been embraced by all.

The reason the solution must first be embraced by all is that misbehavior anywhere acts as an irritant inducing a defensive response. The reaction is like a dye in water, infecting the entire community. To retard this effect, the community must participate together, though the solution lies with each individual. This communal response is equivalent to the unity of universal consciousness. It is this unity underlying the human condition which, once appealed to, is the power to achieve a general healing.

## Thoughts on Creativity, Spirit, and the Ethical Life

The healing is not absolute. There will always be minor failings in a realm of continual change and constant misalignment. That is the material condition of this life. But the appropriate communal response, fortified by individual determination, will smooth unwanted ripples where there is never a condition of perfection. It is the reach toward this condition, not the grasp of it, which is important.

War cannot be ended unilaterally, nor by a bristling standoff of powerful weapons. The limitations of a material, egocentric outlook must be set aside and, in a mutual shedding of fears and national ambition, a cooperative embrace of the oneness of humankind in the unity of spirit can, and in time will, be achieved.

Creativity is the proper use of the ego. Only here is it beneficial and lacking in harmful effects. Creativity imposes nothing upon humankind which cannot be freely dismissed or rejected. Whereas destructive behavior seeks a dominance over others which is difficult to ignore or avoid.

The sexual imagination is a potent and fiery instrument which may not only supplant reason, but twist it into irrational forms. There is no more immediate example of the power of the sensual to utterly, if only momentarily, squelch the transcendental awareness of the self as it is anchored in universal consciousness. For this reason, sexual imagination must always be kept within the bounds of what is reasonable, equitable, and trustworthy.

The destruction of any civil society begins with hedonism and ends in discord. Putting the material self above all other considerations sows divisiveness. It is in this way that the grounding of personality in unity and inclusiveness is overthrown.

Can it not be understood that tyranny of any kind limits creativity? Let the oppression come from either a too restrictive or a too liberal policy, this is what tyranny is: a stifling of the creative impulse. For the sake of order, or as a result of disorder, change is suppressed. Be it science, philosophy, art, religion, or morals, further insight and progress are diminished.

A complete lack of order and discipline impedes creativity just as effectively as too much of these does. For creativity, however free in its imaginative origin, must obey reason. And reason is orderly. Imagination and reason together are both free and orderly. Hence the eternal problem for humankind is to determine how to find and maintain a balance.

Societies come and go in their search for this solution. They inevitably fail in the end. Yet the effort continues because there is a sense of unity within each person which demands it. Furthermore, the destiny of humankind is often only vaguely, and therefore not clearly, understood to be both dynamic and holistic together. For it can be neither stagnant nor fragmented. If stagnant, it does not produce. If fragmented, it is productive to no end.

## Thoughts on Creativity, Spirit, and the Ethical Life

Quantum mechanics compares to classical mechanics in the following manner. If a person were to study the wind with sufficient exactness, she would discover that it is composed of a number of little drafts, each with its own characteristics and peculiar orientation. Thus each is only in partial accord with its fellows. Yet these drafts also decompose into even smaller mutually alienated elements. This is what an attempt to approach the absolute reveals: one must pass through a thorough separation of forms and their relations prior to a realization of the one form which is none of these.

O. Henry does not exhibit great insight, nor is his play of language particularly enlightening. In fact, it can be quite annoying. But his sympathy for ordinary people is unmatched and represents a core expression of the American character. It is by this means, this deeper look at the source of inspiration, that such a writer should be evaluated.

Art must always be approached with an attempt to discern the spirit which suffuses its creation. Only after this is done should its disparate elements be singled out for appraisal. The spirit out of which a work is born, which the artist barely comprehends and the critic almost never does, is the work's transcendent power. It is by this means alone that it will live or die over time.

Laissez-faire capitalism is a condition in which the pursuit of profits outweighs moral considerations. It is a turning away from a unified vision of humankind toward a drawing of values from personal interests set in opposition to one another.

This occurs when it is accepted that external regulation of the business sector is economically harmful. But it should be recognized that a lack of such interference is harmful as well. For it transgresses upon the interests of a majority of the people.

It is true that a soaring economy, with its ever increasing productivity, enhances the power and prestige of a nation. For, when sufficiently expanded, such an economy can support a large, well-trained, standing military force. This facilitates interference in the affairs of other nations, thus augmenting national pride.

It is in this way that selfishness and tyranny build upon themselves. Each individual looking to his or her own interest thinks of nothing else in the heat of unregulated competition. And, where personal success may be limited in varying degrees, the collective ego of the nation is nevertheless enhanced. Such is the compensation of the majority of citizens.

But what follows is a loss of personal freedom, both political and economic. An economy unleashed in its aggressiveness narrows its grip. Fewer people prosper materially. And a government which does not regulate becomes regulated. The problem spreads to a competition between nations, as one after another they feel compelled to catch up and compete with the strongest powers. In this way, limited perspective, selfishness, isolation, and enmity are sown universally.

Conversely, a more modest and balanced economy allows a nation to focus upon fairness, both within its borders and without. This serves the welfare and good will of its people and others as well. In such an atmosphere of settled contentment, creative enterprises spring up. These will not only be practical, but will include those which nurture the human spirit. Progress in the human spirit serves the interests of humanity by enhancing an increasing subtlety of awareness, a growing sensitivity to the genuine needs of an expanding mentality, and an inclusiveness of purpose which reflects the unified spiritual ground of life.

Nietzsche's idea of an "eternal return" does not appear to be a simple assertion of a cyclical process. Rather, it is an attempt to sound a clear note, which is that each life is a significant and enduring expression. One should live positively, affirmatively, purposefully, as if this were so. Decisions made and influences achieved in the relatively short span of a life matter. For they are lodged in an eternal awareness.

Do not dismiss Darwin's achievement on the basis of the simplicity of his concept of natural selection. The universality of its application is enough to justify its worth. For a mind capable of seeing in this way presents a miracle of associated insights revealing complex relations. Darwin's vision was indeed broad, its application like a thread woven throughout the fabric of material reality. In its apparent simplicity, it is an expression of the universal principle of flux.

Darwin thought like a philosopher. He was not a mathematician, deriving multiple principles sequentially from one another. But this is not to disparage mathematicians and those whose endeavors are grounded in an unfolding of insights rather than in a single universal perspective. Both forms of intelligence are essential to an ever-expanding awareness. Together they constitute a creative inner growth which fulfills the most fundamental of human needs.

Morality is founded upon both intra- and inter-communal trust. It is person to person, person to community, community to person, and community to community. A social creation, it arises from a desire to institute standards of cooperation and individual security. An act of war, on the other hand, whether considered as perpetrated by an individual or as carried out en masse, represents either a breakdown or a nonexistence of trust. It is therefore outside any sort of communal relationship and is a matter of expedience. This is true even in the case of personal or community defense. For this reason, war is never morally justifiable.

This does not mean that an individual or a community should render itself defenseless. It merely indicates that expedience is not morality. Such being the case, the only remaining moral issue is one of honesty in discussing the nature of self-defense or war. For what is plainly true should not be disguised under pleasing or deceptive terms. The fact is that some human acts do not exhibit a moral character. They are simply acts of expedience.

It is best to be honest in the use of arguments and terms of expression. If this is done, moral sense can reassert itself, once inappropriate attitudes, ambitions, and fears have run their course. For there are always misunderstandings and irregularities in human behavior. But these will fall back in line with the preferred interpersonal and communal harmony, if allowed

## Thoughts on Creativity, Spirit, and the Ethical Life

to do so in light of a recognition of the truth. This is served by the maintenance of a clear distinction between morality and expedience.

Jesus of Nazareth was a giant of spiritual insight, a genius. For this reason, the complexity and depth of his teachings must be explored and brought to light. They are not simple moral maxims, impossible to follow, and therefore largely hypocritically ignored. They, rather than an outside source, explain his manner of life and death, not the other way around.

It has been said that literature raises questions and philosophy answers them. Neither is entirely true. Philosophy is never able to fully encompass the reality it seeks to define. And in its attempt to express a complexity of emotions, literature does raise questions. But these are not its principal interest. Rather, it is expression. So neither literature as art nor philosophy plows a single furrow. Both sow their seeds in a broad field of challenge and response. For humanity, ever the scion of spirit, but unfamiliar with its parent, seeks to engage with it knows not what.

The Christian Bible, composed of old and new testaments, is perhaps the greatest single compendium of moral wisdom in the world. But it also contains notable barbarities and is an instigator for massive compounds of superstition. So what is needed is a critical approach which does not throw out the good with the bad. For much of what is not good has been added through an interpretation of its texts.

But there is also a core of ancient ignorance which must be rooted out, such as the idea of animal and human sacrifice exercised as the means required to set things straight with an anthropomorphic god. Rather, let the insights of the prophets and other writings shine through. And in matters of interpretation, it should be that the motives of the interpreter are examined and challenged at every point. Nor can any ancient precedent be set forth as having settled the matter. This invites manipulative control. Thus a self-examining mind must always remain active and self-pruning.

The Achilles heel of human existence is metaphysical fear. The mind knows itself to proceed from an illimitable consciousness which cannot be accounted for in material terms. It is the struggle between the former and the latter which results in the forced egoism that brings so much ugliness into human affairs.

Release for a moment the hold of the senses upon the mind and entertain the eternal, indivisible timelessness of the pure conscious self, and the many varieties of fear will fall away. In fact, is this not what the greatest art does? It encapsulates material awareness within a more comprehensive, indefinable sense of being. This is what Rembrandt does in the direct and penetrating manner of his later work. It is why his reputation is so high. But there are also others like him throughout the arts.

# Thoughts on Creativity, Spirit, and the Ethical Life

The human ego has a positive employment. And that is toward creativity, as opposed to the diminution or destruction of any person or thing.

There are but two fundamental ethical considerations. One is trust, the other fairness. For a moral relationship to obtain between persons, an atmosphere of trust must be established and maintained. It means that one cannot cheat, steal, defame, lie, murder, or betray in any way. However, fairness is less well defined. For societies differ greatly as to their hierarchies of influence. But, within any stable and generally understood arrangement of social relations, and in accordance with its accepted rules, there should be fair dealing. This again is a matter of trust.

Though faith, or belief, may extend beyond reason, reason is the only guide to faith. Anything else is blind authority.

The question is: what is the definition of art? There have been many practices. At its most fundamental level, it is an expression of beauty. For example, a sunset can be beautiful. Or the murmuring of a stream in a quiet forest can produce a pleasing calming effect. The work of art in this case is framed by the imagination in the mind. But it is the effect which is at issue. How does the thing of beauty affect the emotions?

Some created works of art, like a painting in the abstract form, strive for such an effect alone, without reference to ideas of things. At another extreme, there is what is presently referred to as conceptual art. Here the emphasis is not upon the emotional, but upon an intellectual response. Whatever emotions may ensue are entirely dependent upon the intellect, not the object of art itself.

So what results from these two opposing approaches is a bifurcation of the aesthetic response. For, in much of both the Western and Eastern traditions, the principal aesthetic response has been a simultaneous coordination of emotion and intellect. Within this tradition, the matter is clarified. For it is in the fullness of its aesthetic character that a work of art produces a combined emotional-intellectual response.

The key to the issue lies in the term "aesthetic," in which a reaction occurs that is both felt and necessarily thought about as the work is responded to with feeling. In fact the feelings generated cannot be understood without an accompanying idea. And the idea cannot be realized without a suggestion of feeling.

The recipient of these impressions, both sensual and emotional on the one hand and conceptual on the other, is moved in such a way as to produce a distinct mood. So the matter to be investigated is the character of a mood. A mood, in the aesthetic sense of the term, is a state of mind which orients the recipient toward an attitude. Such an attitude is a direction of response.

This is not to say that the person is impelled to act. For the attitude is self-contained. It is no more than a state of mind. It does not lend itself to immediate action. But it is nonetheless decisive. There is a turning, an orientation involving the object in question. For the object sets the tone of the mental

## Thoughts on Creativity, Spirit, and the Ethical Life

attitude. But the attitude is entirely within the person. It is not in the world, though it is in some sense about the world.

At a later time, when the aesthetic effect is no longer in full possession of the mind, its shadow continues to linger, throwing a sheen over subsequent practical experience—a little more here, perhaps a bit less there, depending upon the relationship of that experience to the original aesthetic insight. It is the manner in which things are now to be seen.

Of course, none of this would occur if only an emotional response were engendered. It would not matter what was thought about it later. For the thought would not be part of the experience, but only subsequent to it. It would not produce much of an attitude, a weak one at best. Nor, if an intellectual idea were to be entertained prior to and independently of any emotion, would there be an enduring reorientation of personal vision, which is the nature of an insight. Any subsequent, independent emotion engendered by such means would be weak. For it is only thought and emotion working together which have the proper effect.

They are a collection of related emotional responses centered about and dependent upon an idea, the idea, in turn, being aroused by this variegated emotional response. Such is art at its fullest, in its most effective and enduring form. Other forms of beauty or of intellectual interest may occur. They have their place and moment. For many things have fallen under the label of art. And they have their attractions, however momentary. But they are not aesthetic. They are at most pleasing or interesting.

## George Lowell Tollefson

Art is the nearest thing in human experience to universal consciousness. For it involves an intemperate exercise of the unlimited potential of spirit. Though it works with and is limited by material considerations (which are its means of expression and its source of motifs), and by the inclination of the artist as well, yet the artist does not know precisely what will be produced until it has been done.

In addition to this, the viewer, hearer, reader, or appreciator in whatever way of the work in question has his own individual response. This is guided by the artist's intent. But it is not bound by it, due to the same intemperate exercise in potential which was carried out by the artist. The appreciator is free in mind and spirit to flow with the suggestions of the work, which are unlimited. Thus art is creativity always in becoming and never quite realized. Is this not life itself? And is life in its mystery not an expression of spirit?

There is a rhythm or pattern behind the material structure of existence that is difficult to see or understand. What faintly shows through worldly events is a spiritual-emotional orientation. To offer some crude examples: Why did the lives of Shelley, Keats, and Byron end early and within a few years of one another? Why did the post-impressionists Van Gogh, Toulouse-Lautrec, Gauguin, Seurat, even Cézanne, lead tragic, tumultuous lives? Social factors of the time certainly contributed to these coincidental events. But there is more.

There are veils of light and dark, of clearing and storm which pass rhythmically and seamlessly over the surface of events. It is as though spirit breathed its own separate emotions through things. Do these emotions fit together as in a painting, a drama, a musical composition, exploring relations and motifs in various ways? Is life and matter in some sense a single organism pulsating in realization of a deep inner being? It cannot be known. But neither can it be ignored.

Charles Darwin's *The Origin of Species* started a scientific revolution which has kept the flames of controversy going for more than 160 years. But what has often been overlooked is the fact that Darwin was a naturalist and that there are many beautiful and fascinating descriptions of the natural world in the book.

For example, there is the "Cell-making instinct of the Hive-Bee." Anyone who has seen a display behind glass of honey-bees at work within their hive will appreciate his remark, "He must be a dull man who can examine the exquisite structure of a comb, so beautifully adapted to its end, without enthusiastic admiration."

He further points out that, "Granting whatever instincts you please, it seems at first quite inconceivable how they can make all the necessary angles and planes, or even perceive when they are correctly made." He is speaking of "a crowd of bees working in a dark hive," fashioning perfect hexagonal cells, fitted together without any loss of space. He says that the bees "have made their cells of the proper shape to hold the greatest possible amount of honey, with the least possible consumption of precious wax in their construction." Every side of each cell is the side of another cell.

He uses this information to support his theory of natural selection, pointing out that "the comb of the hive-bee, as far as we can see, is absolutely perfect in economizing labor and wax." Making an effort to show how simple instincts might have developed in such a way as to determine the shape of the comb, he offers the added benefit of a visual experience.

Universal consciousness is the fundamental ground of reality. Everything emanates from it. But a distinction must be drawn between "consciousness" and "conscious of." All things material, even a rock, emanate from spirit. But a rock, though a direct expression of consciousness, is not conscious of anything. It simply *is* within the universal state of consciousness.

A plant or a single cell of a complex organism is chemically and perhaps electrically aware of its neighbors, but not more. Some insects, particularly those which are social, may be much more intricately aware. But such awareness can be likened to emotional responsiveness: much, but not all, of it instinctive.

A bird and a non-human mammal are both emotionally and imaginatively aware, some approaching reason in that awareness. Human beings do reason, or at least have the capability of processing mental input by means of language. Perhaps beyond this is an immediate, comprehensive awareness, complex without the aid of reason, but with its advantages and more.

When spiritual insights make their presence known, they are generally not accompanied by a comprehensive awareness

## Thoughts on Creativity, Spirit, and the Ethical Life

embracing them in full. Rather, they are followed by an equivalent development, painstakingly worked out through the exercise of imagination and reason. This is because material circumstances are cripplingly bound by a necessary expenditure of time.

Material awareness of anything must be incrementally revealed. But the mind is not for this reason shut out from the proddings of spirit. For though universal consciousness is wholly present in each material mind, limited only in what it conveys, it may also be found to be separately communicating with it.

It cannot be said more plainly: reason, a weak instrument greatly limited in the tools at its disposal, is yet the means of understanding any truth, of making it accessible to a finite intelligence.

All right, there *is* something mystically grand about the color-field paintings of Mark Rothko. The mind is released to wander among veils, open vistas, and shades of dispersed and clotted feeling. This would not be possible with anything representational. It is a release from the material, a glimpse into a realm of pure emotion, where it is possible to understand feeling as independent of forms and limitations. Pure emotion is the kaleidoscopic nature of spirit. But how can this lead to organized thought? It cannot. It should not. That is the wonder of it.

Clearly, this is a man who has crossed the line. His art does not support any recognizable object. Yet it refers to something concrete in human experience: a complex, floating web of emotions—emotions rising from feelings which are not encountered in the physical world of objects.

Although emotions are generally associated with a body, such an association arises from an unsubstantiated assumption based on physical occurrences coincident to the experience of the emotions. Emotions are independent, immaterial phenomena which do not occupy space. Hence Rothko's works simultaneously engender an emotional response and an occasion for thought. But the lack of a pictorial vocabulary leaves the thought wide open, unarticulated in any specific manner.

So why is this work different from other forms of abstraction? Aside from Rothko's mastery of subtle integrations of color, the distinction seems to lie in an absence of a definitive pattern. Though the color fields interact, their precise integration is ungraspable. Consequently, their transcendence into a realm of pure emotion is without suggestion of limitation. It is spiritual mysticism.

Religion is belief without personal responsibility for what is believed. Authority gives it significance. And one is led to believe. This must pass. In true democracy the individual stands face to face with the all. There can be no intermediate ground between a person and his deep self. Out of inner being comes every particular of awareness. And the fibers of faith must be rooted in it.

Prophesy is inner awareness raised to recognition. It is a discovery that the surface of life is a mirror which must be bro-

## Thoughts on Creativity, Spirit, and the Ethical Life

ken into by anyone seeking the underlying mysteries. Universal spirit is the true self. Its reach extends beyond the boundaries of superficial life. For these boundaries are the falsely constructed outer person of hopelessness, dependency, and dread.

There is a true aristocracy, which is neither based on land nor money, but on merit. What is the merit? It is sincerity born of an understanding which is rendered correct by means of a deliberate disengagement with opinion, be it personal or public. Because people do not generally seek this disengagement, nor do they know of it, an initial elevation of character must be brought about through an education which encourages a depth of understanding. This can be achieved as a result of a persistent contact between an individual mind and whatever measure of such freedom has been attained by classical thinkers, writers, artists, thoughtful scientists, composers, etc.

But, though the exposure should be broad, the measure must be narrow. Only that which is free from dull ruminations can be admitted to the formation of a liberated mind. Every classical source must be tested and selected for its ingredients of merit. For, as no one person is a composite only of good, neither are his works. So an improved aptitude for distinguishing true from false can only be achieved in time as a consequence of effort and a product of persistence. Few will do this. They are the aristocracy.

"Original sin" is nothing more than animal nature, which human awareness is gradually and painfully rising out of by means of the agency of culture. But it is not simply a matter of overcoming the physical appetites. It is a struggle to enlarge consciousness, so that it may free itself from the limitations of a material perspective. As long as these perceptive disabilities persist, there is a constant sense of entrapment and a fear of annihilation on all sides, both physical and psychological. These bring about a defensive attitude which promotes envy, distrust, deceit, hate, enmity, and violence.

Spiritual enlargement, which culture slowly achieves by means of an expansion of understanding into the greater domain of consciousness, comes by degrees. The process of cultural enrichment is often misunderstood. For it is thought to be an enhancement of the material perspective, while in fact it is a transformation. In time, the spiritual core of human awareness will arrive at self-recognition. It will then be fully understood that culture is pivotal to evolution. What was once entirely physical will have become more purely mental.

But this does not mean that human beings will have achieved perfection. As physically limited, they will remain such throughout life. Though inextricably bound up in the material, grand vistas of spirit will have revealed themselves to them. For the first time in a long, difficult history, joy will surpass pain, though it cannot eliminate it. It will be akin to the joy of childbearing, in which the memory of pain is sufficiently overcome to induce a repetition of the process.

It is only at critical moments, when a person encounters a threat or major difficulty, that he turns his attention toward the underlying spirit supporting all things and says, "Help me."

## Thoughts on Creativity, Spirit, and the Ethical Life

But in truth, every breath, every step is underpinned by spirit. For it, there is not one or another incident which is a greater need. What is more, human beings do know this. They choose to ignore it, so they can entertain a false sense of independence. Yet an individual is never more free than when recognizing, in the deepest sense, that he is spirit and that his life is its expression.

The interstice between an individual mind and universal consciousness is unfathomable. Can it ever be known? Human beings discover and promulgate natural laws in order to form a deterministic view of their world, only to discover that, upon close examination, the apparent directional uniformity of events upon which they have so depended is riddled with contrary effects. An exactness of view is made inexact. And once again there is a need for new laws.

Determinism is an illusion. And so is free will. It is this contradiction which frames the limits of the mind.

Some say there is a god. Others say there is not. Can any meaning be attributed to these words? A tree flourishes but does not worship its roots. Nevertheless, it cannot do without them.

Universal consciousness is neither a he, a she, nor an it. All such terms are a form of idolatry.

Ah, prejudice! Wherever there is prejudice in religion, there can be no uniformity of spirit in human beings. Better to let go every ineluctable fact, every defining feature of a faith, than forgo the unity of spirit.

Religion has long been a political instrument, instilling a peculiar ethical conformity. It is good for forming communities and nations. But these have their boundaries, outside of which are those they oppose. Universal life in the spirit is without such bounds.

The great horror of the philosopher lies in the recognition that, for all he purports to know, he knows nothing. The strenuous efforts of philosophy, science, and art remain embedded in mystery. Surrounded on every side by the ineffable and the unfathomable, the human mind strains against the walls of its knowing and cannot perceive what lies beyond.

Yet humanity presses on, occasionally secure in its self-imposed conceit that it can overcome its limitations. But intermittently it knows better. For every effort to move outward finds another wall, and beyond every wall a new mystery. So why is it that this spirit persists in human beings? It is because beyond the limitations of the mind, it knows its boundless nature. Pushing outward into material experience, it seeks what lies within itself.

There is a connection between emotion and image which must be plumbed. When this is found, the path between universal consciousness and the individual self will have been revealed.

## Thoughts on Creativity, Spirit, and the Ethical Life

How is it that a great painter knows what to paint, how to organize color, line, and image; a sculptor where to chisel?

How does the novelist, story teller, or playwright search the depths of feeling and arrange them in a contrapuntally expressive balance which suggests more than reason can encompass? How does the musician orchestrate sound in terms of emotion and measure to obtain something beyond either? These are questions which cannot be causally answered because their source does not lie within the articulate mind. The mind suggests, but it is the heart that knows.

Some people spend their lives looking over their shoulders to see what other people think. They are but shadows of themselves, exhibiting the gravitas of a feather in a strong breeze. Substantial being is within. And, while a person can learn fragments from others, the erection of a solid edifice of vision she must do for herself.

Each individual is a cosmos expressing her unique outer form from within. She is consciousness, which is prior to its content. She is, in a way she cannot materially understand, the creative origin of her experience, the source of what is known to her. It is for this reason that she is mistaken in thinking that self-knowledge can be discovered among physical things.

The images of the mind are the root of reason. But they have no movement without the faculty of evaluation. Value is an expression of emotion. Or it is sometimes but a feeling. When applied to an image, it sets one thing in its proper relation to another. Only subsequent to this can reason place these images in its mold.

But where do the least anticipated of these feelings originate? What moves the mind unexpectedly into an original mode of seeing, one exhibiting no connection to a previous thought or train of emotion? It is consciousness, the hidden resources of which are more comprehensive than the mind which contains them. Its subtle proddings come like thieves in the night, illuminating a day of creative thought.

The human mind is often bound by the chains of material existence, so that it cannot see. But it has set those chains itself and can therefore remove them. For they are of its own making.

The problem with worshiping a god is that people never truly do so. They reverence an institution. When they prostrate themselves before any symbol, whether of a god or a god's power, they are submitting to the practices of an institution. Thus it is the institution and its rituals they bow down to.

They cannot worship spirit in this way because it is their own awareness, their consciousness. In attempting such a practice, they would fall into the love of their inner self and of all things in their experience as emanating therefrom. As a result, they would find that to love is not to worship. Rather, it is to embrace. This is why the spirit within cannot denigrate its character by prostrating before itself.

If it should be suggested that a person may better pay obeisant homage to an abstraction cleansed of all material defects—for this would appear to be beyond representation—it should be noted that the abstraction is an idea. An idea is a product of the mind. It is a thing, though without physical expression. It is a thing of the mind, yet material because it must express limitation in order to be represented in the mind. Consequently, it is no less an institutional idol for being abstract.

To love the material world is an imperative. But this is not a love which omits giving notice to faults. Physical life is limited, painful, stark. It has its momentary joys as well. But these are all too frequently brief and clouded over by troubles. A genuine love of life in its terrifying brevity is a seeing through—a recognition of the spirit from which it emanates. That spirit is universal consciousness. It has no physical limits, no temporal duration. And it loves all things which proceed from it.

Material life proceeds from it. Thus the love of physical existence in its variety is the proper orientation for an enlightened mind. Yet this love ought to have a detached quality, a recognition that what is passing, though quite a show, is not the person who appears to be in the midst of it. That person is universal consciousness.

The pained soul cries out from the crematorium: Why am I here? It is so hot! I am falling to ashes. The crematorium answers back: This is not your place. If it were, you would not see it as you do.

The refinement of the mind is both emotional and intellectual. It is neither exclusively one nor the other. For the mind sees in images which surround an emotion, or set of feelings. But the images themselves are linked together by concepts. They vary in emphasis according to perspective, the mind turning this way and that within the context of its thought. Altogether this is a mood. Or it is an integrated set of moods. And these, when set down in sensory form and made permanent, compose a work of art.

This complex layering of articulate awareness can take other forms as well. For example, a system of philosophy is a careful blending, or orchestration, of insights. The insights shine forth in the mind individually as well as collectively. Hence the flexibility of the system. For their variety in luster depends upon the emotional emphasis which they receive. Thus the philosophical tenor of the system, its mood, is a general attitude which holds the varied elements together.

These are the reasons why a refinement of the mind must be both emotional and intellectual. Without insights composed of a subtle fusion of emotional and intellectual elements, it cannot be braced with understanding. Consequently, every mind is philosophical to some extent. And the rigor of its thought is its measure. Thus the understanding is by nature thoughtful and evaluative. For without concepts it is a string without pearls. And where an evaluative structure is lacking, it is devoid of hierarchical meaning.

In addition to this fundamental composition as described, there must be a plurality of perspectives, enlarging the scope

## Thoughts on Creativity, Spirit, and the Ethical Life

of vision. That is, when linked together, the varied points of view form a more comprehensive awareness, a general sense of knowing about the world, which is a conquest and harmonization of experience. Even a systematic buildup of scientific conclusions, for all their grounding in sensory observation and mathematical organization, exhibits these characteristics. It is always growing and diversifying, while maintaining its interrelatedness.

The problem concerning so much of the art of the early twentieth century is that it represents a great extension of the imagination, while exhibiting a closing of the sympathetic heart. In much of its pursuit of spiritual possibility it has shown an advance in sensibility. But it has absconded from a deeper understanding of the mundane. This is a rift between the transcendent and the physical which must be repaired.

As humanity enters more deeply into matters of the spirit, it cannot neglect its rootedness in the material. For the future ought not to become another Middle Age of fabricated dreams divorced from the daily concerns of life. Rather, it should involve a lifting of those concerns into a more enlightened perspective. The way forward is spiritual. But it is spirit in the flesh.

The beauty of nature lies in its suggestion of transcendence. It expresses development: tumultuous change in the midst of stability. Taken as a whole, it runs counter to the sense of limitation generated by its isolated fragments. That is what draws the mind into it and makes it pleasing to contemplate.

It is stated at the conclusion of the Beowulf poem that the hero was "most eager for fame," *lofgeornost*. That is why he fought the three monsters. Yet today the deeds of many such intrepid souls are no longer remembered. So, turning about to look at great painters and their magnificent frescos, panels, and canvases, the question arises: how long can a knowledge of these last? Even though recorded in electronic imagery, how long before the inevitable turnover of civilizations buries them in loss and neglect?

Most great literary achievements from ancient times are forgotten. Only fragments of visual artworks remain. The ghosts of old music tantalize without recognition. For a memory of their composition no longer exists. Clearly, time erodes all, and little endures. But nevertheless there is culture.

It continues to advance by fits and starts. And it is true that old, unremembered influences flavor its workings. For they do live within it. Yet even here there is a limit to their duration, since human cultural history is but of short tenure. It bears the shadow of an ever-present warning that humankind itself may be expected to pass.

So what for the individual does endure? There are two things. One is a condition which resembles Nietzsche's "eternal return," which is a circle's circumference that has no beginning or end. It is a material eternity in which any point on the circle of time, such as a life, is the focal point of the whole, every moment of it as important and enduring as any other.

## Thoughts on Creativity, Spirit, and the Ethical Life

Regarded in this light, life should be lived with the utmost intensity. For it is both limited and absolute. Beyond this consideration, however, there is the eternal ity of spirit, or universal consciousness, from which all things emanate and which takes no note of time, time being of its own manufacture. Here all things are eternal together.

A heart that is gentle and giving is more free. It is not balled up like a fist, clutching hate, envy, revenge. So how does this relate to spirit? What is its connection with universal, creative consciousness? The proddings of spirit can only flow into and through a sensibility that is open. Clotted emotions are not receptive, as they are in conflict with the world.

Can it be held that the principle of life is in the nature of material existence? Causal relations readily apply in macro-situations. Yet they break down under close scrutiny. For this reason, the physical world may be said to be determinist, but not exclusively so. An allowance is made for subtle anomalies, variations in the firmest of relations. Under such conditions, emergent behavior may occasionally result.

An example would be the capacity of living forms to temporarily or partially reverse entropy. There is also a debate over the extent of plant awareness. Darwin considered that carnivorous plants might be classed as animals, since they are sentient. So life would seem to be at the behest of spirit. The spirit creates, then creates again within its creation. It is indeed a flexible universe.

Ernest Hemingway's *For Whom the Bell Tolls*, a novel set in the Spanish Civil War, centers upon three principal protagonists: Robert Jordan, an American expert in demolitions, and Pablo and Pilar, a guerilla band leader and his wife. A few lines of dialog provide a sense of the opposing characters of the latter two.

> "And how is she, the *mujer* of Pablo?"
> "Something barbarous," the gypsy grinned. "Something *very* barbarous. If you think Pablo is ugly you should see his woman. But brave. A hundred times braver than Pablo. But something barbarous."
> "The *mujer* of Pablo reads in the hands," the gypsy said. "But she is so irritable and of such a barbarousness that I do not know if she will do it."
> "...she has a tongue that scalds and that bites like a bull whip. With this tongue she takes the hide from any one. In strips. She is of an unbelievable barbarousness."

Pilar turns out to be warm, loyal, and sensible.

Pablo is different:

> "Pablo was brave in the beginning," Ansel-

mo said. "Pablo was something serious in the beginning."

"He killed more people than the cholera," the gypsy said. "At the start of the movement, Pablo killed more people than the typhoid fever."

"But since a long time he is *muy flojo*," Anselmo said. "He is very flaccid. He is very much afraid to die."

"It is possible that it is because he has killed so many at the beginning," the gypsy said philosophically. "Pablo killed more than the bubonic plague."

Pablo is a coward only in the sense that he is willing to do anything for his own benefit and hesitant to do otherwise. He puts himself above the Loyalist cause and the interests of those who follow him. Pilar's apparent cynicism conceals a deep humanity, just as what others see as Pablo's cowardice reveals an immense brutality. This human dynamic of underlying motives which conflict with superficial appearances is as characteristic of people now as it was then.

Perhaps the most remarkable fact about human intelligence is its tendency to float above the sensory world. It is closer to experience than a heartbeat, without ever fully grasping it. In this way, philosophers have struggled against the grain of practicality to enclose their world within the lineaments of abstract systems. They have generally succeeded in some measure, but have also failed.

Either they paint themselves into a corner, as did Locke in his inability to connect the workings of the mind to external reality. Or they cannot sufficiently brick the wall of logical inclusiveness to fill all gaps. The mind recoils from such unsuccessful attempts and tries again, compounding new principles into new systems with the same results.

In recent centuries, the exact sciences have arisen. They carefully observe events and construct their edifices slowly, securing gaps with considerable precision. But this is accomplished at the cost of their practitioners being fitted with blinders. For them, the course appears to have been successfully run because the track is designedly narrow. But, being limited to the evidence of the senses, their work ignores a broad range of experience, such as is exemplified in the arts. Thus they make such preposterous proclamations as "the emotions are not objective" and "consciousness is an epiphenomenon."

Organized religion, the oldest of systematic speculative enterprises, appeared in the earliest flowering of settled life. It developed as a composite of emotional and intellectual experience, imagining forth a unified body of explanation. Its work was admirable, but costly. For it forced a more rigorous concept of revealed truth upon the multitude.

Such truths were of necessity interpreted by a small body of the initiated. Thus a few were assigned to do the thinking for the many, while these many were enjoined to cling by faith to their pronouncements. Thus was produced a tiny cluster of active minds among those utterly numbed intelligences who had originally been gifted with reason.

What is the meaning of these errant acts of the will, stumbling forth in chaotic manner? Is it that a hope of universal success must be disregarded? No, it is not. All the many failures have succeeded in one thing. They have shown progress. The indomitable human race presses on. Reason may at times glimmer shoddily over its limitations. And imagination may run afoul of any focus. But together they are advancing nonetheless, closing in on the many gaps in understanding.

And, though they are unlikely to erect a perfect edifice, there is the continual advance. Ignorance grows increasingly less menacing, while reminders of it remain present as a foil to hubris. Is this not the signal mark of human freedom, that it must be purchased in this way at the price of uncertainty?

Creativity would never occur if it were simply a product of knowledge. It is a gap in knowledge which allows imagination to seep through, bringing something new.

Undisciplined imagination is riotous and spendthrift. But, when brought under the control of reason, yet allowed to go its way, it mounts up to the highest possible limit of awareness.

There is an obscure impulse in the mind, a thin emotional prodding, undetermined in its origin, which leads imagination to places it has never before encountered. Here is the true source of human progress. Often unacknowledged, it is immaterial in its nature.

The ideal and the real are meant to be inseparable. The mind thrusts the ideal outside the real in order to clearly see it. But the ideal is ultimately the harmonization of the real. For they are one.

For those who look deeply within, there is a self which is not created for public perusal. Yet many are lost in the public self, while but a few cultivate the other. Both selves constitute clusters of emotion, the one hurried about by the exigencies of life, the other no more than passively involved in such matters.

Now, the success which the inner self exercises in curbing the distancing of the outer self from spirit depends only in part upon its efforts. For the public self, being increasingly constituted of impenetrable intellectual convictions gathered both by exposure and choice, may deviate so far from inner awareness as to lose its connection with it.

This is unfortunate. For, as a facet of universal consciousness, the inner self endures. Whereas the public self, having become independent of spirit, partakes only of the fragmentation and short duration of the material. Consequently, it passes into nothingness. It is in this ephemeral character that the Buddha likened it to a flickering candle flame, soon extinguished.

It is the external self which experiences pain, both physical and emotional. The internal self simply takes note, regarding it with equanimity. However, as it is exceedingly difficult for a person to extricate her mind from material influences, she

## Thoughts on Creativity, Spirit, and the Ethical Life

generally succumbs to them. This is what brings about the initial distancing of the outer from the inner self.

A defensive posture is assumed and built up, like the shell of a bivalve. The person, locked safely inside, understands the world only in terms of what nourishes or threatens her. Thus she is enclosed in such a manner as to limit her experience of life. Yet it is only the extent of her exposure which enriches her inner person.

It is evident that universal consciousness, or spirit, does not exhibit an image of humankind. Being of a more extensive character, its operations are beyond human understanding. Conversely, there is an element of validity to be found in the assertion that humankind is the image of spirit. All thinking beings participate in the awareness of the one universal consciousness, while differing in the extent and depth of that awareness.

Having learned to traverse the distances of time and space by means of thought, a human being calls upon spirit as upon another of its kind. It is as though there were an intimacy between them. But how can this be? How is it that a limited mind may presume to find common ground with the unlimited? It is on the basis of an interpersonal relationship. Though spirit is not a person, it is the source of personhood. Thus a nexus is formed which brings them together.

Little is known, though much is to be known. And though much is to be known, it is but a little distance that the human mind can travel in what, to it, is a limitless void.

For the future of humanity, a respect for intelligence is absolutely essential. But this does not mean that the products of the intellect should be worshiped. Reason has its limits and often admires itself into folly. Yet so is an absence of a balanced regard for reason a problem. Throughout recorded history, the many have been duped by the fictions of those who would gain and retain power over them by encouraging non-thinking.

There have been many arguments regarding the transcendent: there is or there is not such a thing. But in the final analysis this is a question for the individual heart. Whatever the transcendent may be, it is likely that it smiles equally upon both the believer and unbeliever. Together they are part of a general progress, or evolution, toward a greater understanding.

Throughout biological history there has been physical evolution. So the rocks and the panorama of selection reveal. But in at least the last ten thousand years humanity has opened a new era. The principal instrument of evolutionary change among human beings has been culture. It is through the works of the mind that human existence has mounted higher and spread farther through the world.

There is a class implication in this. A widening gulf is developing between the educated and thoughtful and that broad sea of ill-formed prejudice which has exercised the greater number of humankind. Both cannot prevail. The old standards of wealth, birth, religious hierarchy, and sheer numbers must pass away. In their place is growing up the plant of higher intelligence devoted to fairness and understanding.

## Thoughts on Creativity, Spirit, and the Ethical Life

So great is the difference between this slender, delicate plant and its heavy-limbed forebears, that it is developing into a form of cultural speciation. Those who are thoughtful and those who are mired in the fury of opinion cannot communicate. The one does not know the other. It is like a form of speciation in which there can no longer be an interbreeding. There is a separation into classes. And this distinction is more important than all previous means of determining such.

Notwithstanding their direct descent from dinosaurs, songbirds are the jewels of the earth. They are the moving blossoms of field, forest, and sky. Through their beauty one may glimpse the eternal, as through a porthole into another world.

The point to be noted is how little a person is conscious of and how restricted his acceptance of what can be known. But when the material limits of his mind fall away in death, he is freed from impediment and rendered capable of understanding more than he could have imagined. This turns out to be the full extent of his consciousness.

It is not the rudiments of intelligence alone which have lifted humankind to its present exalted position. These are possessed in varying degree by other life forms. What makes the difference is the development of language which, by means of its concepts, has given to imagination the necessary restraint of a firmly articulated structure.

In terms of aesthetically conceived philosophies, creative literature is principally concerned with moral issues, music with emotional complexities. Thus it is the plastic, or visual arts, which come closest to a metaphysics that can be sensuously and emotionally conceived. This is no doubt because human beings think in terms of mental imagery. And these images are predominantly visual. Hence, there is a greater comprehensiveness of suggestion in the production of a painting or a sculpture, though these governing ideas are less determinate in conceptual articulation than are those of either literature or music.

In his art, Michelangelo projects a visible force through the material substance of his work. That force is a living soul. It is within, but not of, the material representation. Rather, it is limited by and stands in opposition to it. In another case, Rembrandt's work exudes a deep spirituality, not only in the facial expression and physical gestures of a portrait like that of himself or St. Paul, but even in the clothing and insentient objects represented. For such a living element is understood to lie deep within all things, from which it glows with a visible presence.

    These characteristics are the essence of great art. They are the halo with which the artist is able to envelop his depiction. That halo is transcendental. It is a fusion of emotions expressing an idea. But from whence does such an insight originate? How does the artist come to know what he wishes to express? He cannot say. Neither can the viewer who receives the work's

## Thoughts on Creativity, Spirit, and the Ethical Life

impression. This is the mystery of art, the nearest approach to the ineffable nature of spirit, or universal consciousness.

How does Paul Klee so gently evoke a sense of humor amidst such a weight of integrated form and color? It is his childlike playfulness, arising from a serious demeanor of artistic control, that is the beguiling appeal of his art. This is not to say his method always works. It does not, as is the case with any artist.

But when it does, it succeeds very well, transporting the viewer into a lighter, freer dimension of seeing. It demonstrates that there is more to awareness than material experience. And it also reveals a manner, one of many, in which the emotions can be wrought to a level of transcendence. What is then expressed cannot be encountered in terms other than itself.

In the cool of the evening, when the mice are at play and the mind is limpid and clear, purity of thought occurs.

Is it not strange that an artist, who is often ethically confused in the conduct of her life, should in her work have so much perception and insight, even of an ethical nature? It is as though something higher dwells in a person, whom it generally cannot influence in practical matters. But in the art there is promise. For it is that towards which the human race is striving.

When mathematicians encountered the criticism by Berkeley and others that the infinitesimal in calculus was a nebulous and inexact expression, they rose to the challenge by rectifying their terms. It is in this way that the infinitesimal became an indistinguishably small but whole number. Yet the problem was not fully resolved by this means. For, under the guise of a function's approach toward a concrete limit, this infinitesimal slipped surreptitiously unseen into the general inexactness of all numbers. It is one of these which in any function supplies the limit.

Thus arises a fundamental disagreement between two different and contending states of mind, the philosophical and the mathematical. Each presses its thesis towards the bounds of its domain and locates the other outside it. But neither domain is transcendent. For any purely conceptual train of thought is rendered subordinate to the imagery of the mind, which must be drawn exclusively from material experience.

The persistent need for concrete representation leads human beings toward anthropomorphism in their attempts to form a relationship with the transcendent. For they find a lack of any tie to a greater power unfeasible. People are inherently vulnerable. And they feel their limitations. So in times of crisis, the greater number of them need to align themselves with a power beyond their natural means.

For this reason, Jesus of Nazareth introduced the concept of a spiritual father. This was not intended as an anthropomorphic figure. But neither was it lacking in those warm attributes which are associated with a father. However, people being

## Thoughts on Creativity, Spirit, and the Ethical Life

what they are, the attributes soon found a corporal body and a narrow personhood in the imaginations of Jesus' followers.

The strong wine of an intellectual pursuit flatters the ego. But if it is a product of the ego, it will soon turn to vinegar.

Creativity inhabits many forms. What they all have in common is the extension of a person's influence over something detached from herself, be it an idea or an object.

From a cultural standpoint, the entire twentieth century, in the arts as well as philosophy, represents one massive retreat from reality. There are individual exceptions, of course. But these are like stones in a rushing stream, overwhelmed by the moving water.

Mathematics is one of the arts, beautiful in the purity of its imaginative productions, which are entirely fictional. Yet it acts as a supposedly real backbone of the physical world.

Out of spirit, truth. Out of this truth, all the lies of superstition.

One of the great unacknowledged houses of superstition is modern science. Originally built upon a foundation of observations and simple insights, it has grown into a monolith of overweening pride and prognostication.

By its very nature, the human mind is incapable of seeing all, knowing all. This is the case with every human endeavor, including the revealed insights of scriptures. For the door is always open to new revelations and insights. And no science, not even mathematics, can be airtight, in spite of its seemingly incontrovertible logic.

Consequently, it should not be said that a philosophical system is final. Philosophy must learn to proceed progressively, like any other field of knowledge or expression. It is natural to propound a system of thought *as though* it were final. Otherwise, it would appear to be inconsistent and incomplete. But always there is the lurking encroachment of new minds, new perspectives. This is as it should be.

Unreflective people are the vast majority of humankind, even among the educated. This must change because human beings are spiritual beings. And spirit is the only means of access to the accumulated wisdom of a genuine understanding. A future peace and prosperity of the race depends upon this understanding.

Reason is a fallible instrument. But it is all human beings have for setting and clarifying the terms of a judgment. Imagination is essential. But in matters of judgment, it is not more important than reason. For reason is necessary to form a judgment. Neither is faith more important than reason. Rather, reason is more important than faith. This is because reason supports faith, when faith is judged to be reasonable. Unreasonable faith is folly.

# Thoughts on Creativity, Spirit, and the Ethical Life

Humanity has only recently emerged as an independently reasoning species. This condition of independence exhibits a capacity to reason apart from circumstances. Hence time can be understood as not just a before and after, but as a thing apart. Even so, the mind is a fragile instrument which is easily submerged under the compelling forces of an emotional and sensual nature.

Evolution is the only scientific theory this author openly embraces within the context of his philosophical thought. It is included within his representational viewpoint. But it is superseded by his more encompassing immaterial perspective. Insofar as it is embraced in the former case, it is the Darwinian view which is favored.

The so-called "modern consensus" of the nineteen thirties and forties is too mechanistic and therefore overlooks some of Darwin's intuitions, such as those making allowances for some degree of Lamarckism and consequently for a communication between somatic and generative cells. These could not be demonstrated at the time of his investigations. But perhaps, when the body is better understood as a mutually interactive array of intercommunicative cells, the matter will be clarified.

Will humanity ever emerge from the darkness of confused thinking? It seems to be such a simple thing to accomplish. Yet thousands of years of concerted effort have produced only glimmers of light. Still, to continue the struggle to expand and sustain a domain of clear understanding seems more than reasonable.

Any conceivable transcendent power can only be understood to be reasonable in character. Should it not be so, it would be chaos. For chaos is not a power, but the destruction of power. Power is organization to a purpose. And that involves reason of one kind or another.

Change is vitality, life. Eternity is stillness, death. Yet change implies the departure of what was, eternity the duration of what is. Can one be had without the other? If there is no permanence in life, it is without meaning. And if there is no vitality in duration, it is also without meaning. Therefore, there must be change in eternity. And there must be something of the eternal in life. This juxtaposition is difficult for the human mind to grasp. Yet, in one way or another, the mind has struggled with the problem throughout its earthly sojourn.

The terror of death is a fear of having failed at attaining some purpose in life. And it is also a fear of leaving an emptiness for loved ones. Yet purpose is not always understood when it is achieved. And can a life filled with all the creative variety of one's presence be called an emptiness, even when it is but a memory?

Art fills the heart in a way that little else can. Yet it is an illusion passed from one mind to another. It is immaterial in its essence, vanishing once its effect has been accomplished. Unless, of course, mind is what truly endures.

## Thoughts on Creativity, Spirit, and the Ethical Life

The ceremony of life is thought and emotion. And in human beings neither of these is ever independent of the other. The heart generates thought, which again reaches to the heart.

If a curved universe can be both finite and infinite, it allows the mind to combine in an exactness of expression the unlimited reaches of observed phenomena with their causal interrelationships. Hence the practical appeal of this idea. On the other hand, quantum behavior undermines causal explanations.

It reminds the investigator that causal relations do not fit tightly together. A recognition is forced concerning the fact that any human attempt to create a nonporous blend of relations does not work. It is a reminder of the mind's limits. For it is the mind which is at question, rather than the phenomena.

When the Nazis destroyed monuments and public sculptures, they put out one of the eyes of universal consciousness and rendered the human race partially blind. It is the business of spirit to see through the human mind, thus enlarging the mind's access to experience and giving it transcendental power.

How small the mind is. How tiny its world. Yet how great its inner resources!

In northern France in the second half of the nineteenth century the industrial revolution was underway. Industry needed raw materials, especially coal, to build its new world. To get that coal, men, women, even children must spend their lives deep in the earth. Emile Zola's novel, *Germinal*, about a miner's strike is the story of these people—their poverty, hopelessness, and craving for justice and love.

There is young Étienne Lantier, who has ideas to fill men's heads with dreams of a worker's paradise. And there are simple, good people like Maheu and his wife Maheude, who, inflamed with this hope, cannot understand the forces that hurl them and many others like them into a war between Capital and Labor.

Opposite the striking miners, yet caught beneath the weight of big business is Deneulin, the small mine operator who sees and understands:

> Another fortnight of the strike and he would be bankrupt. And in the knowledge of this certain disaster he no longer felt any hatred for the Montsou hooligans, but rather was conscious of universal complicity, sins shared by all for generations past. Brutes they might be, but they were brutes who could not read and were dying of starvation.

In the midst of this struggle unfolds the story of Étienne Lantier and Catherine, daughter of Maheu and Maheude. Theirs are the emotions of the young and inexperienced, the yearnings of untempered hearts.

## Thoughts on Creativity, Spirit, and the Ethical Life

There are descriptions of mob violence, passion, fear, hate, and embarrassed moments of understanding and tenderness. To read this book is to feel what it is like to choke on coal dust in tight, dark, sweating galleries five hundred meters underground and to experience the seemingly unimaginable dream of returning to open air to breathe once again under a sun.

If it were possible to create a species possessed of an unvarying wisdom, that species could not have come from animal origins. Woe is humanity, that it must shed the muck of materiality while praising the vision of beauty, even in itself, which it has painfully wrenched from its earthly beginnings.

There is a perfection in Keats which is hard to match: stately, steady, yet with passion. But he only lived to be twenty-five—a distillation of transcendent seeing in so short a time. Others take many years to mature in wisdom. Can it be that the elastic which holds the two bookends of life together—birth and death—is tuned to an inner resonance oblivious of time?

As a corollary to the *fundamental theorem of arithmetic*, the following can be stated. If every prime number above 3 is either one more or one less than a multiple of 6, and if 6 is a multiple of the primes 2 and 3, then every prime number can be factored into a 2, a 3, and a multiplier of these which either is or is not a prime, the final resulting prime being dependent upon that one unit which is either added to or subtracted.

As to those multipliers which are primes, they are derived in the same manner as the primes of which they are components, making the overall process iterative. And those multipliers which are not primes (i.e., composite numbers) can be factored into primes, which are again determined in the same manner. Primes and composites together comprise all the natural numbers.

So, at the root of these operations lie the primes 2 and 3, and the unit 1. Hence every natural number above 3 can be derived from the digits 1, 2, and 3, with those primes above 3 being derived in the recursive manner described. Consequently, all the counting numbers are a function of the first three. Such is the creative simplicity of the mind's operations.

The human race is beginning to explore the solar system, while pushing its instruments of curiosity further into the cosmos. For this reason, it cannot afford to be irrational in the understanding of what it is, its strengths, and its limitations. To do otherwise would be to spread infection beyond the home wound.

Light is the fastest carrier of information known. So all other physical relations have been built around it. But this does not mean that these relations cannot be understood in another way. The advance of knowledge is a progress of the mind. And it is hard to see what the next paradigm shift will be prior to the mind's readiness for it.

## Thoughts on Creativity, Spirit, and the Ethical Life

The emotions, though closer to the animal, are more fundamental than reason. As a result, they are nearer to the transcendent. Yet it is reason which informs the mind of the connection. Thus it is this discursive faculty which has lifted humanity to a higher plane, albeit that the plane itself is lodged in the deepest emotional recess of animal nature.

When an artist uses imagery to create her emotional complex of music, form, line, color, or language, she is summoning forth an awareness which, if drawn from the deepest springs, may not exist in material experience or thought. Rather, it is drawn from her innermost person, that emotional base which lies within the foundational self and not within the self that has been created and adjusted to environmental and social conditions. This is why it is spiritual. For it is seated in a consciousness which is an expression of the universal.

The subtle emotional proddings which emanate from spirit are sewn as a delicate thread into those human emotions which are associated with life. Once recognizable as an artistic vision, these elements are brought together under a conceptual organization. And it is this which is the emotional complex that is transformed into a transcendent work of art.

The working of Providence comes quietly and generally takes on an appearance of coincidence. Yet it is on the mark, a ready fit to circumstance, so that only the most obtuse intelligence can ignore its character. Thus it is here, more than anywhere else, that the rise of animal nature toward spiritual expression is felt.

Unreflective natures receive its gifts without concern or question. Only an active mind is apt to confront it. For it is such a mind which examines it in reflection. This is the leading edge of humanity: reflection, not mere reception. For it lends to nature a self-awareness, lifting it into the spirit whence it came. Amidst the suffering and joy of humanity, there is this: a separate and independent knowledge of both self and Providence in the mind of the willing recipient.

Van Gogh's art, with its flaming cypresses, swirling clouds, pulsating suns, and writhing sunflowers, is not just the product of a highly wrought, nervous temperament. Such may be the case. But in addition, this work is an expression of an awareness of the living spirit in all things: a life force which begets, energizes, and brings meaning to what would otherwise lie inert and forgotten, to be trod underfoot. The artist felt it in his limbs, transferring it to all things in his pure religion of spirit.

When Gauguin liberated color to become an expressive force, he made manifest that what is encountered is more about what is felt than what is seen. Consciousness of emotion took precedence over sense. More than that, emotion was singled out as the essence of sense. For what is sensed begins in feeling, rather than form.

Matisse's use of color and form expresses peace and restfulness almost as if these were independent of reference, but not quite. August Macke, on the other hand, fixes color to form,

## Thoughts on Creativity, Spirit, and the Ethical Life

thereby to reference, raising the mundane to spiritual appreciation. If spirit is free, all things immersed in spirit are free.

Rothko's representational reductionism has uncovered the mystery that color is emotion and emotion is color. The same can be understood of the music of Mozart, Beethoven, and Bach. Sensation and emotion are in unity, each born of the other. The universe, a kaleidoscope of color and form, exhibits the emotions of spirit.

Emotion, supremely hierarchical, evaluative, is not arranged on a plane, but in terms of elevations and depressions signifying meaning through progression and development. Without emotion, there are facts of no consequence.

Faith does not believe. It does not organize ideas in regulation of events. It releases the mind into possibility. As an act of creation, it welds mind into spirit, its home.

There is no register of right and wrong in spirit. That record is in people's hearts, where it perishes with the material self. What remains, more or less and according to its rightness, is that portion of the eternal self which has been translated into acts.

At some time in the multi-millennial past, humankind became aware of a more heightened understanding of itself, perhaps through the use of language. This resulted in a condition which Christianity has labeled a state of "original sin." It marks a bifurcation in human identity, in which people have become conscious of themselves as spiritual, yet continue to be driven by animal appetites and fears.

As this problem has become more acutely articulated, the attendant fears have also grown proportionately, particularly in matters of interpersonal and social relations. They have become the bane of humankind, producing wars, hate, murder, cheating, and slander. In fact, there has appeared to be no end to the ills which arise from them, no way out of them. People, feeling themselves to be thus limited, do not acquiesce to the limitations, their animal and spiritual natures remaining in perpetual conflict within themselves and with others.

Evolution by cultural means, raising itself up in the face of this dilemma, offers an increasing hope of spiritual dominance over material being. But to become such, to become spirit in the flesh willing to acknowledge an enduring nature within a perishing shell while embracing the ambivalence, is a formidable undertaking.

What is required is a society in which every individual is held to be sacred. Each person, as a direct expression of universal consciousness, is spirit. The individual is a son of God. These statements do not imply the possession of deep spiritual insight in every person, as was the case with Jesus, the Buddha, and others. This is to come, a wave of change in the human condition. Nevertheless, such potential lies in the womb of humanity and is deserving even now of respect.

## Thoughts on Creativity, Spirit, and the Ethical Life

Many people do bad things. Few are evil. The misdirected intellect is prone to shortcuts. And that is the source of most wrongdoing. What is evil is deliberate malice. Nevertheless, the whole is involved in the human movement toward spiritual liberation. So spirit can be understood to smile upon humanity with compassion. For all things emanate from spirit. And these will in time reach their transcendent home.

The veil between individual and universal consciousness is at times so thin as to be almost transparent. But for the most part it is opaque. Both conditions exist in varied proportions in each individual. Thus it is this alternating condition which sustains the struggle between doubt and belief concerning the transcendent. It is a situation which informs life with a high-strung tension. Until the body gives out, yearning never ceases. Though it is often firmly denied.

To gaze hourly into the dimly lit reaches of infinite space is no different from looking inward with close scrutiny into the obscurest chambers of the heart. It requires patience and determination. This is the reason for the small number of astronomers and for the even fewer people who can be honest with themselves.

Cash register honesty is easy, absolute self-reckoning nearly impossible.

It is the ability to search one's heart and form a judgment about it that sets humanity apart from other sentient minds. A heavy burden, it is, yet for many, too much to bear.

Wisdom is the recognition that whatever meaning there is in life is more to be sought than attained. For it is not the articulation of meaning that matters. It is the search.

Instead of drawing upon the creative transcendent for insights that elevate the mind, and doing so without injury to others, many seek power by means of manipulation, deceit, and force. The result of such a widespread misdirection of will is division with its attendant attributes of injustice and hate.

War and strife will never cease so long as humanity is mired in this kind of material blindness. Generally ignored is the deepest inwardness, the true person. Without this, an upright character is at best glimpsed through a fog. It is as though a person were intoxicated from birth until death. Moreover, parents unwittingly pass this condition on to their children.

The mind expresses abstractions in words. Abstractions are concepts. Thus language is the instrument of conceptual thinking. But the mind thinks in images even when thinking in concepts, however obscure and unnoticed the images may be behind the concepts. So images inevitably lie, sometimes invisibly, behind words.

Because the mind's foundational tool for all thinking is the image, and because purely imaginative thought occurs directly in this way, there is a greater store of images in the mind than concepts. This is so, even though there can be a concept for any image. For images are produced spontaneously, concepts by deliberate design. Thus concepts merely suggest the full range of imagery at best and are unable to express that completeness of experience which requires the immediacy of images.

This is the reason that the visual arts are able to exhibit subtleties which are beyond verbal articulation. Many visual representations, once expressed, cannot be adequately defined. For they can only be converted into abstractions with considerable difficulty and by means of a roundabout approach. Such is the explanation of a Velasquez, a Cézanne, a Matisse, a Macke, or any other such work.

Due to the influence of the ego, much of the human pursuit of sustenance both physical and spiritual is given over to the race for social eminence. Gradually such a stifling self-enclosure of purpose works to produce a thoroughly unsatisfactory world. For the greater part of one's effort not devoted to physical maintenance is committed to social placement, leaving little opportunity for self-examination resulting in an enrichment of general awareness.

This is a loss which is damaging to both the individual and his society. If it is subsequently repeated generation after generation, example reinforcing practice, it is spiritually devastating. Yet, even in the most extreme cases, there are exceptions to be found in those who devote themselves to an intrinsic self-awareness and growing spiritual consciousness.

These are the means which bring cultural evolution to a higher state of being. In time, such efforts may self-augment to a transposition of human purpose. For it is not unlikely that a level might be reached which would convert the whole to a higher pursuit. But at present, this must appear to be only a hope.

The human ego is a default setting of spiritual consciousness, which is brought about when the higher view cannot be sustained. Rather, it is converted to material ambition. What should have been a liberation of the mind is thus committed to a hopeless blindness of endless striving for what no one can satisfactorily attain.

Consciousness is the supreme reality. It is not an epiphenomenon. Neither is it a passive whiteboard upon which experience is written. It is the fomenter of experience, the medium through which it comes. And it is its organizer. Consciousness is life. All else is appearance, except insofar as it is understood as an expression of life.

For this reason color, shape, line, sound, and every kind of sensation and material organization is an instrument for the awakening of the inner resources of consciousness, which are bodied forth in emotion. The subtle impulses which call forth the profoundest of these emotions are the inner heart of consciousness, giving it a vitality and peculiar movement unfamiliar to unmotivated matter. These are ensconced within the states and divisions of consciousness, which are respectively the separate frames of mind and the individual persons which are its multifarious being.

A lack of a sense of the transcendent leads to most human evil. Blindness to the unity of spirit within plunges a person into an environment of fragmentation, where one thing impinges upon another and all is perceived to be in a state of enmity and conflict. Under such pressure, the only available response is self-defense.

Self-defense invites preemption and offense. The tools of these are lies and a subtle underhanded opposition, which lead to counteractions of a similar nature. And, as this sense of fragmentation spreads, there is a mounting alienation of multiple minds from the peaceful transcendence which lies undetected within.

Sexual desire is a fearsome appetite. For it not only has the power to captivate and distort reason. It demands satisfaction in the physical embodiment of another person in disregard of her spirit. This is why promiscuity is socially inadvisable. It is the use of another person for gratification. Any interest in spiritual character is put aside for a moment's pleasure. Such an attitude is habit-forming. And, when extended throughout society, it can lead to a loss of cohesion and an eventual dissolution.

Gentleness goes hand in hand with courage, as cruelty with cowardice. An unwarranted brutal act toward either animal or person arises from an individual's need to put something beneath him, so that he may feel empowered. There is no more obvious indication of a lack of personal confidence than such a disposition.

Bullying and ostracism are one and the same. They arise from the need to make another feel inferior. A fragmented spirit, having lost sight of its inner unity, does this.

Jesus was spiritually anointed, which is to say, spiritually grounded. This is made clear by his character, exhibited in his teachings and healing ministry. But the notion that he is, or ever could be thought of as, one facet of a trinity is the result of an ad hoc solution to a difficult problem which was worked out over the course of the fourth century C.E. It has introduced the popular idea of an anthropomorphic deity.

Spirit is universal consciousness, infinite but self-limited into multiple material persons. Sentient life expresses consciousness, exhibiting differentiation through the content of each mind. Furthermore, humanity, by means of the faculty of language, has been rendered capable of self-understanding, lifting it apart from its material experience. But only in the sense of a grounding in spirit can any person be conceived as a son of God.

Institutions are necessary for the regulation of human affairs. But institutional bondage is wrong. The regulation of human affairs, being largely a material matter, is greatly facilitated by institutional norms. But the universal spirit expressed through

## Thoughts on Creativity, Spirit, and the Ethical Life

every personal consciousness cannot be made subordinate to material concerns.

It is for this reason wrong to render obeisance to an institution, regardless of what it is done in the name of. This applies to whatever may be the institution's holdings, findings, or representations. Universal spirit is not its property. Neither is it that of its trained officials. It belongs to each individual and must be reckoned, saluted, and adored by an individual alone and independent of external authority.

Is it not strange that a lizard on one's garden wall—simple, cold-blooded, and dependent on the sun—is also an expression of universal spirit, similarly blest as any human, though not in the same way? It too, having joyfully absorbed the warmth of the sun into its innermost being, will pass from this life. But it will not depart out of the spirit. That is its home. So much more is it the case for those of greater awareness.

Death seems incomprehensible. People learn of it by observing the dissolution of all material things and by noting that they have no active memory prior to sometime after birth. But the cessation of consciousness itself is inconceivable. It is this peculiar circumstance which suggests belief in an afterlife.

There can be questions about the duration of the content of consciousness, which content is the substance of a material existence. So, if that content is perishable, what is beyond material existence, if anything? And prior to it? What enduring element might surround each small individual stain on the unfolding life fabric of history? Something beyond time and the material? Incomprehensible. So what is to be said of it? It is a question which is impossible to abandon or resolve.

The reason a visual work of art can be said to be metaphysical (or epistemological when considered in reference to the mind) is that its foundational elements are line and color. These are spatial in character when employed in an art work. In other words, a painting is built up spatially with line and color. Even the use of color without line, or the exercise of a monochrome palette varying in tone but independent of line, is spatial.

A sculpture, as generally conceived by the modern world, is limited to line alone. And that line is clearly geometrical. That is to say, its varied orientations are spatial. So it is that in either case, painting or sculpture, be it a delineation of physical objects or not, no visual representation can occur without a suggestion of space.

Space can be represented with line, color, or both. But either one or a combination of these means must be employed. Otherwise, no conception can take place. Concepts are supported by images—even concepts of pure color relation, or of nonrepresentational linear form. For imagery lies behind every concept, however subtly it may be concealed behind a verbal expression. These, like any other representation, are spatial in character, one image of independent hue, tone, or line orientation, being set against another in the mind.

Color is emotional in its impact upon the sensibility. In a myriad of conceivable combinations, it exhibits throughout a composition the highs and lows of emotional response. Linear representation does the same thing and can be combined with color for a heightened effect. So the entirety of possible material experience can be brought into mental focus by these means. This is why the visual arts are held to be metaphysical (or epistemological) in character. For they are expressive of mental awareness.

Jane Austen's *Pride and Prejudice* begins with the statement, "It is a truth universally acknowledged, that a single man in possession of a good fortune must be in want of a wife." Here is an intelligence with the grace not to say, "Money and social position are always an occasion for predatory man hunting."

Pride and misinformed opinion are the central concerns of the novel. Elizabeth, a high-toned young woman, is prone to forming rash judgments from first impressions. And Darcy, an aloof, taciturn man, is one to encourage such a breakdown in communication. He is not in the habit of expressing feelings. So she mistakes his distant manner for pride.

Consequently, Elizabeth does not understand the motives behind some of Darcy's actions, particularly in relation to her sister. As a result, she becomes angry with him and refuses to accept his offer of marriage. And it is only upon her later discovery of the good he has done her family that she realizes her error. There is also, of course, the matter of her having seen his large estate.

As Elizabeth becomes aware of her misjudgments concerning Darcy, as well as of the degraded character of Mr. Wickham, whom she had formerly admired, she tells her sister, "There certainly was some great mismanagement in the education of those two men. One has got all the goodness, and the other all the appearance of it." She realizes that, "the misfortune of speaking with bitterness [in turning down Darcy's proposal of marriage] is a most natural consequence of the prejudices I had been encouraging."

For Austen, the tempering of imagination and emotion with careful observation and reason is essential to good character, as Elizabeth learns. But it should not be overlooked that imagination and emotion are also important when moderately expressed. It is this balance between thoughtfulness and feeling that Austen calls "civility."

Monet painted atmosphere, its many subtle moods and complexities, in fact an entire world of human emotion in terms of atmospheric nuance. He studied the winds and currents, the humidity, the joy and oppression of the air in a manner never before seen. In his later life, he depicted his water lilies as if, at times, they might be detached from any context.

Pissarro painted the peasant milieu. One feels the presence of these country folk even in landscapes which either do not emphasize or do not include people. The people inhabiting the land are always of a dominant importance. The heat of the day, the dust, the cold of winter, inclement or good weather, the sweat and reward of labor—all these are felt where represented and where not.

Renoir painted paint, its texture and light. This was light glowing within color, as opposed to light suggested by color. Through such handling of paint, he beautified whatever he represented, made it glow with a nacreous sheen. So, among these three, great as they are, each in his own way, something

### Thoughts on Creativity, Spirit, and the Ethical Life

other than landscape alone was a matter of emphasis. Especially was this true in the case of Renoir.

Thus it is Sisley who must be designated as the true landscapist, as he was entirely focused upon a harmonious representation of the scene before him. No one element exceeded another in importance in his pictures. Trees, sky, atmosphere, water, buildings, earth forms, are presented as one.

Out of this intra-inclusive world comes a hint, just a suggestion, of human activity, an intimation of unfolding story. But it is never brought to bear upon the scene at hand in such a manner as to dominate it. So, when considered in these terms, it must be Sisley who is granted the title, purest landscapist of the four, though, of course, all are equally great artists.

Human wrongdoing and wrong thinking are the source of much unpleasantness and suffering. But it would seem to be obvious that these cannot be the cause of natural disasters like volcanoes, earthquakes, and tsunamis. Yet, when the close association of consciousness with material experience is considered, such an assumption may be called into question. Can it be that there is a subtle link between the content of the mind and the will? For it is within the mind, and only within the mind, that these things are experienced. If so, would not material reality be in some degree responsive to human mental states, good or bad?

Perhaps in a manifest but indemonstrable way, human selfishness and waywardness do contribute to an undesirable enhancement of overwhelming physical events. It may be less than a full causal relation. But there could nevertheless be a power of disturbance which intensifies the presence and harmfulness of large scale natural processes.

An understanding of this relationship between mind and nature might therefore be modified in the future. But who can know with any certainty, short of testing the assumption by means of a collective attempt at the correction of evil? Is humanity willing to rise to this occasion? Or is it presently stuck in a stew of its own making, boiling at an unpleasant temperature?

Socrates is recorded as having observed that, if a person knew and understood virtue, he would do no wrong. However, it must be allowed that this observation should be modified according to Aristotle's principle of akrasia, or weakness of the will. One example of this is a smoker who knows it is unhealthy to smoke, but who goes on doing so. Clearly, intellectual knowledge of the good is no guarantor of its pursuit. Something more is needed.

There are many liars and cheats. And the majority of these know what they do is wrong. But they affix themselves to their wayward course, some in small, occasional ways, others with determination and conviction. Each of them knows, if and when he thinks about it, that what he does is wrong. But so many others do the same, why should he not preempt their harmful efforts to his own advantage? He believes that virtue in such a world is sure to be trampled underfoot. And there is no benefit to anyone in that.

This analysis applies to the smoker as well as to the liar and the cheat. The smoker's pleasure is immediate, as opposed to

## Thoughts on Creativity, Spirit, and the Ethical Life

any far off health concerns, just as the others see benefit in their combative readiness to confront wrongdoers on their own deceptive ground. Some never suffer from these acts. So why not encounter the risk for the benefit? Life is short and ought to be lived in full. Moral principles are long and full of ambiguous results. This is the kind of thinking which motivates the majority of the human race.

So what can be done if upright convictions are so easily dismissed and conveniently placed out of mind? What is the bulwark to prevent such a strong tide from sweeping humankind to a barren shore? It would appear there is nothing. Certainly, by the greater number of people nothing has been done.

But when all has been surrendered in defeat, there remains an inner prodding, ever so subtle and conveniently ignored. This itch—for it is no more than an itch—if caught hold of and inflamed, placing candle wick to candle wick, could revolutionize the world. But it is a chain of events which has yet to occur. Should all the human race, if only for a moment, share in one vision, the transformation could be accomplished. There would then be no going back. For none would venture to return to the unhappiness he had previously and so grievously misunderstood.

Science is a noble and accurate pursuit. But it is an inscription on the outer surface of a box. What is within remains to be revealed.

The starry universe is a vast array of twinkling lights, as revealed to human beings from their earthly position. When they probe outwards into it, its configurations change, experience being magnified before them. Is it the same reality? Does it matter? The initial perspective stands. A subsequent is added, providing, it would seem, a more exact and complex interpretation of the original. Thus experience is a varied phenomenon. What is constant is the consciousness which displays it.

That consciousness holds fast when the brittle realm of experienced things is removed. For these latter were but an expression of it. There may be many other such expressions, since the resources of consciousness are of an inestimable plenitude. What matters is not the show, but the audience. The audience, viewing, hearing, seeing the show, is what endures.

The spirit can be approached by means of prayer or meditation directed toward Jesus, Mary, the saints, one's ancestors, a deceased Bodhisattva, or any other such departed person or persons. The problem with this practice can, and often does, lie in losing sight of the fact that it is universal consciousness which is being invoked, not a person.

In life, every individual is a limited expression of universal consciousness. When that person is released by death from material constraints, he or she assumes the character of universal awareness, while yet retaining the inner uniqueness (as opposed to the outer personality) which made him or her an individual. But it is not the inner uniqueness which is being approached by prayerful petition or meditative union. It is universal consciousness: that which creates, informs, and embraces all things, even those things which lack a faculty of discernment, such as a stone.

# Thoughts on Creativity, Spirit, and the Ethical Life

The true realm of causation is spirit. It is not material appearances. In spite of their powerful effectiveness, their impressive predictive capability, the causal relationships between material events break down under close observation. Thus one is left with probabilities, and, beyond that, mere anomalies. But the unfolding of events arising in spirit remains mysterious and beyond dispute. The future is what it is. And no ascertainable material entity controls it.

Events are as they occur, seemingly coordinated in the manner of their appearance in experience. But it is the fact that they happen at all which is of the greatest interest. It is only beyond this that the multitude and consistency of their relations captivates the attention. What is marvelous, an occasion for wonder, is that these are not absolute. Under careful scrutiny, they vary and become individual, rather than universal. A recognition of this should be enough to forestall any hubris concerning scientific achievements.

Why does life appear to be unfair? Is it because nature has not distributed its resources equitably? Or is it because individual people, in their attempt to get the better of others, go to great effort to make their victims feel the full impact of whatever lack they may encounter? It is both. But surely the greater weight of the burden lies in the misuse of advantage on the part of human egoism.

So much pain and suffering are caused by this behavior, it is a wonder people do not see it and strive to change the situation. Perhaps they do not wish to see it. For so many, when they do acknowledge the problem, prefer to dismiss it as inalterable and go on to magnify the evil. But how can any of this be brought to a close, if it is always embraced and never challenged? Why is courage in such matters so little valued? This indeed is cowardice!

Jesus of Nazareth was a man of great understanding and spiritual insight. His parables and sayings are transcendently beautiful. Filled with common sense and worldly experience, they nevertheless illuminate what is not easily recognized. But, in spite of the beneficial effect of his words, Jesus did frequently exaggerate. He did so for rhetorical purposes.

This must be acknowledged in getting a proper sense of what he meant. Otherwise, all is superstition and meaningless impracticality. Read his utterances carefully. Taken collectively, they are filled with profound wisdom. But considered separately and at face value, they offer little more than an excuse for manipulators to distort people's faith and bring their behavior under a harmfully deceptive control.

The belief in an afterlife originates in consciousness, which lies in the depths of human awareness as an encompassment of experience. Though an encompassment, it is also a center. For it has an independent life of its own. It is this independence which results in the conviction of an afterlife. Such a determination cannot be gainsaid. And it has troubled humanity throughout its history. In fact, the heightened self-consciousness arising from it might be said to be the origin of recorded history.

## Thoughts on Creativity, Spirit, and the Ethical Life

From the setting down of its actions for further reckoning, human awareness has become more richly articulated. There has been an increase in self-awareness and general inventiveness. Science, for example, was born out of this improved articulation, or separation of awareness from its material experience. But so has an increasingly murderous warfare and environmental exploitation.

What should be recognized is the fact that, though increasingly divorced from its material content, consciousness remains responsible for it. For in cooperation with universal spirit, human beings make their world. Consequently, they can change it for the better. But to do so, they must act together as a unified organism, sharing in the center of awareness which encompasses them all. This can be accomplished in a more meaningful and effective manner than is presently understood. It is not magic, but intelligent proceeding.

It might be difficult to understand how human attitudes could have an effect on the seemingly compact and inseparable relations of material causation. But it should be remembered that the roots of causation lie within the realm of spirit—i.e., within universal consciousness. As each human being is a direct expression of the fullness of spirit, and as a universal (or nearly universal) consensus in attitude removes any (or most) contradiction from the human community, spiritual causation may give life to unexpected material potentials.

This is not to assert that human beings can independently, or even collectively, *will* material change on a colossal scale. They cannot. But it is the case that the present waywardness and mutual obstruction in human attitudes and behavior impedes the unified functioning of spirit. The inherent good of the transcendent is confounded in the free, contradictory actions of its multiple human centers of expression.

Nevertheless, the faculty of personal self-awareness which has been granted by reason provides a ready access to the spiritual core. And this can be exercised for better or worse. For it is this access which involves, and has long involved, humanity in its material and spiritual destiny. The only question is how much such a human consensus would affect non-human events. This not having been put to the test, it is hard to say.

Food nourishes the body. The body supports the mind. Yet it is the life of the mind which is of the greatest importance. For the mind embodies spiritual life. Here is the justification for feeding the body. Does this not adequately express the spiritual depth and potential of human existence? So let it be that human nature should rise above its animal state, and that this should be done without ascetic extremism.

The physical appetites ought to be enjoyed in moderation and exercised with a considered discipline. But the approach to spirit through the mind (within the admitted limitations of the latter) is the proper destiny for humankind. Let this be universally acknowledged and its pursuit taken up with conviction.

An intense intellectual life may not be for all people. It must be pursued in accordance with the natural distribution of gifts.

## Thoughts on Creativity, Spirit, and the Ethical Life

And the paths of mental life are many. But good will and an upright heart are open to all. They require no special cultivation of gifts. They need only be decided upon.

There are many approaches to universal spirit. Meditation is one. Mystic unity another. But it is prayer which is the most common approach. A prayer takes the form of a petition and is generally submitted in expectation of a response. Moreover, it is addressed to a person. But person, by its nature, is a form of limitation. And there can be no limitation regarding the infinitude of spirit.

Yet it is within spirit and by its means that all things have been made manifest. So person lies within spirit as potential. It is this which is petitioned. And it is from this that a response may be expected. However, a desired response must be conditioned by the greater purveyance of universal harmony.

Is there an afterlife? Was there a fore-life? The former is yet to unfold. And the latter cannot be recalled anymore than a person born and bred entirely in the dark can remember an expansive blue sky. The conditions of spiritual preexistence do not coordinate with physical experience and would be summarily rejected as fantasy by the material mind. Thus, even if a fragment of such a pre-life were encountered in thought, it would appear to be no more than a dream.

To live is to kill—for food, for self-defense, for whatever reason. Those who pause in thought over this may be concerned with it. But they should not be overcome by the illusion of material life and its accompanying illusion of death.

Life is art. If lived purely, it is like a singing bird. Whatever has brought the melody forth, the result is beauty.

The apperception of beauty is the nearest approach the soul has to its sequestered self.

It is not nature, but imagination, which makes nature beautiful. Granted that nature supplies an abundant complexity of material to imagination's workshop. Nevertheless, it is the imagination alone which apprehends harmonious relations and recognizes suggestions of unity. As the flexible image-forming faculty of the mind brings various features under purview, reason fixes them vis-à-vis one another and holds the pattern for the satisfaction of the mind. Yet none of this is rigidly determined. Rather, it varies according to perspective, allowing for that richness of regulated suggestion which is the power of art.

International wars are often a product of vanity, either on the part of whole peoples or that of their rulers acting with the support of a majority of the people. Usually it is the latter case. In a pattern of unbridled arrogance and retribution thousands of lives are lost. Often in the course of the same, civilizations are wrecked.

What lies at the root of this? It is a desire to dominate. Or it is a determination not to be dominated. These two manifesta-

## Thoughts on Creativity, Spirit, and the Ethical Life

tions of egoism—for they are the same—move back and forth like a lumberman's two-handled saw, until the tree of moral restraint is felled. To put an end to this endless undermining of decency, the will to dominate must be set aside.

Individuals and nations should turn to creative activity to satisfy their need for recognition. Nietzsche's Übermensch (overman) is not a boot-stomping Nazi. He is a Michelangelo. And there are many kinds of Michelangelos. So creativity need be neither great nor small in its influence. For it is not a matter of degree, but of orientation of the human spirit. Perhaps the most enduring such creative expression lies in the formation of a sound moral character.

Should the infinite consciousness deign to speak, it would say, "Today I will pick up my brush and add another stroke to the composition of beauty. There are times when my efforts do not achieve harmony. But they lead to what does and are therefore as necessary as those which do. Yet it is neither this material element nor that physical thing which makes the composition. It is the emotional wealth rising from within as an epiphany.

"A successful painting is not communicated by means of this color or that line or another. It arises as a harmonious expression, a meaning, of the whole. I the infinite consciousness, like any artist, love my work. I am enraptured by dabs of paint, markings, and lines which must then be removed. For they suggest and make possible the final result. Every life, every thing, is a manifestation of the whole. Where each is sentient, it can be said to have a will. But such a will scattered amongst so many, like so many points of light, is the free expression of one will, my will.

"I have said that the final expression is emotion. For it is emotion which endures in the heart of my being: a warming of the eternal spirit in multiple expressions. This is not a matter of sequence. Sequence is merely a laying out in finite dimensions of the unlimited woven complexity. There is but whole cloth, inscrutable in texture and variety.

"Every life is my life. Yet it is complete in itself. For the individual is a focal point of the greater means, the entire weave a harmonious backdrop to each personal interest. Thus no emotion can be entertained alone, no set of emotions made independent of all others. Together they are a lake of fire, sending off flames in all directions, exhibiting heat and light as does a sun. Therein is the heart of infinite consciousness. Therein is the meaning."

The growing sum of emotional states in a human life is never static, but continually generating new states, one following another, the former forgotten in its successor. But these are together timeless and imperishable when considered as existing beyond their physical expression. For this reason, they cannot be understood spiritually as an evolution, but rather as subsisting transcendentally whole and complete in full richness and complexity of interrelation.

In addition, beyond the veil of material existence, each of these personal complexes of emotion is linked to others, flowing into and out of them in ways which are unseen. Consequently, together they are one, though individual, each being the focal point of all. So a sense of joy can be found in the fact that all are united, yet individual, sincere love for another person being yet a form of self-love.

Conversely, and unfortunately commonly, it is through a narrow focus upon physical life that the mind becomes estranged from its fellows. By means of an acquired condition exhibiting an emotional lack of inclusiveness fostered by an increasingly limiting material awareness, alienation descends upon the person. For the interconnectedness is then unfelt and therefore unseen.

Yet in the most intense moments of isolation such a solitary individual continues to long for a unity which he senses lying beyond recognition. Conflicting emotions are produced by this juxtaposition of an inner need for connection upon an attitude of alienation and enmity. And it is this which results in the manipulative desire to be admired at the expense of others.

A thought is never complete if entertained without a recognition of its origin and a consideration of its consequences.

Anger proceeds from a sense that the space between walls of physical or psychological limitation has been narrowed to an intolerable degree. So the bounds must be forced away, as did Samson with the pillars of a Philistine temple. Thus anger is a restoration of an assumed right of personal expression. In this way, Samson regained his moral dignity. Again, fear is not flight. It is pursuit in reverse, much as repulsion is attraction to some other condition—in this case the more desired condition. Thus fear is a pursuit of the condition of safety.

It can be seen from these remarks that the apparently negative emotions need not be understood as wrong in themselves. They may be viewed as positive expressions in which a redirection of purpose has been considered appropriate. For there has been an apparent obstruction in the original arrangement of their objects of attraction.

This discussion might appear to exhibit the character of a tour de force. But its purpose is to indicate that, insofar as the individual is concerned, the emotions always run true. Now, in a larger social context, a strictly personal orientation can contradict other emotion-generating values. For example, an expression of anger may appear in a communal context to be unnecessarily disruptive or destructive. And an exercise of fear may exhibit cowardice. So there is an evident conflict in commitments. One is to the individual, the other to another individual or a group. It is only this juxtaposition of opposing expectations which renders some emotions negative. For no emotion is wrong in itself.

Thus a higher purpose is made manifest: there is a moral law which is above the exercise of individual interest. That law is the practice of good faith. Human beings are social by nature. For this reason, they form commitments to others. The commitments give rise to both interpersonal and communal expectations. And those expectations are founded upon trust. It is a breach of trust which leads to the sense of wrongdoing.

It is impossible to demonstrate that there is a free will. Yet it is equally improbable that it can be proved beyond a doubt that the will is not free. Upon this dilemma rests the whole of philosophy. For, where there is the slightest hint of freedom, there is a hope of transcendence and perhaps even an afterlife. The chains of causation having been undone in the smallest conceivable sense open wide the doors of possibility, where a ghost of human duration may slip through.

Mark Twain is a master of the tall tale. The "stretchers" of fact that are contained in these stories are as broad and free as the continent was in his day. Here is an excerpt from one of two examples:

> My beautiful new watch had run eighteen months without losing or gaining, and without breaking any part of its machinery or stopping. I had come to believe it infallible in its judgments about the time of day, and to consider its constitution and its anatomy imperishable.

This story, "My Watch," is quintessential Twain and tall tale. The employment of animated words like "judgments" and "anatomy" give personality to the object. This personality changes course because the watch turns out to be an ornery cuss with a mind of its own. Twain forgets to wind it, after which it runs both too fast and too slow. When repaired, the repairs make it worse, until Twain declares:

> I gradually drifted back into yesterday, then day before, then into last week, and by and by the comprehension came upon me that all solitary

and alone I was lingering along in week before last, and the world was out of sight.

In his story, "Tom Quartz," a miner's cat of that name has a bad day, which begins by its falling asleep on a gunny-sack on top of a blasting charge about to go off. When the charge blows,

> ...about four million ton of rocks [*four million,* mind you] 'n' dirt 'n' smoke 'n' splinters shot up 'bout a mile an' a half into the air, an' by George, right in the dead center of it was old Tom Quartz a-goin' end over end, an' a-snortin' an' a-sneez'n', an' a-clawin' an' a-reachin' for things like all possessed.

Then

> ...it begin to rain rocks and rubbage, an' directly he come down.... One ear was sot back on his neck, 'n' his tail was stove up, 'n' his eye-winkers was swinged off....

The cat was thoroughly disgusted by this turn of events. And, as Twain puts it, "after that you never see a cat so prejudiced agin quartz-mining as what he was."

To surround oneself with art and beauty is to wrap the universal soul around oneself. It is that oversoul reduced to an individual human expression which seeks itself in beauty, art.

## Thoughts on Creativity, Spirit, and the Ethical Life

The ugliness which is expressed through the blindness of individual human nature is healed and forgiven in universal spirit. Thus, with the advent of death, this transcendence from a lesser to a greater state is as though the spirit had awakened from troubled, fragmentary dreams.

Heraclitus' example of a river presents no eddy or current which is exactly repeated, while its flow continues uniformly over the same stony bed. So why do people not apply this to themselves, when over the generations they are drawn to similar stories with recognizable emotions? Like the river's informal, meandering run, while remaining true to course, their individual responses are ever varying in the moment, but collectively unchanged over time.

The immortal element in each person is universally apparent in the arts. For the enduring spirit in these does not substantially change. Generations come and go in appreciation of this.

An educated person can learn facts. And she will embrace formulas. But a cultivated person increases in inward awareness. There is no measure common to them both. The one is informed, the other enlightened. Thus it is not education alone which will improve the human race. Rather, there must be an ennobling of heart and mind together. For a mind on fire with pure flames of well-directed emotion is eternal. Whereas a mind replete in cold knowledge is an ice-clotted sea.

George Lowell Tollefson

What will finally convince humanity of the supreme importance of an empathetic nature? Nothing but the removal of fear. For this is a darkness which sucks energy from living growth. Fear arises from a sense that one is cut off, alone. Human beings flourish in unity rather than division. Oh, but that this simple truth could be recognized and understood for all time!

People look with envy upon other animals, regarding their seeming simplicity as an indication of happiness. Yet animals also quarrel. But what is notable is that their quarrels are not translated into vindictiveness. Thus a human mind half-formed through poor instruction resembles a lesser creature in understanding but not in capacity for evil. Here it is superior. But, alas, why is it that there are so many such minds?

How much good a person has encountered is not as important as the amount of evil experienced. For evil forces good into contortions which serve its purpose.

Is it not strange that there can never be a length of peace which will not be disrupted? This is as true of nations as of individuals. For the disturbance begins in an individual heart and spreads like a prairie fire until it consumes the whole.

Freud thought the human longing for peace was a pining after death because he saw life as activity. And activity arrives at cross-purposes and conflict. But he was mistaken. Peace is not oblivion. It is a tranquility which has its birth in the heart. Only the inclination toward conflict is a movement toward death.

People pray at cross-purposes to their god, failing to realize that pleading narrowly in pursuit of a solution to one problem raises the unforeseen circumstances of another.

The educational process does not end. If the case were otherwise, the mind's development would not truly have begun. On its own merits, classroom instruction is good. But it is only training. The mind is an organism which must experience a steady intake of knowledge to nourish its understanding and keep it healthy. Thus the purpose of a strictly formal education is to tone the intellect, causing it to become accustomed to feeding and growth.

This resembles newly hatched chicks learning to search the ground for food as they see one another or their mother doing. Granted there is an instinctual impulse to do it on their own. But this is assisted by example. The result is growth, an increasing confidence, and eventual independence.

The last instance—independence—is where formal training leaves off. But the process so instigated must continue. In either case, human or bird, an idle mind reduced to repetition without enlargement of awareness is death. But in human beings, unlike the birds, the body can outlive mental death and often does.

August Macke, though short-lived, was an artist of intense color potency and grace. The power in his use of color is obvious. It brightens the canvas with an internal light. But his faculty of grace is less easily understood. For it is like the subliminal energy of Michelangelo's figures. Herein lies the mystery of genius.

All the enduring religions are based on a mixture of truth and imagination. The problem is that most believers never search beyond the imaginative ornamentation. They thus fail to grasp the underlying insights into the nature of spirit.

There is not one son of God. There are many: all of humanity. And the more appropriate term for God is spirit, or universal consciousness. That one consciousness is the consciousness of all. But where there is human individuation, universal consciousness is self-limited in its content. The present task for humanity, therefore, is to discover its closeness to spirit.

Human beings are not in any way separate from spirit, except in their own conviction, born of the illusion of limitation. To transcend the material and its consequent physical divisiveness in order to reaffirm the unity of spirit is to discover the integrity of existence. The apperception and affirmation of this discovery is what will lead to social harmony—an end to wars, poisonous social relations, adversarial individual disagreements, and all the folly that has clouded human history. When such obstructions are removed, the horizon of human understanding will reveal a clear and united vision. And a new age will have begun.

## Thoughts on Creativity, Spirit, and the Ethical Life

What constitutes a true work of art is not some great difficulty encountered in understanding it. Nor is its eminence the result of whatever interest scholars may take in it. Their labors cannot add to its value. For that value is intrinsic to the work. A work worthy of long term appreciation must stand upon merit.

For example, it may be that Homer is read today largely by scholars and by students in a classroom setting. But the value of his work lies in its ongoing life. The moral principles expressed in the *Iliad* and the *Odyssey* may seem foreign to a modern reader. But that is unimportant. It is the truth to human nature which matters. Because of this, alien mores, seen through the eyes of those to whom the tales were originally delivered, can yet be relived.

This is why Aeschylus, Sophocles, and Euripides can still be staged. Though unfamiliar in their attitudes, they continue to live in the imagination. Shakespeare, Cervantes, Tolstoy, and Dostoevsky will likewise become foreign to distant readers. But they will live for those who go to the trouble of experiencing them. They will do so because of their truth to human nature.

In Spain, near the beginning of the seventeenth century, there was a popular poet named Góngora. He chose in later life to make his work richer, but also increasingly obscure and difficult. This became a fashion. And literary Spain eventually fell into what some consider an eclipse of obscure writing. It is an unfortunate fact that preciousness in art is lethal to its wide appreciation and perhaps eventually to its long term destiny as well. Every writer, painter, sculptor, and composer should be mindful of this.

T. S. Eliot was a gifted poet. But what was the purpose of the introduction of foreign languages into his verse? Was it to impress? To impress whom? Surely there are none who would be edified by such an unnecessary obfuscation. Whatever strengths there may be which gird his work and give it power, they do not come from this obstacle to immediate understanding. For it does not serve the purpose of arousing insight or inspiring emotion. Rather, it is an unfortunate exercise in vanity.

It is also true that Goya and Bruegel unveiled the seamy side of human nature. But a tragic strength and beauty arises in the first and an insightful humor in the latter. However, for those determined to paint ugliness for its own sake (they will not be named here), let them understand that this is not an aesthetic practice. A mountain of skill cannot raise up beauty where it does not contribute to what is ultimately a positive response. Such art will not live beyond the misdirected fashions of its time.

Good supports good, positive purposefulness undergirds expressive power. Ugliness for its own sake is negative and sinks into a morass of weakness and irrelevance. For it represents a withdrawal, a retreat, from the challenges of life. How can this inspire? What would it inspire, though it should momentarily prop up a cowardly age? The return of vigor, love of life, and courage will sweep it away.

## Thoughts on Creativity, Spirit, and the Ethical Life

O. Henry (William Sydney Porter) lives and will continue to live because he knows the human heart. His story lines are generally slick rather than adroit. But for all this he is grounded in a genuinely sympathetic emotion which any sincere and unpretentious reader will recognize as her own.

The beginning of wisdom lies in an ability to discern the difference between shallow intellectual display and genuine insight. So beware the philosopher whose language smothers rather than reveals his meaning. This is mere show. It is not substance. It is no more to be admired than clouds which cover a blue sky and block out its light.

Now what is certainly true is that some ideas are exceedingly difficult to express. Language is not a thin, transparent film over reality, but of a clumsy, obscuring density. It is also true that some eminent thinkers may not be skilled writers. Allowance must be made for these considerations. The clear-sighted and practiced reader is generally capable of the distinction. He will almost unfailingly ferret out the genuine from what is bombast and deliberate obscurity. But on certain rare occasions, it can sometimes take generations to sort this out.

If it is said that imaginative literature is moral philosophy, it is in contradistinction to ethics that the statement is made. Ethics concerns itself with general principles, while imaginative literature is occupied with a delicate counterbalancing of emotions and wills. This is what must be studied if an emotional intelligence is to be developed.

It is in reference to personal feeling that the behavioral patterns of others can be understood and a ground for social norms set forth. And it is imaginative literature which explores behavior in these terms, whereas a determinate establishment of the social norms falls under the aegis of ethics. Thus it can be seen that a study of moral philosophy should precede the development of an ethics.

The desire to surround oneself with beauty is an attempt to achieve the concordant relations of the transcendent. Within a purely material framework, beauty is estranged from experience. Yet its representation must be sought in physical harmonies. But these do not reveal themselves without the participation of the heart. The spirit knows its own character and seeks to project it upon external things, though they be alien to its feeling. For no person can grasp the ineffable beauty of universal spirit, except through the heart, which is its expression.

Moral harmony, like the refinements of great music, is rarely attained and much to be sought.

War is an expression of egoism. Alas, human beings are almost universally egoists!

Humankind at large resembles a child building a sand castle and destroying it with glee. An entire city of great edifices might have been built were it not for this.

## Thoughts on Creativity, Spirit, and the Ethical Life

Cultures come and go, not because people outgrow them, but because they pass beyond themselves. Losing sight of what they were, they cannot discern the original meaning of what was.

Employing material means and knowing only these, why does the imagination seek worlds beyond its experience? Is it not that there is something within the human heart which is immaterial? This something is the indestructible unity of spirit, or consciousness. For herein rests the origin of striving after the mind knows not what.

Now what is to be made of such an awareness which will not subordinate itself to the divisions and limitations of physical experience? Should this seat of emotion subordinate itself to what is alien and repugnant to its desire? It cannot. And all the wounds of experience and fabrications of the intellect will not make it so.

The character of a prophet does not necessitate prediction. This may or may not occur. Principally, a prophet acts as a moral witness, much as an imaginative writer of merit does.

In imaginative literature, anything which deepens or extends insight lends itself to greatness. But an expressive device which merely occludes or muddies thought without further penetration represents nothing more than a submission to fashion. This will pass into obscurity.

For an individual to ignore his spiritual core is for him to become hollowed out and brittle in self-awareness. So it is with a society as well.

A true philosopher has a vision of life, like an artist. He does not create philosophy by much thinking, but rather by deep thinking. His vision should encompass the whole of existence and cover it with meaning.

Philosophy was once thought to be the love of wisdom. This does not imply that the philosopher has achieved wisdom. Rather, it means that she pursues it and embraces it insofar as she is able. For wisdom is not some grand esoteric secret. It is simply an understanding of the relationship between a human being and her experience—that is, her broadened sense of the whole of experience, not just her own.

What is egoism? It is the acceptance that the self is material and therefore limited. It is also a thrust against that very acceptance without its relinquishment. Thus egoism is a paradox, the stumbling block of human existence.

Consciousness is imperishable. Only the appearance of it within a material context is perishable. For it is not the consciousness which is limited. It is only the context of limitation which makes it appear so.

Happiness is having an imperishable purpose. This can be as simple as living a good life. Practice generosity of spirit. And

## Thoughts on Creativity, Spirit, and the Ethical Life

that spirit will grow the practitioner to those dimensions which are fitting to him.

The legacy of science is both its power and its narrowness. The power cannot be disputed. For it is determined by it effects. But the narrowness results from the fact that, aside from its mathematical formulations, science operates entirely from the senses. Yet there is much in human experience which is not a product of the senses.

Throughout history, human beings have always attributed the dark side of their nature to the physical appetites. While it is true that the physical appetites play an important role in human waywardness and deception, there is something deeper. That something is material-mindedness. Until humankind learns to adopt and put on spirit-mindedness, it will continue to wander in darkness.

A woman of the twenty-first century does not live in the context of the time of Napoleon. Therefore, she thinks she did not exist then. But this is not so. For every person inhabits a timeless realm of universal spirit. All are coexistent in this. They only differ in the particulars of material experience given to them.

It is presently held that the material universe is both finite and infinite. But it is not infinite. It is indeterminate. The universe is finite because it is material. And what is material is an expression of finitude, or of limited things. But the universe is indeterminate because it comprehends not only all that is material in experience, but all that is materially possible, without extending beyond finitude.

There are laws organizing such phenomena in certain ways because the mind requires order and will discover or produce it wherever it ventures. But there cannot be a closed system of the finite, lest both material possibility and the flexibility of the mind be cut off. That is why the material universe is indeterminate.

Spirit is universal. But as self-limiting, it expresses itself through each individual person and each individual thing. Science demonstrates that the earth is at a far, insignificant corner of the universe and that humanity appears at a distant moment in earth time. But in spirit human beings are like the spokes of a wheel, each fastened firmly and directly to the hub. Though this is true of all things, as all things are expressions of spirit, the fact remains that each human life, while mentally unaware of it, is consciously rooted in timeless eternity.

To experience a great work of art from the past is to experience the artist directly, soul to soul. And, what is best, all the pettiness gained from a material life of toil and struggle is left out of the relationship.

The beginning of wisdom is, first and foremost, for each person to see herself as a living intelligence.

### Thoughts on Creativity, Spirit, and the Ethical Life

A great artist in any medium exhibits two characteristics: superior insight and superior craftsmanship. Both are important. And both are looked for by the connoisseur, in fact by any person of educated taste and sensibility.

Causation can only be assigned where there are clear conceptual relations. Where these concepts and their relations become unclear or confused, causal thinking is inhibited. The only way through this impasse is to clarify the concepts and their relations. This can require the abandonment of old concepts and the adoption of new ones. The new ones will have different relations more fitting to the situation.

The mechanical interpretation of classical physics breaks down at the level of minute investigation. When a bullet flies through the air, its "instantaneous" velocity can be determined at any point or instant because it is reduced to an infinitesimal at the same time that the calculation of it is reduced to a limit. But, when matters are consistently observed at this minute level, as in quantum mechanics, then the classical conceptualizations break down altogether.

Truth ought to prevail. And truth is an ever-moving target. Therefore dogma is the enemy of truth.

The reason human beings seek recognition and remembrance, even to the point of death, is that they recognize their grounding in spirit. They know that their consciousness is not like their body or the material world around them. It is indivisible and indestructible. But there is no other evidence for this in their material experience. So they seek recognition and remembrance.

Every sentient creature, particularly the higher forms, is centered upon and aware of spirit. But only human beings, so far as is known, have the combination of imagination and intellect which makes them capable of projecting themselves out of themselves into a quasi-material state of immortality. Though they do not have a clue as to what this might be.

Is there an afterlife? Impossible to know. Is there no afterlife? Very difficult to accept. Is there something not subject to dissolution and extinction? Yes, consciousness. Not consciousness of this life. Just consciousness. The hope is that something of this life, a preservation of personal identity at least, can be carried over the boundaries of material disintegration.

Imagination is the seedbed of reason.

Reason is disciplined imagination.

Consciousness is the only indisputable fact.

The senses can lie because they must always be interpreted.

## Thoughts on Creativity, Spirit, and the Ethical Life

Faith is the willingness to set foot on indiscernible ground.

The knowledge of God is subject to revision. But it is not the knowing which is revised.

Facts belong to one another more than they belong to the human mind.

The root of free will can never be discovered because, if it was, it would no longer be free.

Good character can only be discerned on the common ground of good character.

The intellect—i.e., reason—is a product of this world. It may be understood as a creation of evolution. And imagination may be seen to work like a kaleidoscope, endlessly shuffling the particles of material experience into new combinations. But what pushes these processes forward into previously unencountered realms is not a product of material experience. It can be simulated in thought. But it cannot be precisely accounted for by reason and imagination, the very instruments it so adroitly employs.

In art, beautiful expression and inventiveness are important, but only if they reveal a deeper meaning relevant to life.

Emotions and physical needs cannot easily be ignored. But to live only for them, even largely for them, is to live a purely animal existence.

The human mind, purified of ego and appetite, is the instrument of spirit. But this does not mean that it *is* spirit. For it is only the material means, enabled under these special conditions, for it to look into itself toward spirit.

Not just the first time a person looks at Cézanne's work, but every time he does, Cezanne shatters his vision and then puts it back together again.

Van Gogh's paintings are expressions of the universal spirit of God, present and burningly alive in everything.

Velázquez put the entire emotional and intellectual history of humanity into every face he painted.

Rembrandt painted material things with such loving fidelity, it is remarkable to conclude that he saw it all as an expression of spirit.

Hemingway's shorter short stories exhibit an unrivaled perfection of form and depth of insight. Yet he is principally known for his novels.

Scott Fitzgerald's longer short stories, like *The Rich Boy, The Diamond as Big as the Ritz, The Bridal Party, The Last of the*

## Thoughts on Creativity, Spirit, and the Ethical Life

*Belles*, and *Babylon Revisited* should, along with the novel *The Great Gatsby*, be the principal reason he is known and admired.

The brevity of the Japanese haiku exhibits a Zen-like focus on timeless experience.

Emily Dickinson was a profound metaphysician who expressed her philosophy with the apparent simplicity of a child. To encounter the natural imagery of her poetry and not recognize the deep thought is inexcusable.

Only when human beings rise above what they know to encounter what everyone is sure they do not know do they achieve the essence of what it is to be human. This is the spirit of *Don Quixote*.

It is fascinating to remark how nature periodically defies classification. It makes a person wonder: does the classification originate in nature or in the classifier? For example, are Venus flytraps and sundews more of the character of plants or animals? Why in quantum physics does causal thinking break down, if not for an increasing lack of clarity as to classification? And do not irrational numbers defy the classification of numbers? Even the efforts of Georg Cantor only partially restore a sense of successful classification in this case.

So it would certainly seem that classification is an effort of the human mind to organize that which only partially cooperates with it and which at regular intervals defies the effort. It makes no difference whether what is being subjected to such organizational labors is apprehended through the senses, like the behavior and structure of carnivorous plants or the experimental results in subatomic research. Or whether it is conjured through the inventive faculty of the mind, like mathematics. For classification in either case can neither be entirely intrinsic nor totally extrinsic to whatever is under investigation.

Spirit in its own intrinsic nature does not yield to material classification. It cannot be understood in this way. Moreover, what it submits to human awareness in the form of material experience, it submits in such a way as to be only partially amenable to classification.

Philosophy is an art form. Though it differs from the arts in that it seeks a direct, rather than an indirect, expression of the truth. In this it resembles the sciences, though it is not limited to the material.

In John Steinbeck's short novel, *Of Mice and Men*, a reader can hear the still, sad music of humanity. It is the story of two men looking for peace in a world where meanness of spirit is often the rule.

George is "small and quick, dark of face, with restless eyes and sharp, strong features." Lennie is best described by the fact that "his arms did not swing at his sides, but hung loosely." He is severely mentally challenged but possessed of great strength. As George says of him, "Lennie ain't no fighter, but Lennie's strong and quick and Lennie don't know

## Thoughts on Creativity, Spirit, and the Ethical Life

no rules." Of their past troubles, he observes, "All the time he done bad things, but he never done one of 'em mean." George travels with him to watch over him and keep him out of trouble but sometimes wonders, "God a'mighty, if I was alone I could live so easy."

They have a dream: to buy a small farm and live outside that circle of meanness, of low-spirited humanity they have come to know so well. But as itinerant farm laborers they cannot avoid coming in contact with what they would rather avoid: a man like Curley, who loves a fight he thinks he cannot lose, and Curley's wife, full of too much loneliness and a need for any kind of attention.

There are good people in the book, like one-handed Candy, the swamper, who dreams of peace and security, and Crooks, the Negro stable hand, who longs for the human society he is consistently denied. Among them also is Slim, the jerkline skinner, who is "capable of killing a fly on the wheeler's butt with a bull whip without touching the mule." There is "a gravity in his manner and a quiet so profound that all talk stopped when he spoke."

Steinbeck understood the struggle of modern man, so often caught alone and exposed without community. His major characters long for compassion and decency. Fundamentally hopeful and good, they are like a brook that sings in the mountains, unaware of the hot, dry country that lies ahead.

Ideas are the vehicles of human thought. But in themselves they are limited and imperfect because, when unaided by other sources, they must rely strictly on material experience. However, certain kinds of insight can be deeper, arising, as they occasionally do, from spiritual influences on emotion. The emotional reorientation following upon such influences then creatively enhances the development of what are often surprisingly radical new ideas.

Mathematics is strictly a creation of the mind, with the exception that its development is initially suggested by physical experience. Its capacity to be employed in an understanding of nature arises from the fact that the mind is also involved in the conceptual apprehension of the physical world, albeit that it does not create the order of physical events and is only partially employed in determining their relations. Nevertheless, the mind's activity in both mathematics and perception is what makes it possible for them to be wed in a functional union.

With the exception of its experience of pure consciousness, the human mind can only encompass limitation, or the finite. Thus it can conceive an indeterminacy, as in an unending progression of natural numbers. But it cannot conceive the infinite. For any definitive look into the progression of natural numbers discovers only finitude. It is for this reason that the extent of the universe must be said to be indeterminate, rather than infinite. It is also for the same reason that a particular line segment cannot be understood to be divisible into infinite points. Rather, its divisibility is imaginatively indeterminate.

What is at issue here is a peculiar characteristic of the human mind: it can transcend its own functional limitations by imagining a limitation beyond any already determined limitation. Therefore, it is assumed that this can go on without end, which it can—mentally. But this is an imaginative sleight of hand. For finite conditions are never transcended in the process. They are merely repeated through a progression of mental associations.

It is impossible to experience nature without interpreting it. It may be experienced sentimentally, copying the attitudes of others. Or it may not. But an encounter with the natural world will always find a place in the mind within a framework of imagination, emotion, and a final conceptualization arising from these two.

Even familiarity with some aspect of nature, or a preoccupation with something other than nature, cannot remove this inclination, deliberate or otherwise, to interpret it. Nature is never lodged cold and indifferent in the mind, except that it be deliberately conceived as cold and indifferent, which, of course, is an imaginative and emotional approach to it.

The reason for this invariable reliance upon interpretation is that nature is complex and mysterious. Not only is it so. But it is vitally important to human interests, no matter how remote and sheltered from it those interests may appear to be. For human beings experience themselves as a part of nature. They coax their sustenance from its seemingly kinder side. And they proceed in wonder, sometimes fear, of the other side. Altogether, it is perceived as an extension of themselves, or they of it. So they must continually invest it with meaning.

George Lowell Tollefson

All things, including personhood, arise from universal spirit. But this does not mean that universal spirit is bound by personhood. It is not a person, though personhood should proceed from it. Rather, the fact that personhood has its origin in spirit indicates that spirit may in some sense be understood to be capable of responding to a person in a personal manner. Thus human beings can relate to it on a personal basis.

There is no need to deny the possibility of reincarnation. But there is good reason not to emphasize it. For an emphasis upon it becomes an expression of egoism. It creates a differential (even deferential) sense of status. What is important is that a person should fulfill her purpose in life. To discover that purpose may require an extended and labored search over many years. Or it may not. In either case, the realization of one's innermost being, and a drawing of one's life purpose from that realization, is what matters.

Language is exceedingly opaque. To translate the imagery of mind into words, sentences, and paragraphs generally requires a considerable effort. It is an effort to close the gap of inexactness to a minute level. So beware of the first attempt. It may not express what is truly meant.

It is a curious thing to consider animal intelligence at its various levels. There can be no doubt that the higher forms of sentient life feel pain, fear death, even experience grief. What seems to set humanity apart—and this can only be a matter of speculation, not certainty—is its power of looking forward and backward in time in an abstract manner. Also, in the cases of pain and death, there is an increased imaginative working up of complications in the matter.

So it may be postulated that humanity suffers more—suffers more than the particular experience would indicate, were it not imaginatively augmented. Could this, then, be a reason to suppose that there is more in store for human beings—an afterlife perhaps? Why the added misery, if there is no compensation? Did human awareness evolve simply as a plaything of an unlimitedly cruel universe? Why must it be supposed that the universe is inherently cruel any more than otherwise?

If the universe is governed deterministically by a mechanism of material laws, perhaps cruelty is the answer: human bones ground up in the iron gears of a merciless necessity. But there is much that is not explained by a material mechanism. And it is here that any hope for a better explanation of human destiny may repose.

A closed system of thought can be described in terms of a Euclidean circle. Any point on the circumference of that circle is a function of all the other points. But no point can be distinguished until one is arbitrarily designated. The one point having been designated, the other points can be described in relation to it and to each other (with an ultimate reference to the original point).

In general, human knowledge rises out of experience in this way. The experience is a chaos, which is equivalent to nothingness, until something within it is made a point of reference.

Then other aspects of experience are organized in relation to the point of reference and in relation to each other with an ultimate regard to the original point of reference.

What has just been described is, of course, ideal. Oftentimes knowledge is organized in isolated eddies in relation to unrelated points of reference. But the goal is the same: complete organization within a closed system of mutual reference. Why has this never been achieved? It is because such a closed system is to be developed within the mind of a person or persons.

But the disparate information which appears within that mind cannot be guaranteed to be entirely systematic within itself. Following the systems of thought already formed, there may always be anomalies which do not fit their pattern, not to mention the concepts with which the patterns are constructed. For concepts, however concise, are also patterns with relational references within themselves and to other concepts. So the mind spreads its web of ideas concerning that of which it cannot be certain will fit its ideas or the web of relations they inform.

Now a closed system—say classical mechanics, the theory of gasses, or the theory of relativity—may be verified repeatedly by experiment. But this does not guarantee its stability. For, as the science progresses and advances the technology of its investigations, it encounters new experiences which bring unanticipated impressions to the mind. These impressions may not submit to the existing closed patterns of thought. Therefore, a new pattern must be created. And it will be isolated to relations which fit the new impressions. This is the case with quantum mechanics.

But what then? Shall, say, classical mechanics, the theory of gasses, or the theory of relativity be explained in terms of the quantum relations? Perhaps. And perhaps one or another of these, say the theory of relativity, may be used in conjunction with the quantum relations. But, as the sea of contrarily eddying systems becomes ever more complex, it must reach a point where the continual recurrence of anomalous impressions on the mind weakens the whole. Here it becomes obvious that the idea-forming mechanisms of the human mind lag behind the input of its incoming impressions of experience. There may be corrections and reorganizations. But in the end the limitations of the mind are revealed.

If one carries an intellectual investigation far enough into the most minute recesses of thought and observation, be it a matter of physical phenomena or a question of free will, the result will be the same. Cause-and-effect relations and other means of classification will break down. For the mind cannot settle these issues with anything approaching an absolute finality.

It is incumbent upon any person to find the principle of joy which lies at the core of her being and live by means of it. This only appears to be difficult because the false facade of the material self stands between the true self and the individual whose nature the true self is.

Universal spirit, or universal consciousness, is good, not because it satisfies individual wishes or even the collective wishes of humankind. Neither is it good because it fulfils a conception of perfection concocted by a materially limited mind. It is good simply because it exists and because all things emanate from it. In this sense, it can be understood as good for each individual person because it is who that person is.

Life in the spirit is perilous because to achieve it a person must learn to balance himself upon the thin edge of a razor. It is simply too easy to fall to one side or the other into a state of material-mindedness.

It is not the afterlife which should be sought, though it may well be the case that there is one. The goal is an absolute life, a life truly lived in all its potential. This material life extends beyond either limit of its span. For it partakes of the timelessness of its essential being. And it is this timelessness which gives it its meaning.

When rightly understood, it is not wrong for a person to dislike her own personality. The personality is a shell formed from the hard knocks of material experience. It is not the true person. But the true person can be felt. It sits back and observes the passing show of physical existence, sometimes with indifference.

As a person approaches a deeper understanding of her immaterial self, she is freed from the limits of the material. She understands that her personality is a flawed construction, patched over with sticks and sharp stones to make an impermeable covering. She sees in the spirit, in the depths of her own consciousness, that peace, joy, and freedom are her true heritage. This is who she really is. It is where she needs no protection, no impermeable shell.

For this reason, she draws apart from her human personality. She understands the accumulation of culpable misjudgments which have encrusted it, causing its creation of the shell. It is true that she cannot discard the shell during the tenure of her physical existence. But, knowing it is not who she is, her heart becomes light, her mind cleared of its burden of misrepresentations. Misrepresentations there may need be. But they are not a death warrant.

Human beings do not know what love is because all human love is based on a core of animal selfishness. Every altruistic act is so based. Empathy is no more than a placing of the love of self in another's situation. Human love is founded upon the experience of personal limitation. Consequently, to attribute such a thing to universal spirit, with its lack of limitation, is meaningless. Material and spiritual things alike emanate from universal spirit. They have their being in this all-embracing consciousness. Therefore, "all-embracing" is a sufficient term for the relationship of spirit to humanity. It is advisable to leave any human conception of love in its limited domain.

In a universe of continual flux and limitation, perfection is a meaningless concept. No one thing is sufficient either to itself or to the whole. And, if the whole is sufficient to any limited thing, it cannot be known by the limited thing. Neither can it be known by the collective plurality of all things. So the idea of perfection is no more than a human chimera.

A genius is someone who combines the open intelligence of a child with the determination and focus of an adult.

A high intelligence quotient can be useful, if there is imagination and discipline to go with it.

Unbridled egoism is a sign of low intelligence, except where there is a necessary defensiveness against injury.

The wastefulness and frequent impotence of war make its ineradicableness seem ridiculous.

The most profound lesson of war is that, while in the midst of fighting it, a soldier must restrain any impulse toward empathy. He may indulge a "bleeding heart" before and after his immersion in the acts of war, but not while carrying out his soldierly responsibilities. This necessary restraint of emotion does not authorize unwarranted acts of cruelty, though war is inherently cruel. It merely illustrates the otherworldliness of the experience. It is something no thinking combatant ever forgets.

No person can find her authenticity in another person. That is too much. A limitless gulf separates each material person from another. But a person can locate her authenticity in the unity of

## Thoughts on Creativity, Spirit, and the Ethical Life

all persons, provided it is the unity and not the persons which is emphasized. For all persons together are one person. And that one person is the true self of each individual person.

For a material mind, the greatest mystery is a plurality in one, in which each member of the plurality is not a part but the whole of the one. It is like dividing a loaf of bread into twelve slices, in which to devour one slice is to devour the entire loaf.

In quantum physics the concepts of complementarity, non-locality, and the uncertainty principle provide excellent examples of the breakdown of the human mind's categories of understanding. For they seem to challenge the mind's construct of space and its dependent property, incremental time. It appears that the idea of distance, upon which space and incremental time depend, no longer applies.

For example, take complementarity. This principle, put forward by Niels Bohr, holds that physical phenomena at the particle level may be understood either in terms of waves or particles. In other words, they may be described by means of wavelength and frequency, or by means of energy and momentum, but not completely by both means at the same time.

Wavelength includes the concept of space, while a particle does not. A wave occupies space inasmuch as it is conceived to be extended in space. But a particle, when being conceived as a particle, is not extended in space. Insofar as its physical presence is concerned, it is treated as a point mass, something which may be conceived to exist *in* space but is not *of* it. So space (as distance or location) is handled differently in the two cases. This places spatial concepts themselves in question. Do these phenomena occupy space? Or are they merely observed in space?

Again, there is the case of non-locality. If a beam of ultraviolet light is split and two lower energy beams of red light issue from it while being directed toward different locations, entanglement occurs. Whatever one photon in a particular beam does, the other photon in the other beam simultaneously mimics in some way, as if there were no distance, or separation, whatsoever between them. So here at the microphysical level apparent distance does not indicate separation. The two beams, or the two photons in question, are one. And location is irrelevant.

What is peculiar is that this occurs in carefully observed experiments. The impressions on the mind which result from this observation must be judged to be *real*. Thus a clear explanation is that space and its dependent property, incremental time, are constructs of the mind. These constructs, when introduced into a close observation at the microphysical level, tend to break down. For they are no longer relevant. Or, at least, they cannot be applied.

What clearer indication is there that the human mind itself is the author of space and incremental time? Where the mind's application of the phenomenon of locality is too much "squeezed down" to apply, locality becomes meaningless. Those impressions on the mind, which are the observational points of the experiment, are rendered free of the mind's control.

## Thoughts on Creativity, Spirit, and the Ethical Life

The same is true of the uncertainty principle. Because incremental time is a function of space, or distance undergoing change—insofar as time is measurable, or incremental—a momentum and a location cannot be simultaneously observed. For to identify a location implies a state of rest. But there are no states of rest in a momentum. So it must be one or the other.

So, yes, when observing the results of experiments in particle physics, the impressions on the mind are definitely real. But they are of necessity observed outside the envelope of spatial and temporal structure created by the mind. There is, of course, still a temporal sequence accompanying these events. But it is non-incremental in character. It is so because, within the experiment, there is no comparative spatial reference by means of which to measure it. Nevertheless, it can be tentatively referenced to those incremental temporal events within which the experiment takes place.

Though a person may at times dislike a number of his fellow human beings, he should acknowledge that he and they are together one spiritual body. And that is God.

Spirit is fully expressed in every individual human being. Thus the actions of every person, however reprehensible in appearance, are acts of God. In all people collectively, there is one great movement toward the final good.

Were there only an experience of things and events, there would be no need to posit a consciousness. One could simply speak of experience. But consciousness is also aware of itself apart from things and events. Therefore, it must take itself alone into account.

Every philosopher is a cripple insofar as she is a philosopher. For she habitually neglects the cunning aspects of the world. This is to say that the majority of human beings move about in this world on the crutches of dissimulation and deceit. Yet it is the philosophers, hobbled as they are in practical matters, who will gradually lead them to deliverance from themselves.

Human beings have always prospered by having good memories. Thus they are enabled to study and apply formulas received from others. But this can lead to a slavish imitation and repetition. It is only original deep thinking that builds upon the learned recipes.

Unimaginative people often think imaginative people are stupid because they, the unimaginative people, do not understand them. In varying degree, the unimaginative people pertain to the great majority. It is for this reason that they have so effectively retarded intellectual progress throughout history. Nor is it a protection for the progress of imagination that many people be well educated. For education is no guarantee against this problem.

There is something unique and penetrating to be gained from the pictorial arts which is characteristic of those arts alone. Rembrandt's painting, *Bathsheba*, is a nude. She is sitting

## Thoughts on Creativity, Spirit, and the Ethical Life

down and has apparently just read a letter King David has had delivered to her. Expressions of doubt, hesitation, and desire are in her face. The king, who is her husband's military commander-in-chief, is tempting her into adultery. He is, after all, the monarch. And her husband, Uriah, has not been a caring spouse.

That is the Biblical story. But there is more here. It is a beautiful image. The woman is attractive, but not in the idealized manner of representing flawless skin and body. She is real, a faithful representation of a living person. Nothing is hidden. But her nakedness is the baring of sensitivity, the revelation of a soul in the complexity of its vulnerability and contradictions. The result is intimate and tender, honest and fully developed.

There is much which can be gained from this painting and others like it: a deeper sense of what it is to be human. Because of its unblinking realism and extraordinary insight, Rembrandt's work is Christianity at its best. Vincent van Gogh, another Dutch painter, once remarked that there is a little of God in Rembrandt and a little of Rembrandt in God.

When the development of an idea has not completely formed itself in the mind, it will continue to elude it. It flickers in and out of thought like a scent of roses, no sooner carried in by a breeze than wafted away. This is perhaps a safeguard against an ill-formed thought gaining a hold on the mind before it can be properly utilized.

It comes as a surprise to discover that old age is not a time for a carefree disregard of life. There is, if anything, a greater clinging to it. Projects, which were disregarded in youth, suddenly emerge with a greater urgency. Were it not for a reliance on the will of spirit, and a belief in the fulfillment of its purpose, this sense of urgency could take on the characteristics of a panic.

In any political system, especially a democracy, there should always be a well-educated, open-minded, intellectually creative minority. The people at large should be taught to respect, though not worship, this minority. Thus, over time, its best insights will filter through the entire population.

This is the way in which a society may be entrusted to evolve toward a greater understanding of and absorption in spirit. It may also work to impede the confusion and downward spiral of idle minds. For an increasing immersion in egoism, sensuality, the cruder elements of emotion, and triviality of thought has long been the fate of most nations and nearly every democracy.

People have often been inclined to confound consciousness with intelligence. They are not the same. Consciousness is fundamental and without precedent. It is contingent upon nothing but itself. Intelligence, on the other hand, is an adaptation of consciousness to material experience. As such, it reflects the character of the material and is conjoined with it. To perceive the material is the beginning of intelligence. It is also what intelligence subsequently builds upon. Whereas the faculty of awareness alone is consciousness. It is prior to anything of which it might be aware.

Any development of a new concept directly involves mental images. To accomplish this in the midst of an ongoing process of reasoning, the concepts under consideration are first reduced to their supporting images. This is done in order to free the images from their definitional constraints. For definitional constraints are what combine the images of properties into a concept.

A definition makes a concept inflexible by asserting the precise nature of its properties. It is for this reason that the definition is removed from the concept. And the freed images are restored to their flexible status. Once rendered flexible, these images representing properties are enabled to be interchanged. So it is at this point that they are recombined to create a new concept.

But, prior to such a creative change, there is the matter of recognizing an association of properties between the original concepts. This is what determines the logical relations between them. The logical relations suggest the insight which brings about the creation of a previously nonexistent concept.

Thus, in the syllogism

> All men are mortal.
> Socrates is a man.
> Therefore, Socrates is mortal.

there are the individual statements, "men are mortal" and "Socrates is a man." These statements are concepts incorporating other concepts as properties. In other words, within these two greater concepts, there are the lesser concepts, "man," "mortal," and "Socrates," which are referred to variously as the subject and predicate terms of the propositional statements. It is these which function as the properties of those statements.

When the two statements are brought together by an association of their properties in the above syllogism, they are both subsumed under universal quantifiers. In this way, the properties within them, "mortal" and "Socrates," have been brought into association through the property "man," (or "men") which is contained in both statements. As a result, the associated properties, "Socrates," and "mortal," are removed from the two original statements and incorporated in a new statement. Thus the concept, "Socrates is mortal," is created.

Far from being a ham-fisted artist, Van Gogh was a superb draftsman. Examine his sunflowers, his early drawings of Borinage mining folk, his portraits and self-portraits, his boots, his chair with a pipe on it. These pack extraordinary expression in a few lines. If there was no grace, delicacy, or refinement in his work, it is because there was no artifice. His vibrant, pulsating color was like his drawing. His brilliant landscapes were thought and felt with an intensity that compares with an act of creation from the movement of will alone.

# Thoughts on Creativity, Spirit, and the Ethical Life

A person must commit to an idea in order to form one. But such a commitment to ideas increasingly limits the capacity to progress beyond them. Hence the painstakingly slow development of civilization. Einstein was committed to a Spinozistic view of the world. This material objectification of reality made it impossible for him to accept the Copenhagen interpretation of quantum phenomena.

The only way a person can know anything well is not to know a lot of other things. This is one of the great disappointments in life. However, it is also paradoxically the case that any genuinely creative fertilization of the mind requires a crossing over from one body of knowledge to an unrelated one. This is what happened when Darwin read Malthus.

Reason is a fallible instrument. But it is what human beings have. When they do not reason, they let others control their minds.

Cunning and wisdom are opposites. For this reason, no ruler can be completely wise. It is possible for a ruler to combine cunning and wisdom to a certain degree. But they remain separate within her as opposite states of mind. And, given the nature of rule, cunning must be dominant overall.

Faith falters. An honest and sincere heart is steadfast. Therefore, the latter is greater, even when it is agnostic or atheist.

Honesty and sincerity are closest to the ground of being, since they attempt to touch upon what it is.

Genius is not talent. Talent is necessary to genius. But talent alone is insufficient. Focus of mind and purpose, arising from determination and drive, fix genius upon the consciousness of the world.

In philosophy, to express unclearly anything that can be stated clearly is wrong. For a deliberate act of obfuscation is an attempt to mask a thesis insufficiently thought out.

To love guns for the power of destruction they convey is to not have seen what they can do or to lack the intelligence to understand what has been seen. Weapons are sometimes necessary. But they must be possessed and handled with a full regard for what they ought not to do whenever possible.

Democracy is an instrument of voluntary social harmony. It is based upon personal discipline as opposed to external coercion.

Hatred leads to an increase of personal isolation. The greater the hate, the greater the isolation. Infinite hatred is self-immolation.

Intolerance leads to ostracism. And ostracism is spiritual murder.

**Thoughts on Creativity, Spirit, and the Ethical Life**

Not all acts can be tolerated. But, where this is so, the acts must be disapproved without a rejection of the person.

To become aware of another person's conscious nature is to recognize an infinity which is already familiar within the observer.

Great natural catastrophes unite people. War is a manufactured catastrophe. But rather than unite, it can destabilize a republic by shifting its center of interest and power to a war-making effort. For in such a situation, individuals do not matter.

All laws, sacred or profane, are made for people, not people for the laws. But, while blind obedience is to be avoided, a change in law is a weighty matter and should not be taken lightly.

To worship anything is to worship human institutions. To embrace something with all one's heart, mind, and soul is not to worship it. It is to love it.

Universal consciousness—spirit—is more fundamental than a heartbeat.

Life is ephemeral. As a fowl is plucked from the barnyard, so is a person removed from material life. Nevertheless, few would forgo their moments of physical existence.

Love life. But do not be consumed with it. To do so is to lose perspective, to become self-centered, to work toward a fragmentation of society.

It is wrong to persecute, to openly disapprove of another person's orientation. But an even greater evil is to be enslaved to every form of appetite.

A life without meaning is a life without purpose. A life without purpose is a life without direction. Material limitation narrows possibility and demands direction.

An independent sense of time sets instinct and impulse aside.

To be aware of things independent of their material origin is to recognize the source of human misery and joy.

Complexity and subtlety of emotional response are the essence of great works of art. They are the justifiable reason that life, amidst its pains, limits, and frustrations is thrust upon its often unwilling participants. Out of the struggle of material existence comes an enriched awareness—the intellectual appreciation of an emotional life which transcends physical experience.

All people are motivated by a desire for power and influence. There are no exceptions. But the desire is expressed by means of varying alternatives. Some want to control others. The pursuit of money is such a case. For wealth is power. And even a philanthropist is exhibiting such power. He decides how the money, removed to his possession, should benefit those without it. The nature of political power is obvious, though it can sometimes be devoted to service. Artistic, philosophic, and scientific creativity are also expressions of power. But they channel the grasping instinct into influence rather than control.

People who cannot dominate will often associate themselves with those who can. They cling to associations, ethnic groups, nationalities, religions, and military service. Because power is distributed within such organizations, the vanity at its center is somewhat nullified in appearance. But these are the most lethal of all the means of suppression. For their numbers trump the advantage of personal vanity and obstinacy.

Time gets shorter with age. This is because a person measures a span of time against a total accumulation of it in her memory. The greater the accumulation, the shorter a particular span.

Natural rights exceed democratic practice in importance. The first of these rights is to know the truth.

A common attitude is: if I cannot rise to the top, then I will pull the top down. This is why it has been said that Shakespeare did not write his plays, Euripides was a bad poet, Van Gogh was mad, Poe wrote as an alcoholic, and Emily Dickinson was an uneven poet.

George Lowell Tollefson

Democracy is not founded upon reason. Clear and independent thinking is a rare virtue. Were it the foundation of democracy, democracy could not exist. Rather, democracy is based upon the personal discipline of self-restraint. But, when a society becomes rich and powerful, its people turn inward towards self-indulgence and hedonism. Self-governance is lost. And popular government becomes distorted and dysfunctional.

The inner person is sacred. Yet the outer parade of personality often destroys it.

There is much bitterness in the human heart—a seed which rankles in what should be nurturing earth.

Two legs or four: a bundle of vanities encircling a core of appetite.

No one is exempt from the evils of humankind. Would that it were otherwise.

Living is difficult because mental fulfillment is continually thwarted by pettiness and wounded vanity.

The sensitivity of a child is soon replaced by the hardness of an adult. An innocent mind seeks every avenue. The adult, imprisoned by social concerns, peers through a very small aperture.

## Thoughts on Creativity, Spirit, and the Ethical Life

Much of speech is idle, back-biting, and self-adorning. But a child's naïveté begins in freedom.

Why fear gentleness and kindness? Where else, in the midst of so many thorns, can beauty, simplicity be found?

Fear of physical death ushers in a death of the spirit.

Who can hold to the simple emotion of kindness in a gale? The plant withers from too much drying.

People often strike out to counter a blow they have not received.

One person bent on increasing his power has more resources than the many who are merely free.

Financial increase is political. A free people should guard against its extremes.

Lawyers and capitalists are necessary evils which should be kept under strict control.

Though selfishness and greed infest capitalism, there are also positive results. Keeping the latter uppermost is the problem.

The founding fathers were largely of the moneyed class. So they failed to put a firewall into the Constitution between money and political practice.

Lawyers do many useful things. But there is little ethical restraint upon their actions. This should be corrected, and severely so.

A respect for the integrity of other nations, whatever their internal organization, should be a hallmark of a democratic republic. Markets and special interests should not govern its behavior. For these are a danger to its freedom. Unfair external relations with other nations corrupt the internal affairs of a republic. It was so in Rome and Athens. It is so now.

A person of few words and consistent action exhibits gravitas.

A people must choose between military power and political freedom. Rome chose the former and gave up its republic. The choice was brought about by greed in milking the provinces.

No one accumulates wealth for the sake of the toys it may buy. Money is power.

A demagogue draws power to himself. A true leader confers it upon others. Anyone can rule by command. Only a few can lead.

## Thoughts on Creativity, Spirit, and the Ethical Life

Not all issues can be resolved by agreement. Hence the need for tolerance.

There is one truth. But there are many understandings of it.

Agape, or universal love, is nothing more than a respect for others. It is not an emotion.

Intolerance loves tyranny.

Tyranny in the interest of overcoming tyranny is still tyranny.

Once intolerance is accepted, tyranny is affirmed.

Political opponents deceive one another. But they should not deceive the people. This is a thin line, almost impossible not to cross. So it should be made subject to repeated correction.

A free press should distinguish between fact and opinion. The temptation to blend the two enslaves it in emotion.

An emphasis on profits leads to market expansion. Market expansion characterizes a consumer economy. This brings on heavy advertising. Advertising exploits sex and egoism. The public becomes preoccupied with physical appetites and vanity. It is a turning away from others and common social goals. Hence social division and enmity. Hence the breakdown of a republic.

Democracy nurtures individualism. But if individualism leads to selfishness, the democracy is ruined.

The senses are material. Feeling and emotion evaluate. Reason judges. Thus a three-way tug of war is created in which the quality of life hangs in the balance.

Modesty is an expression of self-respect. It is not a loss of self-assertion. It is self-assertion grounded in honesty.

A lack of self-restraint is a sign of weak character. To be in command of oneself is to be in command of one's circumstances.

Empathy and compassion reflect intelligence.

Democracy thrives upon empathy and compassion. It withers in the absence of it.

A sharp tongue cuts with ferocity and little skill.

Insults shatter social cohesion and harm the perpetrator.

A demagogue can be recognized by his appeal to emotion and not to reason. He knows that if a person is encouraged to think, that person will not submit to being controlled through her emotions. She must be appealed to on her own rational terms. She does not indulge in the excitement of the mob.

## Thoughts on Creativity, Spirit, and the Ethical Life

Religion provides democracy with moral weight. But it cannot govern the state. For it demands a suspension of reason.

In Mark Twain's *Adventures of Huckleberry Finn*, man's inhumanity to man is a point of interest. And another is personal responsibility for that inhumanity. In chapter sixteen Huckleberry Finn and the slave Jim are on a raft on the Mississippi River, attempting to free themselves from the vices of civilization.

Huck's conscience confronts him. It is in a state of confusion: the heart rising up against social convention, as in the play *Antigone*. Huck has been brought up in a society which leads him to believe a slave is property. And to understand that helping one escape amounts to stealing. So he ruminates, " I got to feeling so mean and so miserable I most wished I was dead." He decides to secretly turn Jim in at the first opportunity.

As he pushes off from the raft in a canoe to go ashore, Jim says, "Jim won't ever forgit you, Huck; you's de bes' fren' Jim's ever had; en you's de *only* fren' ole Jim's got now." Huck relates, "I was paddling off, all in a sweat to tell on him; but when he says this, it seemed to kind of take the tuck all out of me." When Huck is fifty yards out, Jim adds, "Dah you goes, de ole true Huck; de on'y white genlman dat ever kep' his promise to ole Jim."

"Well, I just felt sick," Huck continues. "But I says, I got to do it—I can't get out of it." At that point, a skiff comes along with two men on it armed with guns. They stop. And one of them says to Huck:

> "What's that, yonder?"
> "A piece of raft," he says.
> "Do you belong on it?"
> "Yes, sir."
> "Any men on it?"
> "Only one, sir."

The men are looking for runaway slaves. But Huck cannot betray his friend for the sake of his conscience. So he lies.

Experiencing this story, the reader finds herself asking, What is more important, the dictates of a community or the demands of personal feeling? It is not a simple question, since a response from either source may be an expression of superficial reasoning. Yet it is the same heart which must be examined to determine and weigh whatever truth may lie in both.

Deregulation and laissez-faire economics destroy the middle class. Without a middle class, democracy destroys itself.

People who have not learned to reason carefully, or have learned to set reason aside in the interests of belief, tend to support demagogues.

Science is reasonable. But little understood science is not.

Too much wealth and power in one sector of the public undermine discipline in the other.

# Thoughts on Creativity, Spirit, and the Ethical Life

A focus upon consumption increases appetite. And appetite enslaves desire.

Factionalism suits a person divided against herself. Heal the inner division and social harmony will prevail.

Demagoguery fears change. Yet change is a fundamental principle of life. So demagoguery supports the suppression of thought in order to insure that its manipulation of opinions and emotions will not change.

Democracy depends upon thinking things through. Opinions are a drug designed to prevent this.

Intoxicants diminish true courage. Their consumption exhibits an unwillingness to confront life and solve its problems.

Anger masks fear. An angry society is afraid of moral courage.

Know when the way within you is right. Know when it is wrong.

Beware of cunning. Limit its use. For it pushes wisdom out of the mind.

An animal nature must be brought under control if a person is to become human.

Slaves seek guidance and self-control from without.

A heart on fire with enmity is at war with itself.

Each person is a cornerstone. The inner strength of the cornerstone builds the castle.

Fads in opinion are silent destroyers.

What a person is must be born within him, not borrowed from the advantages of others.

Intelligence recognizes goodness. It is not a formula or a creed, but a condition.

Envy works to suppress others without increasing the merit of the suppressor. An elevated moral character does not seek to suppress.

Vanity knows no limits. So put it into creative work. Do not use it to limit others.

Low social station often seeks to make other people fools in a fool's opinion.

Lack of respect creates a sense of oppression. Avoid showing disrespect.

# Thoughts on Creativity, Spirit, and the Ethical Life

Free speech can be broad in application. But it need not be uncivil.

Sincerity is the only definition of truth. There is neither a fact nor a law of nature or life that may not be put into doubt. But sincerity does not pertain to particular facts or laws. Rather, it concerns the nature of an individual's relationship to whatever situation, fact, or law may be at issue. Thus truth is principally a matter of relationship between a human being and whatever he surveys. And sincerity is the means of determining it.

The particular circumstances which require a sincerity of approach are those which compose the relationship of a human being to something. For all circumstances must be relegated to a human relationship when they are brought under human consideration. If the situation involves human action, the matter may be one of practical ethical interest. For such a relationship may express how a person should act toward another individual or behave within a social environment.

On the other hand, the character of the relationship may be intellectual. It may concern an approach to certain facts or to a physical law, where no immediate physical action is required. But in either the ethical or the intellectual case, the human position, if it is to be one of truth, must be one of sincerity.

For example, a person who is involved in a situation should clearly apprehend the circumstances. He must be sincere about what they are. For if the circumstances are vague, his determination of how to deal with them will be vague. Where his determination is vague, he will not be sincere. He will not be in truth.

He must also desire a truthful outcome. Such an outcome is to be reached by the shortest path. Sincerity is that shortest path. For it involves no deviations. There cannot be an insincere approach to a sincere outcome, since it would lead away from the outcome. There cannot be a dishonest approach to the truth. Sincerity and truth, which are the same, are a matter of conduct. Sincerity is an act, be it physical or mental. Truth is the goal. In other words, sincerity and truth may be considered a means of transport in which the vehicle and destination are the same.

This issue of sincerity holds firm in art, a discipline sometimes thought to demur in matters of truthfulness. For a work of art is generally understood to be an independent object of a purely inventive character. But, though the artist does leave his work to its independent destiny, he leaves the stamp of himself upon it.

This results from the fact that in art there is an enduring relationship between a creator and his created work. So for others the value of such a work depends upon its truthfulness. And the truthful quality of a work of art depends upon the honesty of the ideas and emotions expressed within it. It also depends upon the penetrating insight of the artist. For not only honesty, but penetration of mind, are products of sincerity.

They are interrelated, as more can be seen where the seeing is accurate, clear, and deep. The more seen and seen correctly, the more a sense of truthfulness is gained. So sincerity is the guarantor of insight, accuracy, and clarity. In these there is no sidestepping of any issue but a going straight to the truth. For their role is the removal of vagueness.

## Thoughts on Creativity, Spirit, and the Ethical Life

For instance, in a painting, the motifs, lines, and colors are merely so many instruments of expression. Alone they have but neutral value. So, to achieve penetration and power of insight in what they convey, they must be employed in a manner that is deeply sincere. They must be arranged with a profound honesty of intellectual proportion and with emotions carefully pruned by reason. In short, they must be true.

Sincerity applies to philosophy as well. It determines the verifiable and the unverifiable. For even the most unverifiable speculative concepts, such as are found in metaphysical thinking, ought to conform to reason and experience, however indirect and tenuous that conformation may appear to be. In other words, even the most abstruse metaphysical speculations should not be in conflict with what is rationally and experientially verifiable.

For this is what philosophical concepts do. They provide an intellectual fulfillment, or at least a greater comprehension of relations, where completeness of such relations derived by means of induction from experience is unachievable. They bring about a rounding out, as it were, of those gaps which are always encountered in the employment of the limits of human understanding. In this way, they allow for a greater integration of human understanding. What they should not do is fabricate an utterly alien world, which has no roots whatsoever in the trial and error of thought and action.

Finally, when it comes to the relationship of the scientific investigator to the facts or laws he seeks to uncover or formulate, sincerity is his assurance that any fact or any law which he puts before the world is promulgated in naked and honest simplicity. This sincere approach is what makes science universal and useful, not the supposed enduring value of the revealed facts or discovered laws in themselves.

For these latter may be subject to change. But, once certain facts or laws have been set forth and verified by experiment, the sincerity which has set them forth brings with it an assurance that those facts or that law may be depended upon until further research carried out in the same manner reveals something better.

If human beings teach themselves and others that their actions are separate from the concerns of the material world, and if they see spirit as unconnected to life, then they will buffer themselves with possessions and search exclusively for physical comforts. In this frame of mind of insulated self-regard, they will continue to damage themselves and the earth.

So people must come to an understanding that the material world is an expression of spirit. And they should acknowledge that every form of sentient life possesses a ground of awareness similar to their own. Each kind of animal differs only in the apparatus with which it processes the information it receives from its environment. All are conscious. And all may even have a sense of self, albeit not articulated in symbolic or abstract terms.

If humanity were to give up its intellectual arrogance and assume its place in nature, then the question would not be, why are human beings spiritual in aspiration? It would be, what is it in nature which makes them so? When people un-

## Thoughts on Creativity, Spirit, and the Ethical Life

derstand that human intelligence is not different in kind from that of other animals, but only in degree, they will be at a beginning. They may go further and ascertain that imaginative life exists in other beings as well.

There is no mystery of the human mind. The only mystery lies in the character of awareness. Human awareness is a product of both spirit and nature—that is, of consciousness and its content. But the content is also a product of spirit. Thus it is spirit alone which is the origin of human awareness. Whatever mystery there may be lies within spirit alone.

Instinct alone cannot provide a means of coping with the unlimited variability of environmental circumstance. For this reason, all or most sentient life, even that of an ant, must possess some measure of independent awareness which it can act upon freely. In other words, it must act upon more than instinct or reflex, sensory or chemical response.

For example, an ant behaves in a manner for which instinct would be an inadequate explanation. As has been observed, an ant, being isolated in a bathtub in which the sides are too slick for it to scale, finds a wooden-handled rubber plunger in its path. So it climbs onto the rubber bottom of the plunger and circles it repeatedly. But finding that these efforts do not improve its situation, it climbs up the wooden handle.

Arriving at the top, it circles it, reaching out in all directions with its forelimbs. Finding that this does not produce the desired result, it descends the handle and begins to circle the rubber portion of the plunger again. Still unsuccessful, it repeats its ascension of the handle, at the top of which it intermittently stretches out to its body length, forelimbs grasping at nothing, probing in this manner at varying points of a 360° circumference.

In these circumstances, the ant not only exhibits an instinct for survival and a persistent desire to continue its foraging expedition. It demonstrates incontrovertible evidence of its being in a state of confusion—a confusion of which it is conscious. It cannot solve its dilemma. Yet it persists in repeated attempts to do so. That a faculty of reason is little evident cannot be denied. Nevertheless, the ant is clearly aware of its predicament.

It does not persist in a single course of action. Nor does it follow a fixed sequence of variants. Rather, it freely adjusts its actions within the limits of its capabilities. And when these do not work, it repeats them in new combinations. Particularly remarkable is its extending itself into open space in the hopes (dare it be said) of discovering something upon which to fix its grasp. Clearly, this is a creature exhibiting something more than the rigid mechanisms of instinct.

The environmental impact of a specialization in reason is great. For it has made humankind the dominant species. So, in light of the mind's nearly exclusive focus upon a material context, and in consideration of the fact that people are spiritual beings, a form of empiricism is suggested which would consider both consciousness and the phenomena of sensory input as originating in one source.

# Thoughts on Creativity, Spirit, and the Ethical Life

The spiritual and material elements within human awareness are thus seen as components of one unified experience. For a mental awareness, as well as any phenomenon of which it is aware, is grounded in spirit. This applies to all of nature's expressions, whether considered together as a whole or as independent objects apart from the whole. A human being is firmly rooted in spirit, as is a bird or a horse. Moreover, since material phenomena in general arise from spirit, a plant or a stone cannot be denied this dignity.

Argued from an evolutionary viewpoint, where did sentient life get its will to survive? Instinct? But why does it have this instinct? Evolution? Then how did evolution select what was not originally in existence? Would not a survival instinct already be necessary for natural selection to preserve it as a favorable variation? A creature must first will to persevere in the face of environmental constraints. Otherwise, selection could not occur. Or at best it would have occurred up to the present time with the greater uniformity of plant life.

Clearly there is more to the human spirit, to the animal spirit as well, perhaps even to plants, than simple mechanics. Some greater underlying unity must decree the evolving harmony of being. In living things it is the unity of spirit. Spirit supplies the unity of matter. This unity is recognized by means of laws because there is a unity.

The human mind initially perceives all things in unity because the mind is a unity. Unity is *a priori* to the mind, since consciousness, which is a unity, is prior to its content. Because consciousness is a unity, the study of nature must begin with an acknowledgment of this unity. Only subsequently should an understanding of the various modes of differentiation be undertaken.

No animal operates within a rigid structure of instinct. Such a creature would lack the flexibility of action necessary for survival. Thus an ant makes choices which lie outside the domain of instinct. And to make such choices requires an associative capacity, however crude. Without such a capacity, no interpretation could be given to events and no meaningful choices could be made. Thus, in having the ability to make choices, both a person and an ant are on common ground, separated by the degree of development in their breadth of awareness and power of association.

A human being is more than her physiological makeup. She is a person. For she interacts with her environment, both internal and external, in complex ways. But a materialist would insist that a lack of knowledge of all the causes which lead to a decision is no excuse for assuming that a deterministic explanation of a person's actions is unobtainable. And certainly from an isolated causal perspective this would seem to be the case. But the question is: is it possible to know all the determining factors in such a case? And is it feasible to discern their variable relations?

Let a plethora of desires and fears affecting a decision be imagined. Consider ever so minutely the vaguest impulses originating in a response to both memory and immediate circumstance. If they could be put together without an omis-

## Thoughts on Creativity, Spirit, and the Ethical Life

sion of any of them and be measured like kernels of corn in a bushel, a person might arrive at a mechanical summation of the whole. Or they could be divided into positives and negatives and thrown upon a set of scales to reckon the greater weight. Thus might a decision made by a person be preconceived as causally determined.

But, not only might a person respond to a problem with a complex of impulses great and small. She would also be reacting to the impulses as they occurred, and to her responses to those reactions as well, arranging the whole in ever-increasing combinations, then subtly reorienting her mind to them.

All this nearly instantaneous mounting up of determinations and responses is not a matter of simple additions of vectors of will and emotion. It is a dynamic building of a cloud of multidimensional complexity. The result may appear to be predictable. But not the process. For that is indecipherable.

Can the precise location of a bullet be determined while it is in motion? Can an instant be reduced to zero duration? The bullet is continuously moving against its background. Precise measures of motion and time are conveniences of calculation, not realities. The situation is no different with interrelated fragments of will and impulse.

In the physical world, processes which are closely scrutinized in what are inevitably crudely observed circumstances, are prohibitively complex in their hidden details. It is true that impressively accurate predictions can be made on such a basis. But they are nonetheless rough and inexact.

In matters of thought and behavior, the process is organic. A living organism is more subtle and complex in its interactions within itself and with the world than is the relationship of a speeding train to the background it moves against. For an organism, particularly a thinking organism, is a dynamic complexity which is more than the sum of its parts.

When Euclid asserts in his fourth definition of Book I of the *Elements* that "A straight line is a line which lies evenly with the points on itself," he means this: Given the flat, two-dimensional Euclidian plane, a straight line's points can be duplicated in the plane. Then, given any two points on this line, when these are matched with any duplicate pair of points on the plane, all other such points on the line and in the plane would coincide to the extent of the line's length.

Moreover, if the line were to be further extended in both directions, the additional points on the line and the matching points within the plane would continue to coincide. Whereas a curved line might be lain upon two of its duplicate points within a Euclidean plane in a manner in which the remainder of its points would not coincide with its duplicate points in the plane.

What is the purpose of a third dimension? It is the means by which a human being conceptualizes himself as a separate existence. For it is the mental act of withholding from general objects those sensations which are equated with the self that accounts for the division between objective and subjective awareness.

# Thoughts on Creativity, Spirit, and the Ethical Life

From this form of distancing, a person extrapolates a sense of depth which he applies to himself and to the variations in shape and relation pertaining to those external objects not equated with himself. For they thus assume a relationship to him of varying depth. And they have the same relationship to one another. It is in this way that a third dimension can be understood in distinction from two dimensions. Hence the experience of three-dimensional space as human beings know it.

If a work of art is meaningful, it is a moral object. For a moral object is judged according to an emotional standard. In other words, it is evaluated. Moreover, the combination of varied emotions united under a concept, which constitutes the expressive character of a work of art, is what provides it with meaning. This meaning informs a mood which, in turn, is reflected in an attitude. So what an artist is attempting to convey is an attitude. Attitudes are moral in character.

Much (though not all) of modern art is thick in invention and thin in meaning. It would appear that too much of one dilutes the other. This works in either direction.

In the nineteenth century Henry David Thoreau described "the mass of men" as leading "lives of quiet desperation." What did he mean by this?

A twentieth century American poet provides an answer. The poet is Theodore Roethke. And his response is expressed in the thirteen line poem, "Dolor." He states, "I have known the inexorable sadness of pencils,/ Neat in their boxes, dolor of pad and paper-weight,/ All the misery of manila folders and mucilage." This heavy-toned description of inconsequential objects makes a reader want to laugh.

But continuing, he speaks of the "Desolation in immaculate public places,/ Lonely reception room, lavatory, switchboard." It is the deadening routine and orderliness of modern life, particularly at the clerical and secretarial level of employment. There is an undeniable loneliness and emptiness in it. It is "The unalterable pathos of basin and pitcher,/ Ritual of multigraph, paper-clip, comma,/ Endless duplication of lives and objects."

The modern world, especially at the blue and pink collar level, yet also in the professions, is a world which has forgotten what beauty and life mean. It has become a place where "dust from the walls of institutions,/ Finer than flour, alive, more dangerous than silica" sifts "almost invisible, through the long afternoons of tedium,/ Dropping a fine film on nails and delicate eyebrows,/ Glazing the pale hair, the duplicate gray standard faces." It is the world Thoreau was referring to, but in its more recent form.

Fear of death comes from believing in a fragmented self. In letting go of that self, a person does not cease to exist. For he is not that fragmented self.

All things are referenced to oneself. Oneself in all things.

## Thoughts on Creativity, Spirit, and the Ethical Life

Philosophy stands midway between poetry and science.

An attitude is a confluence of emotions bound within a concept.

There is no truth that does not have its opposing truth.

A love of peace demands that people fight for it. How then peace?

Consciousness is indivisible. There is but one consciousness.

An inner life is the outer radiance of spirit.

Truth yields its secrets slowly and always beneath a veil.

Thinking makes people intelligent. Reflection makes them wise.

Fear is the source of "original sin."

Fear springs from limitation.

A person who lives or dies for others lives or dies for a larger self.

A science of the mind must begin with the question of consciousness.

It is impossible to be entirely benevolent. Nature would not have it so.

Love is respect. Anything else by that name is either concupiscence or mere sentiment.

War begins in a single mind. When it is unsuccessfully waged there, it is carried into the world.

A life without meaning is a life without purpose.

A life without purpose is a life without definition.

The beauty found in nature and art is found in oneself.

The ideal of democracy is to give reason command over vanity and appetite. Where the market governs, vanity and appetite have command over reason.

Knowledge knows the world. Wisdom knows its worth.

The stars fascinate because the night sky keeps a safe distance.

Cruelty proceeds from the pain of a sense of personal limitation.

Democracy begins with the truth of equality and ends in the illusion of sameness.

## Thoughts on Creativity, Spirit, and the Ethical Life

One thing's distinction from another can only be understood by means of the other.

It is said that a bird sings to declare its territory, and not for joy as the poets had originally thought. Yet it sings with all the might of spring in its heart.

Consciousness is the greatest miracle.

A healthy appetite for life demands obedience to its limits.

A contemplative life is well lived though no word of it should ever get out.

A concrete wall is neither boastful nor belligerent. But it will not do to run into it.

Turtles are not slow in the water. One must carefully choose one's medium of expression.

The sky would not appear to be overcast if there were no sun. It is expectation that makes the difference.

Rebellion is the hallmark of youth. Individualism comes later.

It is not the work of genius that matters. Nor is it the genius. It is what goes into the making of such.

To see an experienced fighting man freeze under fire and behave bravely in the next crisis is a lesson in modesty.

False pride is wrong. No pride is self-defeating.

The human ego cannot be suppressed. It can only be displaced to something or someone other than oneself.

The knowledge that red, round, and sweet go together to make an apple is in the mind of the perceiver.

All events are external to the self. Death is an event.

People cover themselves in knowledge in the hope of being warmed by the truth which has always been within them.

There is more strength in soft manners than there is in the finest steel.

Unrefined iron will not hold an edge. Neither will an undeveloped mind.

Human beings desire good and do evil when they desire good only for themselves.

There is no such thing as energy. There is only change and proportion.

## Thoughts on Creativity, Spirit, and the Ethical Life

The theory of evolution is final-cause thinking. It asks: how does A fit into the larger context of B? In other words, what is the purpose of A?

The body perishes. But the inner spirit endures.

A neglected mind is like driving at night without headlights.

A good poem will incandesce into meaning.

Insight is the stored up treasure of the mind.

The school of war has no graduates.

All religion tends toward a spiritual state. But it also degenerates into social control.

If it does not lead to insight, logical thinking is sterile.

Democratic republics are generally short-lived because people become so self-engrossed they lose respect for one another.

The rights of a people demand self-discipline.

A free market cannot become a free-for-all and remain free.

Where wisdom fails, only the cunning survive.

## George Lowell Tollefson

A sense of beauty arises from the discovery of a striking exception that does not offend the harmony in which it is found.

Irregularity is the essence of life, the very rise and distinction of it. Yet every living thing longs for the peace of regularity.

The trouble with a period of great social unrest is that it is so difficult to tell whether it represents the birth pangs of a new order or the death agony of an old one.

A clean heart, a clear mind—the essence of a noble character.

Pleasure leads the mind toward serenity. Pain focuses the mind and withdraws it from a complacent serenity.

Success or failure are relative. But a sincere effort is always the same.

Islands are separated by water. But beneath the water they are connected by land. Likewise, judgments of difference and similarity are relative to the penetration of one's vision.

Any attempt to gain historical insight necessitates a willingness to look through an opaque glass.

In an age of frivolous distractions, habits of reflection will have been thoroughly routed.

# Thoughts on Creativity, Spirit, and the Ethical Life

Jesus said that, for those who have, more will be given and, for those who have not, what little they have will be taken away. What this means is that spiritual growth must be fed. Otherwise, it will be starved into nonexistence.

Jesus said that the only unforgivable sin is to blaspheme the spirit. Spirit is both unity and forgiveness. It rights a wrong by bringing it into its own inner harmony. So, if rejected, how can it forgive?

Why are people willing to be gullible fish, responding to every form of market bait that is cast in their direction?

Human beings are capable of being more than spiders spinning and abandoning convoluted riddles.

There is so little evidence of good. Yet there is reason for believing in it.

Science is a good thing, so long as no one makes a god of it.

Worry is like a capacitor. It can store up enough energy for a big bang.

When the works of Plato and Aristotle are considered together, they exemplify the way reason contradicts itself.

### George Lowell Tollefson

Courage is steadfastness of purpose.

When the heart is sincere, there can be no greater risk than belief without evidence, no greater folly than unbelief in the face of it.

When Americans have completely lost their superstition that the Constitution is sacrosanct, they will have lost their political freedom.

Probability demonstrates that things can be organized in such a manner that room is left for indecision and doubt.

The beauty of a flower lies in its chaotic orderliness.

There is nothing like illness to illustrate the grandeur of health.

Money confers the ability to lead without charm.

A person is tense when not in control. He is tense often.

Pity is most convenient when expressed from a position of eminence.

Laughter is the acceptance of what is not right in the world.

Injustice is the norm. To ignore this is to become unjust.

## Thoughts on Creativity, Spirit, and the Ethical Life

Quantum physics is disturbing because it reveals the inconsistency underlying all things.

Human beings live within a bubble of reason. There is nothing more frightening than what lies outside of it.

Shakespeare and Milton can be heard from a great distance, walking in their noisy galoshes of language.

People are best at what they love because they love what they are best at.

To find one's true vocation is not easy. For to do so one must shed the false opinions of others.

The only person worthy of praise is one who is not in need of it.

The only praise of God is to live in the spirit.

Universal consciousness is spirit. Human consciousness is spirit. That is as close as human understanding can get to the matter.

Spirit is indivisible. It is always entirely in one place. The question is, where is that place?

Universal spirit sees the sparrow's fall because the sparrow is universal spirit.

Jesus is universal spirit. He tried to teach his disciples that they were also universal spirit. They did not understand.

Universal spirit sees beyond the suffering of this world. Lack of sufficient vision is this world's greatest source of sorrow.

Human truths are relative. They fall back upon human limitation.

A revelation held to be incontrovertible is a blockage of the mind's freedom to enquire.

Never trust final authority. Nothing is final in this world.

It is good not to be blinded by shallow alternatives. There is a danger in such choices.

Science activates the curious and disturbs the complacent. It is restful to neither.

It is a sky full of winds, fast moving clouds, and breaking lights that refreshes. Life is movement and change.

Calm, gently moving water brings peace. It is modulated change that soothes.

Music, like water, can be shattering, glittering, moving in one flow.

## Thoughts on Creativity, Spirit, and the Ethical Life

There is no such thing as time. There is only the change by which it is measured.

Logic is the illusion that one proportional relationship is superior to another.

People who reason much often have little to say. But what they say matters.

Great poets express truths difficult to grasp, even for them.

Philosophers speak truths that fragment over time. But they know their manner of speaking will not.

Universal spirit is outside of time because time is not universal.

By dwelling in the past and future, a person neglects to live in the moment. Yet she is always in the moment.

The enduring self is consciousness, not the content of consciousness. For experience does not beget consciousness. Consciousness begets experience.

The mind of universal spirit is not reason. What it is is unknown.

Human reason cannot transcend its material origin. Yet all things are grounded in spirit.

Socrates said that people would do only good if they understood the truth. But, as Heraclitus pointed out, most people do not want to know the truth.

Ego and the search for physical satisfaction make up the sum of most human lives.

Philosophy is the consolation of the few.

The vigorous style of the Roman historian, Cornelius Tacitus, exhibits, as his translator, H. Mattingly, says, "a lively imagination and a quick wit [in which] he is manly and high-minded, and ... capable of genuine moral indignation." Mr. Mattingly goes on to point out that Tacitus is fond of short sentences and that he is "a great stylist—perhaps the greatest of the Roman Empire." He refers in the same introduction to Tacitus' "somber magnificence" and "mordant wit."

One of the earliest and shortest of Tacitus' works is the *Germania*. Written in 98 C.E., it is a colorful description of German customs, ways of dress, and attitudes about war. The German tribes were never conquered by the Romans, which is not to say the Romans did not try. Caesar Augustus, the first Roman emperor, was often heard to lament the loss to them of three legions in an ambush in Teutoburger Wald in 9 C.E.

Tacitus says in the *Germania*, "The liberty of the Germans is a deadlier foe than the tyranny of the kings of Parthia."

**Thoughts on Creativity, Spirit, and the Ethical Life**

Parthia, now a part of Iran, was a powerful enemy on the eastern limits of the empire. Tacitus compares Germany's primitive vigor to Rome's more civilized and luxuriant laxness, though he acknowledges the superior discipline of the Roman legions and hopes the Germans never discover the usefulness of that discipline. They eventually did.

Speaking of the Germans in comparison to the Romans, Tacitus' wit is evident: "Heaven has denied them gold and silver—shall I say in mercy or in wrath?" Later in the *Germania* he observes, "No one in Germany finds vice amusing or calls it 'up-to-date' to debauch or be debauched." He adds, "Good morality is more effective in Germany than good laws in some places that we know." In this, it is worth reflecting upon the present age.

Human beings often forget that they are destined to be fertilizer. Nature is a family.

The use of money generally cloaks theft under commerce.

The "state of nature" is a condition which resides near the core of every human heart.

Scriptures are inspired, but not immutable.

It is not in triumph but in distress that wisdom is gained. Suffering is a gift to mind.

Fear finds refuge in a crowd. Courage is solitary.

The mind cannot entirely reveal itself.

The pursuit of truth is an activity in which human beings are designed to live.

There is no past or future. There is the present and its illusion of loss and gain.

In human affairs, good is to evil as a mirror is to its silver backing. One cannot be without the other.

Had there been no life, there would be no occasion for death.

Celebrate life as a kiss: not for its length but for its lingering moment.

A human soul is eternity.

Theorems hide their uncertainties in their axioms, thus allowing their proofs to proceed with certainty.

The human mind gains strength from its ability to gauge the scope of its weakness.

Literature teaches broad thinking. Philosophy teaches deep thinking.

## Thoughts on Creativity, Spirit, and the Ethical Life

Literature is moral philosophy. But its ethical concepts are not expressed as principles.

There is no greater earthly gift than intellect. Yet it is nothing compared to consciousness.

Wisdom is humanity's heritage. But people generally prefer cunning.

There is much richness of experience and insight in organized religion. But there is also a love of self-delusion.

Human beings demand justice because they desire recompense.

Nature has a wisdom of its own: it knows proportion.

Imagination is free. Reason is bound. Without imagination, reason can produce nothing new.

Creative minds imagine before they reason.

Great music must be intellectually complex to counterbalance its overwhelming emotional impact.

Great paintings must be intellectually translucent in organizing the sensuous impact of color.

Great sculptures must be both simple and sensuous of line.

The rigid maintenance of definitions within a scientific discipline is both its greatest strength and its greatest weakness.

The highest life of the mind is ethical.

What is potential in the material realm is actual in universal consciousness. What happens already is.

Universal spirit is not being. It is the power of being.

Religion is philosophy without the argument. It is picture philosophy.

Truth is sincerity of heart.

Personal wealth is not about money. It is about power over others.

Money in the hands of a few diminishes productivity. The few cannot need what the many do. And the many cannot purchase without means.

Truth, though much of it is inaccessible, is worth the pursuit.

Wisdom is not a product of science. For it is more than a sum of parts.

## Thoughts on Creativity, Spirit, and the Ethical Life

The principal gift of spirit is wisdom.

Superstition is belief unrestrained by reason.

To be engulfed in the light of the mind is to be possessed by the fire of living.

The capacity for reflection has given access to spirit.

Good poetry demands powers of reflection. That is why there is so little of it.

It is easier for an elephant to bathe in a teacup than for a philosopher to engage in trivial conversation.

To be healthy in mind is to pursue penetration in thought.

It takes imagination to envision a universe. The breadth of that imagination determines the size of the universe.

The written word allows thought to accumulate and deepen over time.

It is only when people doubt that they trouble themselves to see anything.

Science searches for a cause, philosophy for a definition.

What has not been defined cannot be organized.

How something is defined determines how it is organized in relation to something else.

Human acts are always incomplete expressions of human thoughts.

In animal research, it is important to consider that what appears to be reasoning in non-human subjects is better understood as sub-reasoning, or proto-reasoning. Reasoning in Homo sapiens involves the use of language. And that language acts as a template, or overlay, on imaginative experience.

For example, it is possible to distinguish between a square, a pentagon, and a hexagon by means of imaginative representation without counting the sides. They simply look different. Four pellets, five pellets, and six pellets, when arranged in separate groups, can be distinguished in the same manner.

But when a human being of at least some degree of mathematical development sees these groupings, he places a rational template over them. That template is an expression of the counting numbers. Thus what was a matter of imaginative distinction takes on a conceptual character, which is derived from the concepts of the counting numbers. Concepts are the instruments of reason. And, when these are employed in discourse, they follow the set rules of logic in their relations. This is the reasoning process.

## Thoughts on Creativity, Spirit, and the Ethical Life

Such is the nature of objects distinguished by count. But when an animal not possessed of the complexity of language makes a distinction resembling a count, it is not exercising reason. For it lacks the faculty of conceptualization, which belongs to language. It is limited to a recognition of visual or other representational distinctions.

Of course, this faculty can be carried to a fairly sophisticated level. Whereas man at his most primitive, in possession of a language, but without any sense of number, is apt to recognize only the categories of one and many. For this may be sufficient to his purposes, which is why he does not develop a counting system. Other relatively primitive human social groups, having incorporated the concepts of one, two, and three within a greater idea of incremental progression, will have truly begun to exercise a system of numbers.

Paul Cézanne's paintings are a study of the mind. Their layering of mere patches of color representing form and distance clearly exhibits how fragments of an image function as the barest and most useful representations of properties in rational thought. Paul Klee's use of simple suggestive imagery also functions in this manner. Both are like ideograms. When similar brief representations are employed in rational thought, they can be moved about and interrelated in the mind with the greatest facility, which is why they are the essential instruments underlying it.

This is also what lends the paintings much of their curious power. For the latter is a revelation of the inner workings of the mind, a demonstration of how it is that people think.

Though, as is generally the case, people do not recognize this. For they are apt to overlook the minutia of their thinking processes in deference to an immediate seizure upon the completed thought.

The world is not an airtight causal construct. It is quasi-causal, whether phenomena be ideally understood as originating in the mind, or whether they are investigated though the senses. In terms of its ordinary functioning, the world of experience does appear to be causal. For this is what makes the activities of daily life possible.

It allows for predictions, reasons, plans. But when physical phenomena are examined in depth with precision, it is discovered that experience is not strictly causal. The relations between what comes before and what follows break down in a number of ways, becoming probabilities in many instances and, in some cases, even acausal anomalies. For this reason it can be said that the world appears to be causal, thus facilitating practical and useful responses, but that in its innermost reaches it is otherwise.

So the universe is not strictly causal. But it is consistent enough in the unfolding of its relations to appear so. This is what lends possibility to the daily functioning of all sentient life. Any creature which moves about in search of food and protection must exhibit both conditioned and unconditioned responses which align its activities with external events.

These responses can be either instinctual or voluntary or, as is generally the case, a mixture of both. But there must be such a relationship between a sentient creature and its world which

# Thoughts on Creativity, Spirit, and the Ethical Life

is based on expectation or prediction. For it is in light of it that human beings are equipped with reason, the power to predict, and to plan. Yet none of this obviates the underlying mystery: an indeterminism at the root of things. That is why it can be argued that there is a pattern in the arrangement of phenomena which is not one of necessity.

Philosophy, like any creative endeavor, depends upon imaginative insight. Powers of argumentation only serve the purpose of realizing the insight. For, when the two are reversed in importance and the latter becomes the dominant principle, there is much intellectual show, accompanied by a consequent loss of penetration.

Human beings generally fall over one another in a tumult of self-assertion. But, why is it that they do this? The behavior derives from a superficial drive toward a felt sense of unity within them. They want to bring that unity to bear upon others, or at least gain recognition for having expressed it in themselves. What they frequently do not understand is that enclosing walls do not make a space. They merely separate it from its greater realization. Neither is spirit enlarged by limitation.

Humanity exhibits a twofold ethical nature. A person is social, recognizing herself as an integral part of the larger organism of society. And she is an independent unit in the universal order. Moral fulfillment lies in a complementary operation of these two factors. As the highest form of personal and social activity, this is the enlargement and rectification of conscious awareness.

Such an awareness is broadened through a personal process of extensive and deep thought concerning the limitations and transcendences of life. The resulting increase in understanding produces an expansion of moral awareness, which is passed on to a community by means of art, philosophy, and science, where it enters into the practical realm of virtuous action.

Thus the development is initially individual, originating in a single sphere of consciousness. But when rendered social, it is transmitted to other minds, enriching their thought and moral comprehension, where it is further nurtured and expanded and again returned to the social body. No dichotomy between the independently virtuous character of a creative, reflective mind and the practical, social side of ethics need ever be assumed. For they are mutually interrelated, as any sincere moral act is unabashedly assumed to follow from a deeply held moral conviction. It is in this way that the dual character of humanity is drawn out in fulfillment.

Morality is a maximization of individual life, a creative expression achieved through the productive use of one's faculties in terms of self-enlightenment and a contribution to the increase of spiritual enlargement in others. The development of these capacities depends upon social harmony and material balance.

Social harmony is a cohesiveness attained by the maintenance of trust between individuals in a community. Moral systems seek the promotion of mutual trust, which is a univer-

## Thoughts on Creativity, Spirit, and the Ethical Life

salization of the high regard of one person for another. Anything which breaks the tenor of this fabric is immoral. Material balance is determined by the environment. It is physical security: food, shelter, protection from danger. Here also lie the tools, both in symbol and craft, of all creativity. Where is the poet without nature, where the sculptor without stone, music without sound, the scientist without facts and laws, the philosopher without concreteness of thought?

Material balance determines the relations of social harmony. For it exhibits limitations. For example, in sexual matters the practice of monogamy, polygamy, or polyandry may answer to a need as simple as supply and demand in the availability of arable land or the guarantee of an adequate lifetime's provision for members of a disproportionately more numerous sex. Thus social institutions conform their relations of trust to the limitations of physical circumstance.

In the present age, greatly enhanced means of production, healing, and environmental control release humankind from a heightened fearfulness and dependence upon class-bound needs. Social relations which answer to the loftiest ideals of trust and creative expression may now be sought. But it cannot be overlooked that absolute perfection is unattainable to limited beings. Such a goal is not possible under the ever-shifting circumstances of nature. There will always be a need for social change and adjustment. Tolerance for irregularity must therefore appertain.

But wars, pestilences, and famines brought on by economic disparity—those convulsions of the past arising from class strife—can be eliminated. Once the human race has fully experienced and come to a general understanding of the transcendent and nurturing value of this loss of old chains, it will not regress to its former state.

Intelligence is a matter of spirit. Spirit feeds imagination. Imagination is the embodiment of emotion figured forth in material symbols. Imagination is then brought under the discipline of reason. If the initial instigating emotion is subtle, coming, as it were, almost invisibly from the innermost self, it is a precursor to wisdom. But, if it is an expression of the outer, social person—the artificial but often convincing self built around vanity—it is the origin of cunning and most of the problems of humanity.

Cunning is not simply an exercise of the desire to influence people. It is doing so for egotistical reasons. But one must beware the subtlety of ego. For in a competitive and hostile world, it is generally felt to be natural to act out of small increments of selfishness. For this reason, it is incomparably difficult to discern the quieter motivations of wisdom.

A time must come when human beings are able to walk in the light of day, as opposed to navigating a night of murky dreams. For the latter is the path of religion, a realm of Freudian symbols, indirections of representation which represent underlying emotional truths. Rather than this, the truths should be made clear, direct, and uncompromisingly honest.

### Thoughts on Creativity, Spirit, and the Ethical Life

Human beings pass like meteors through the firmament of life, hardly having time to stop for anything. Yet from within their trajectories, they would imagine that the time is long.

What does it mean to speak of "God's love"? Jesus of Nazareth compared this love to what he referred to as the "Father" being aware of a sparrow's fall. But he did not mention a prevention of the fall, nor a softening of its impact. Why is this? When universal consciousness, or spirit, is taken into consideration, rather than the anthropomorphic term "father," the perspective is different.

It does not change meaning. It is a shift from an emotional to an intellectual focus, in which it can be understood that an individual life is engulfed in spirit. For it is spirit. And there is but one spirit from which all things emanate. Moreover, since spirit is one and indivisible, it is fully expressed in each person. That person is universal consciousness, limited only in the content of his awareness.

Thus in a person's deepest inner nature, he is secure. For his suffering can only arise from material attachment, which is an expression of his external character. These torments are insurmountably difficult to shed when viewed from a perspective of immersion in them. But they pass. And what remains is the imperishable awareness of the inner self. It is the imperturbable peace never absent from this condition which forms the protective shield referred to as love.

It is not possible for a person to love humanity. Understood in emotional terms, the concept of agape is nonsense. And its embrace leads to failed effort and hypocrisy. But it is possible for people to practice respect for one another. A personal emotional attachment need not be exercised. For respect is a discipline of the mind.

No political system—autocratic, aristocratic, or democratic—can endure. It will inherently fall into corruption, so long as there is not a collective change of heart in people. The change must come from within. It cannot be enforced, except by nurture and general practice.

A philosopher is a thinker who develops a systematic explanation of human experience which is deep and thorough enough to be fully comprehensive. Yet it must also be open-ended. In this way, others following may extend the investigation in consonance with its original principles. Newton, Einstein, and Darwin were such philosophers, as were Plato, Aristotle, Plotinus, Bacon, Descartes, Spinoza, Lock, Berkeley, Hume, Kant, Kierkegaard, Schopenhauer, Nietzsche, and Hegel. Though much of the thinking of each of these persons has since been surpassed, something of the original pattern of insights remains and continues to be of use.

All others who do not fit this description are certainly thinkers, some quite important. But they are not philosophers. This includes the Stoics and Existentialists, who are indispensable to culture but cannot be included in the above list. For example, the Stoics take for granted the metaphysical background to their position. And the Existentialists assume a subjective perspective which excludes it.

**Thoughts on Creativity, Spirit, and the Ethical Life**

Marcus Aurelius' *Meditations* express a Stoic philosophy which favors an ideal of personal discipline, unaffected dignity, and calm. In one of them, translated by George Long, Marcus Aurelius states that, "In the mind of one who is chastened and purified thou wilt find no corrupt matter, nor impurity, nor any sore skinned over." This is a mind cleared of excessive desire, fear, hate, envy, or malice.

He also says, "Nor is his life incomplete when fate overtakes him, as one may say of an actor who leaves the stage before ending and finishing the play." In other words, death is not to be feared, since it will come at its appointed time in a life lived soberly and purposefully without self-seeking and personal ambition.

These are the reflective words of a man who was a professional soldier. Disciplined, duty bound, and austere, but also aware of the deeper meaning of life, this emperor spent his governing years commanding Roman legions fighting on the northeastern frontiers of the empire. He did it to protect those he ruled and, for the most part, lived the life of a soldier in the field. This was very much unlike the sumptuous indulgences of some of the other emperors.

He ends this meditation with, "Besides, there is in him nothing servile, nor affected, nor too closely bound to other things, nor yet detached from other things, nothing worthy of blame, nothing which seeks a hiding-place." It is hard to imagine a military man whose philosophy could be more in tune with the dangers and hardships of his profession.

It was a philosophy worthy of a Roman, a soldier, and a human being who felt the full weight of responsibility for the well-being of others. He may not have lived up to these ideals on every occasion. Few, if any, could. But he always carried them within him and did his best. For that reason, and because he wrote well, he has been read in the Christian world for almost two thousand years.

If Monet's studies of atmosphere and light strum the chords of an indefinitely broad range of subtleties of human emotion, no two paintings alike in this, then can it not be said that the breadth and depth of his art are beyond compare?

Van Gogh wanted people to "feel" his art. But what is meant by feeling? Certainly it implies a strong emotional response. Yet is it not more than this? Is it not a union of spirit with spirit through the medium of emotion? Emotions, or the feelings of which they are composed, arise within the domain of spirit. Thus their origin is not the realm of nerves and organs. Rather, they are paralleled by these ensigns of a material mind. For they are of a more penetrating and enduring nature.

Time, as understood in *The Immaterial Structure of Human Experience,* is subjective insofar as it is an expression of the input of primary mind, the mental impressions of which are regarded as pertaining to the noumenal precipitate. But, as expressed by means of secondary mind in its development of the realm of material experience (i.e., the phenomenal precipitate), it is objective. This latter is what physical science recognizes as the space-time continuum. For it is a mental projection of a seemingly independent material world. That is to say, the material realm appears to exist independently of the mind.

Thus the fact that subjective time is frequently measured in terms of objective time, making it objective as well, is false for the purposes of an immaterial philosophy. But true subjective time is not readily grasped. For it is an expression of the initial input of the noumenal precipitate and is therefore obscured by the development of the phenomenal precipitate. Hence the incorrect assumption that subjective time should be identified with objective time.

Ernest Hemingway's work might well be referred to as a form of literary impressionism. This is not to say that Hemingway was concerned with such things as atmosphere and light or that he sought to capture a moment's impression. Consider only the general attitude of this writer and those painters. For it can be seen that they have three things in common. They are realists. They embrace the whole of daily life, including its darker aspects. And they go about it with a positive, even joyful, embrace. For they are immediately sensual in their treatment.

Emotion transcends both imagination and reason. For it lies in the deepest heart of awareness. This is so whether the emotion should be an expression of the superficial person which is developed by means of social interaction, or whether it should arise from that inner self which is prior to material awareness.

As a coalescence of feelings, emotion is always a direct expression of the mental impressions which constitute the foundation of the content of consciousness. But those feelings which derive from the innermost self are prior to the other. For they are of greater significance, as they are reflective of the character of spirit, or universal consciousness. Yet, as a guide to life, they are so subtle as to be generally ignored.

Living in the spirit does not imply an avoidance of material well-being. It requires that life should be conducted perceptively. A person should be sensitive toward herself and others, recognize inner feelings, their susceptibility to wounds, and respond with respect and consideration. This requires vigilance and is not easy to accomplish. For it demands a fully developed intelligence involving emotional finesse, reason, and spiritual insight.

Responding aggressively to an accusation that one is stupid or ignorant is a mark of that condition. For an intelligent, well informed person ought to feel no threat from such an insult.

The sense of clarity and peace wrought by an early morning blue sky reflects a well-tuned mind. When a storm gathers, it is always an indication of a disturbance introduced from another quarter. A strong temper controls its own weather, keeping any such disturbance at bay. Nevertheless, this state of mind is more easily spoken of than lived. For, to accomplish equanimity of this kind, a mind must rest upon a foundation of its transcendent inner core, its spirit.

## Thoughts on Creativity, Spirit, and the Ethical Life

In contrast, the external social and material self is ever rife with irritations. These are entanglements beyond the necessary scope of inwardness. Embrace the works of great minds, not only for their content, but their quality. For the character of such works is that the petty annoyances of both life and temperament have been largely set aside. And what remains is of an admirable purity.

Upon the earth, it is uncertain that any creature other than Homo sapiens reasons. Intelligent species, such as ravens, parrots, great apes, even wolves in their coordinated hunting, practice a form of proto-reasoning. They follow sequences of mental imagery which they know by experience to produce expected results.

But it is language which has facilitated an elevation to reason proper. For it allows sequences of thought to flow independently of experience. This has arisen from conceptual development. Words, denoting concepts, bring mental images into obeisance through definition. The mental images thus come to indicate the properties of things defined. These in turn allow for precise associations by means of said properties.

Such associations determine the exercise of grammatical syntax and logic, complicating language and lifting it out of its original physical context. Thus a person can think of things entirely abstracted from her environmental experience in a manner in which other animals cannot. This is of course assuming that the order of Cetacea, or some other such creatures, does not possess an extensively developed communication system.

The development of an artificial mind resembling that of humans can only be made possible by a combined mastery of logical sequencing and association, creative imagery, and a capacity for refined emotional evaluations. Anything short of this will fall short of an achievement of independence in motives and thought.

It is important to recognize the role of imagination and emotion. Animals exercise these in varying degrees. And it is as an animal that human beings exist and possess knowledge. For without imagination there can be no innovation in thought. New ideas are initially represented as free images. Nor is it possible to orient, or prioritize, a sequence of ideas without emotion. Such an orientation by means of logical input alone is as meaningless and dead to life as is a complete absence of evaluative preference in decision making.

Human beings may be thought of as three-dimensional creatures in a two-dimensional world. Due to the restricted vision of a consciousness confined within material limitations, the phenomenon of ego has arisen. For it is viewed as an instrument essential to self-preservation. But in fact it augments the restrictions imposed upon awareness, thus contributing to flawed judgment.

This is a problem universally experienced. It lies at the root of the intense and occasionally embittered human struggle for a better world, as it narrows focus to the self alone. The only means to an overcoming of this added limitation lies in an acknowledgment of the oneness of spirit underpinning its

## Thoughts on Creativity, Spirit, and the Ethical Life

many souls. In this way, the material restrictions of life can be sufficiently lifted as to become bearable.

The material universe is not causally constructed. It is set forth in patterns, which the mind interprets causally. But when examined closely—morally as well as physically—an apparent tinge of acausality among the patterns is revealed. The source of this subtle breach remains undetected because it transcends the material. For causation, or whatever functions in such a manner, is sequestered in spirit.

Human beings do not only participate in determining the outcome of quantum experiments. Generally unawares, they are intimately involved in structuring their daily world, regardless of whether or not they are conducting physical research.

To maintain that God is love is not to attribute a separate and sentimental character to the transcendent. It is to assert that a person is thoroughly moved by and enveloped in spirit. There is nothing in that person's experience other than spirit, though it may seem otherwise. Her suffering, pain, and joy are those of spirit.

The world is neither good nor evil. It simply is. People are what they are as well, becoming slowly but increasingly conscious of their spiritual nature. In the end, insofar as there is such an end, there is only deeper awareness.

Death is the filtering of flesh into universality. Life is the process which acts as the filter. Through struggle and adversity, the artificially constructed social self weakens and decays, while spirit increases and remains. Even so, an individual consciousness, though having been enlarged to universality in the end, is not lost. It remains eternally viable within the moment of spirit, which is neither past nor future.

Moreover, as spirit is intimately involved in all aspects of the material which emanates from it, any individuality retrieved into the whole at the time of death may yet function as a nexus between its reconstituted purity of being and the limited particular. This is why those who pay respect to their departed loved ones and ancestors are not mistaken. Nevertheless, it is the universal spirit which is of greatest interest. For it is the redressor of the momentary but necessary wound of a limited existence.

Because of its conceptual, and thus logical, character, the human mind craves causal explanations. But at the most refined level of material investigation, general patterns are revealed in lieu of rigorously related sequences. For this reason, space and time lose their conventional application. For time is change observed in terms of distance, which is what is involved in sequences of event, causal or otherwise.

Events develop in an order, be this causal, associative, or apparently random. For even in regard to the apparently random, there is an order of time and place. Hence, all such relations having been undermined by a lack of a full integration between patterns, the logic of space-time is distorted.

Therefore, space is dissociated from time, and events do not occur within a recognizable spatial/temporal context. This results in observed anomalies regarding distance and time,

## Thoughts on Creativity, Spirit, and the Ethical Life

where some events appear to occur independently of one another, but are nevertheless linked by simultaneity. An anomaly of this type demonstrates that the observed phenomena are, in fact, identical, or at least intimately related parts of an integrated unity in which distance is not a factor.

It is generally thought that there is no communication between somatic and generative cells. But sufficient knowledge concerning nerve and endocrine messaging is lacking. For example, neuron synapses are both electrical and chemical. So such relations on a larger scale should not be overlooked. They could contribute to acquired characteristics.

Darwin's tolerance for some suggestion of acquired characteristics may not have been in vain. Birds do alter accustomed migration routes in response to prolonged seasonal change or a variation in the availability of food. Yet their migratory instincts would appear to be fixed. Also, some species of cichlid fish, when in schools which are entirely female but for one male, will convert the lead female into a male upon a loss of the original male.

Even if such responses are regarded strictly in terms of immediate chemical or physiological triggers, a physical or behavioral acquisition has taken place. An external stimulus has provoked an internal reorientation. Thus birds may permanently change their migratory pathways. And some species of cichlid fish have made a behavioral and physiological adaptation which may not have been induced strictly by random variation responding to a selective agency.

In fact, is there a clear distinction between environmental influence and internal response, or a complete understanding of the depth and duration of the effect of the former upon the latter? For any variation to occur, is it not necessary that both operate in conjunction with one another? If a creature did not willfully respond to an environmental change, how would a permanent alteration in the organism come about? Factors of apparently random variation and selection are important. But this process is not necessarily the whole. Rather, it is the inheritable permanence of change in an organism which is at issue. Perhaps there is something quite subtle at work here.

Mathematics is an invention, not a discovery. What provides it with an aura of discovery is the appearance of a new logical relation suddenly, and it would seem fortuitously, recognized against a backdrop of previously established axioms. But this is strictly a function of intellectual imagination. There is no revelation from a realm of eternal ideas.

There is no difference between meaning and purpose. Meaning arises from purpose. An inner sense of incontrovertible fitness informs both meaning and purpose in a strong and flexible mind. A weak mind borrows its motivations.

There are a number of interesting and fine works to be found in the modern arts. But many of them register an element of thinness, a sense of too much invention and too little vision.

Time, distance, and mass describe the mechanics of the physical universe. But mass is equivalent to energy in accordance with $E = mc^2$. And energy is measured by the work it does or is capable of doing. Work is expressed in terms of time and

## Thoughts on Creativity, Spirit, and the Ethical Life

distance. So time and distance alone describe the mechanics of the physical universe.

Zero is written as a number solely for the purpose of occupying a transitional position in a progression of numbers. Either it signifies a movement from positive to negative and vice versa. Or it is a place holder indicating multiplication by ten. So, other than the importance of its position, it represents nothing. For this reason, zero divided by one yields a quotient of zero because nothing can be done to nothing. But when one is divided by zero, nothing can be done *with* nothing.

Now an infinitesimal, in spite of its name, is a finite entity, however small. So it is something. And if it is divided into one, it will yield an indeterminate quotient, the number of parts of which cannot be ascertained. But this does not mean that the parts are infinite in quantity, any more than the assumption that an infinitesimal divisor, because it is understood to be indeterminately small, should be infinite in the reduction of its size. Like its quotient, its precise quantity cannot be ascertained. But it is nevertheless a finite entity.

The reason it is possible to perform the operation of dividing a so-called infinitesimal into one is that such divisors and their indeterminate quotients are both finite, however incomprehensibly small the divisor or unimaginably multitudinous in number the quotient. Thus, by these operations, it is made clear that the highly abstract mathematical imagination nonetheless consistently works with numerical entities which are conceived to be finite.

This is true of all arithmetical quantities, including imaginary units and irrational numbers. For in the former case, the square root of minus one is a quantity whose apparent inability to be resolved by concrete finite means has been rendered by the complexity of operations it has previously undergone. To arrive at its comprehensible expression, these operations must be unraveled in the order in which they originally took place. For the order of operations must be taken into account as a part of its character.

In the latter case of an irrational number, it cannot be said to be less finite than a rational. For its indeterminacy is brought about by an indefinite unfolding of finite increments beyond a decimal. These increments do grow progressively smaller. But they do not shed their property of finitude. That is why an irrational number is represented by an unending string of digits, all of which individually and collectively are finite.

Each digit implies finitude insofar as it alone is concerned. Even single or multiple congregations of zeros in the string of numbers beyond the decimal are bordered on either side by digits representing finite quantities, rendering the zeros finite as well. Thus the whole is finite. So the fact that the progression is unending does not negate its property of finitude.

The reason the results of mathematical computation often appear to defy the hasty conclusions of common sense is as follows. Ordinary human thought processes are brief and take little cognizance of complex structure. But mathematics is an invention of the mind which is specifically designed to parallel the spatial-temporal structure of experience. Of course, it does this only in quantitative terms.

The spacial-temporal structure is also a creation of the mind. But it is only partially so. For it is formulated by the

## Thoughts on Creativity, Spirit, and the Ethical Life

mind in cooperation with the sequencing and character of mental impressions received. Neither the sequencing nor the character of mental impressions is determined by the mind.

But much of the resulting formulation of the structure is, at least insofar as the mind makes allowance for the sequencing and character of mental impressions. And it is this parallel between the artificial system and operations of numbers and the spacial-temporal structure of experience which is realized in the complex formulations of mathematics.

People occasionally continue to attempt to square the circle. Yet Archimedes has demonstrated in no uncertain terms that it cannot be done. The problem is pi, an irrational element embedded in the concept of the perfect circle. Pi, being a non-algebraic irrational, renders squaring the circle in finite terms unachievable. The argument in support of this can be found in Archimedes' treatise on the circle.

Wisdom is knowledge enriched by a capacity for thought which extends beyond protocols and formulas. It is characteristic of a small number of people, exercised by fewer than is generally imagined. Formal education is not a measure of it, though it can provide a sound basis, if properly extended by further study and much reflection.

The painter, Camille Pissarro, a man of Jewish descent, was possessed of a Christlike humility. He expressed a kindness and patience which was experienced by all his associates and is recognized today through his paintings. His works induce a gentle thoughtfulness in the viewer. Many of them are landscapes: sun-drenched, mellowed with mist, or fresh with fallen snow.

There is *The Road to Rocquencourt*, filled with sunlight, a blue sky which occupies most of the upper two thirds of the painting, and the violet shadows of a quiet, pleasant day. *The Road to Saint-Germain at Louveciennes* shows the rural calm of a village when the sun has not yet taken off the morning mist. The viewer senses a timeless early morning stillness.

But *Snow at Louveciennes* was painted in another season, later in the day. The scene is wooded and there is a path through the snow, which was busily trodden at some earlier moment and is now covered with long blue shadows from the trees growing beside it and from a single house in the foreground. No one is about, no activity can be detected in the self-enclosed silence of this winter scene.

The artist did a *Self-Portrait* in 1873 that shows his gentleness, acceptance of others, and quiet conviction. He was a man who withstood years of poverty, ridicule, and neglect, yet found the strength to settle quarrels among his fellow painters, teach some of them, and encourage all of them as they labored beside him in the long struggle toward acceptance and public recognition.

All of Pissarro's work—including his portraits of himself and others, the others being mostly hardworking peasants in the countryside outside Paris—expresses a joy in simple people and in common things close to the earth. There is a reverence in these paintings, a deep humility in the artist who stands with palette and brush before the mystery of being, that unexplainable mixture of activity and contemplation, happiness and sorrow known as life.

# Thoughts on Creativity, Spirit, and the Ethical Life

It is sometimes imagined that Shakespeare could not have written as he did due to insufficient formal education. But the school of life, augmented by carefully selected reading, informed company, and sound judgment was ready to hand. Because of this, he was more free from common opinion and social conformity. As for the details—fine language, character insight, and dramatic timing—these were his alone.

The inscrutable paradox of human existence is that all is dependent upon and therefore resolved into consciousness. But from a strictly limited human perspective, consciousness is nothing. Though it is known, it is neither seen nor felt. Within it and beyond material experience, there is neither before nor after. No events arise outside of its sensory content. It is simply being. And such being is readily manifest as nothing at all.

Human beings begin life with the sense of an indestructible self. It is an inner self, a deeper self, composed of pure consciousness unimpeded by material limitations. But all of natural experience lends its influence toward an encounter with dissolution. From this the aggregates of fear mount up, blossoming into egoism and combativeness. Hence the ills and snarls of personal interaction.

    Pride originates in the conviction, uneasily borne but not readily cast off, that the opinions of others greatly matter. For one lives an enlarged presence through others, which suggests an immortality rather small but necessary in lieu of an alternative. This need is expressed by means of a domination of others. For it is to obtain an overweening influence, lest others' consciousness of oneself be overlooked.

This limited, yet overbearing, self-regard is the fomenter of wars of both aggression and defense. Moreover, when found to be self-enclosed within a single community—a government, a coalition of special interests, a majority, a strong and influential minority, any body large or small—it is ever nurtured toward increase, so that all within and without must be continually vigilant of its influence. For it often becomes the case that its only prevention is a recourse to internal broils and civil war.

Language is not possessed of an underlying word order, fixed and out of which all grammatical structures derive their origin. Rather there are associative elements of thought which make any syntactical structure possible. For example, concepts arise denoting activity, transitive or passive, in regard to a fomenter of such actions. Within the association between an action and its perpetrator arises the second class of concepts—that of the perpetrator. These together are subject and verb.

There is in addition to these a class of concepts denoting those things which receive a transitive action. There is also another representing to whom or for whom an action occurs. And there are concepts and phrases modifying a subject or such object. Others color an action in terms of its location and character. Subtleties of language proliferate indicating possession, standing in for a doer, etc.

All these means dwell associatively in the mind. They have no locus other than this. From them derives the process which underlies the many varied grammars of the world's languages.

## Thoughts on Creativity, Spirit, and the Ethical Life

Thus there is no lineal order from which the many variations in structure may be derived. For it is purely a matter of association devoid of an initial backbone suggesting an aboriginal word order.

A recognition of the associative character of language may at some future time suggest a means of deriving a much simplified writing system composed of ideograms, like the Chinese but less complex. Such a script could be read by anyone without recourse to learning a new language. But, above all, it must be kept simple, with a strict regard paid to associative (i.e., logical) relations. This can be accomplished if such relations are thoroughly understood and meticulously worked out.

The most important consideration is a well-grounded understanding of the mind's processes of association. Though these are logical, it is a subtle exercise of logic which is required, emphasizing association and demanding an acute employment of imagination in discerning the relations. This will avoid complicating redundancies. Much study is needed. But the result would be a greatly simplified ideographic system, which could then be made available to the world.

Spirit (universal consciousness) is not a person. Yet all things emanate from it, including the many individual persons of the material realm. This intimate relationship with his origin allows a person to commune with spirit as though spirit were a person. It opens every emotional tie. For emotions proceed from spirit and are thus enabled to acknowledge and return to it.

In such a communication, or intimate dialog, universal spirit takes the form of the other in relation to the communicant. Yet it is the case that the deepest inner self and universal consciousness are one. They constitute a wholeness in which neither is a part. Hence the ease with which love flows between them. For who does not love himself?

This love cannot entertain dread of judgment. For there is no eternal condemnation coming from without. All is within. Rather, it is human beings who lay adverse decision upon themselves and in future generations are apt to derive a curse upon the doings of their forebears. Judgment is thus cumulative.

Hence the fall of kingdoms, empires, republics, and much of the more immediate short-term misery of the world. There is ever a weakening of the social fabric and a debilitation of individual relations by means of an unnecessary opposition of wills. But there is no external punishment coming from a greater being acting in opposition toward what is, in truth, only an intimate expression of itself.

However, there is reward. When the individual self acts within the wholeness of spirit, there is growth and increase of possibility. For all potential is in spirit, all causation rooted in its unlimited resources, all genuine creativity its offspring. Human beings, looking inward toward the universal consciousness upon which their limited individual expression rests, do accomplish a wholeness and expansion of their persons which an exclusive orientation toward the external social self cannot achieve.

## Thoughts on Creativity, Spirit, and the Ethical Life

Suicide is the outer social self attempting to destroy itself. It is the inner self wrongfully at war with the outer self. Wrongfully because the inner self is projected as another outer self. In such circumstances, the total outer self (existing in two separate forms) becomes confused. The new outer self believes itself to be all and regards the original outer self with an alienated feeling.

There is only a single form of valid domination of one person over others. It is that of persuasion through the mind. But this must be a condition in which reason is uppermost, lest emotions have an independent and irrational power to lead astray.

The appetites are necessary instruments of physical life. But they contain within themselves a destructive capacity. For when employed recklessly and without regard to the welfare of individual persons, they annul both the spirit of the perpetrator and abuse the spirit upon whom they may have been perpetrated. This is particularly the case with the sexual passion. For it destroys by a disregard and reckless use of another person, while gluttony only preys upon the glutton and those who may be led by such an example. Yet these can be many.

To approach the question of time, the mind, whether thought to be idealist or naturalist in outlook, must be considered as either having constructed or reconstructed experience within itself. For all experience is known only within it. So it is in this subjective manner that it recognizes time amidst phenomenal change and gives it measure in accordance with the construction or apprehension (depending on point of view) of physical structures registering difference, contiguity, and distance.

Accordingly, time must be considered a dimension of space, which in its special case is a metric wrought by changes in the distance relationships between one object and another and between the parts within an object. As such, it belongs wholly to the realm of material experience, which is apprehended solely in the mind.

Whatever lies beyond the material cannot be time as human beings know it, since it would lack the necessary constructs associated with the physical sense of it. For these render the sense of time as change understood in terms of sequential events occurring among physical objects. Thus the concept of eternity is rendered meaningless inasmuch as such a linear measure is concerned. However, the fact cannot be overlooked that events initially occur in simultaneity in an *a priori* condition of deep apprehension by the mind, being there arranged into a succeeding order by it.

So, whether alterations in the contiguity or mutual distance of objects be set aside as circumstances underpinning a recognition of sequential change, the condition of sequence therefore not appertaining, the only remaining concern is one of a distinction, or difference, between mental impressions, such as red as opposed to blue, hot in contrast to cold, etc. Thus any suggestion of eternity, or eternal bliss as it is generally conceived, must be considered without reference to material experience.

This does not mean there is no such thing as an eternity. It simply cannot be imagined or conceptually represented. For it may indicate a spiritual unity which yet allows for elements of

## Thoughts on Creativity, Spirit, and the Ethical Life

personal distinction. Or perhaps universal consciousness (spirit) is inclined to project another universe, which is not unlike the present material realm in some respects and is a state into which personal lives may pass, extending themselves beyond the condition of their physical dissolution.

Nevertheless, what is present to a human sensibility in such matters is nothing: a void. It is into this that any hopes of individual duration are projected. Though such an inclination arises nonetheless from a strong intuitive sense that this expectation should be entertained. For it is derived from the experience of consciousness, which exhibits no intrinsic marks of limitation.

Every culture is the holistic equal of any other. For each is a well-rounded and complete expression of a people's relationship to their experience of life. But on a technological basis differences in degree do arise. All cultures are then not equal. For some are more advanced than others. Neither are they equivalent in terms of spiritual awareness. For an understanding of the inner life differs from culture to culture, as it does from individual to individual.

It is a disturbing fact that a civilization may progress so markedly in one area, say the technological, that it will neglect another, such as the spiritual. Thus, having perhaps once reached a high point of interior consciousness—embracing a deepened sense of the transcendent—it may then begin to recede from that eminence, as it proceeds upon the development of another focus.

Evil and good mount up together in the human heart from the experience of life. They are a product of stress and ease in each individual person. The character of their combination is always unique, expressed only once in the world. And it can be stated with near certainty that these features are likely to exist nowhere else. For they are inextricably a matter of the human condition.

The term "heart" can be understood as a center of emotional and intellectual awareness. The two work together to flesh out the character of a person, much as they function to produce a mood in a work of art. That mood is the expression of an attitude of the artist, which attitude is in turn an exhibition of her heart. She cannot avoid her own presence in her creation. Only in its depth and purity of truth is it to be distinguished from the work of another. For the profundity of the artist—her originality—arises from the degree to which she has invested her awareness in the subtle intuitions of her innermost self.

The great religions almost inevitably exhibit two qualities: initially a search for peace and subsequently a development of control. The founders, possessed of deep insight whether they come at the beginning or late in the tradition, are the ones who seek to place humankind in a proper accord with its experience of life, aligning the outer person with his innermost intuitions. This is the source of peace, an alleviant of alarms.

But such a contribution is followed by less imaginative interpreters and disciples. These are the ones who, being less intuitively perceptive and thus more inclined to align themselves with received norms, attempt to bring practice into

## Thoughts on Creativity, Spirit, and the Ethical Life

accord with social imperatives. They are inevitably the arbiters and enforcers of morals, dictating practice with an ever-increasing rigor. This results in a condition of mental and emotional servitude, which presents the impermeable façade witnessed in the great religions to the world.

So why do so many people succumb to these arrangements and neglect to burrow their way out of them? Why do they not acknowledge in themselves the creativity and freedom of the founders, blundering on as they do for countless generations in dull, mindless obeisance? Generally, they are nurtured in their faith from infancy, where they are taught to fear some kind of retribution or to harbor a sense of inescapable destiny confining them to their received lot. They take it in with their mother's warmth and the security of the family hearth. It is for them the cushion of life itself and cannot be altered.

In this manner, the generations of humanity plod on endlessly, neither daring to question nor to innovate. Thus only rarely does new insight make an entrance. If it does, an inexorable machinery of social norms, ever at the ready to administer means of oppression, prevents growth and smothers the infancy of thought and conviction.

Occasionally, a few do effect changes. Often it is an individual, whose innovations are seen as fragmentary and a cause of factionalism. So the new teacher is forced to the fringes of the community. And another faith is created, entirely original in its vision and soon to be corrupted by others.

Consequently, a question arises. Can the human animal ever escape its sentient bonds, its suppression by the recurrent egoism of those who broker power, in order to become transcendentally reformed? Thus it is that human intelligence might awaken the spiritual being within. But it has been and continues to be a long sleep. For such an emergence into a fully transcendent awareness is no easy matter.

The formula for the surface area of a sphere is $4\pi r^2$. The radius is the distance from the center of the sphere to its surface. As can be seen, this is squared. And, though it is not expressed as an inverse—for it delineates an area, not a distance—it otherwise suggests Newton's inverse distance squared rule which determines gravitational force at any point beyond a source mass.

That force being calculated from the center point of a mass, it would be evenly dissipated over a spherical surface, all points of which are equally distant from the center. And, as the distance (radius) increases, the surface area will be enlarged and the gravitational force diminished proportionally at any point on the surface as the force is distributed over it. This analogy demonstrates the manner in which the mind structures material reality.

It is for this reason that the inverse square of the radius can be found in physical phenomena determining force distribution in relation to distance, such as is the case with Coulomb's inverse-square law. The mind, in order to proportionately register a distribution of force at equal distance in all directions at once, builds a sphere capable of expansion or contraction according to need. It is the mind itself, and it alone, which does this.

Devotion is of necessity an activity. For it must be expressed by means of the love of a human being for some purpose. But,

## Thoughts on Creativity, Spirit, and the Ethical Life

if that person should devote herself to the vapor of a mere idea, say the idea of God, she would as likely as not produce something nasty. For there must be a source of feeling, emotion, a connection which accompanies the idea, as it delivers a sense of internal peace.

It is only in terms of limitation that a thing can be truly felt. Thus it is for this reason that spirit has limited itself to its full expression in each individual human being. The person, both feeling and cognizant of her feeling, registers within her consciousness, and thus within spirit, the joy and sadness of every emotion and of each imagination and thought so provoked. Out of this arises a universe of multiply particularized awareness with which spirit is enriched.

The physical universe is not deterministic. Neither is it random. It is composed of close-fitting patterns. These are sufficiently exact to be treated as causal at the level of ordinary experience. But they break down into probabilities when closely observed. This much is clear. But what is not fully understood is that there is no sense of time or space as generally understood when the level of observation is minute and exact. For such research burrows under the customary structures of the mind. Here apparent anomalies present themselves, non-locality being chief among them.

So it can be seen that space and time, as normally understood, are structures imposed by the mind. And causation in a deterministic sense (should such be the case) must be conceived as occurring transcendentally beyond the physical. Of course, at such a point it is meaningless and merely illustrative to speak of either determinism or randomness. For what can a mind—all of whose conceptual and imaginative apparatuses are material—know of the transcendent?

The reason a condition like non-locality occurs within a context of the customary world of observation is that the mind structures it that way in an attempt to integrate quantum phenomena into common experience. This is its means of assigning it a position in space and time. Such a condition is not in accordance with normal experience. Nevertheless, what is significant is that the same assignment is always made under identical experimental conditions. This points to the consistent operations of the mind.

The human race is at present evolving principally through its culture. Immersed in technological adaptations and imaginatively interpretive theoretical explanations, people have hollowed out a tunnel universe within their daily experience. But this created world is nonetheless closely integrated with the material.

In this way, humankind proceeds into the future in a manner unlike that of any other earthly species. A significant implication of its progress lies in the field of education. For this sort of learned expansion of the mind becomes increasingly important. So the extent to which it is adhered to may in time produce an unbridgeable chasm between class distinctions. Separate cultural races might be presumed to evolve out of the original one to a extent from which there is no return.

However, there is a caveat. Not all people benefit from cultural resources in the same way. Nor do they in the same degree. This has long been the preserver of an integrated

### Thoughts on Creativity, Spirit, and the Ethical Life

humankind, since however long a division between classes may have been retained, the above circumstances have acted as an eventual leveler. But if this preventative were to be sufficiently compensated for as to be overcome, and a greatly distanced class should arise which distinguished itself from the common strictly on the basis of its enlightenment, then its isolation might be set in stone.

Fray Luis de León, a sixteenth century poet of the Spanish Renaissance, wrote a poem called, "On the Ascension," in which, addressing Jesus, he asks,

> And do you leave, Holy Shepherd,
> your flock in this valley, deep, dark,
> with solitude and tears,
> and you rending the pure
> air, going to the immortal secure

It is the voice of a man who knows how far he is from the comfort of Jesus' presence. He continues,

> Those who before were so enchanted,
> nurtured at your breasts,
> now sad and afflicted,
> from you dispossessed,
> to whom will they turn?

Human beings are utterly alone in the comparative darkness of earthly life.

> Upon what will eyes look
> which saw the beauty of your face
> that will not annoy them?
> Who, having heard your sweetness,
> will not find dullness and misfortune?

Not only are they alone, the presence of glory and hope they long for has been taken from them. Frey Luis describes the world as,

> This turbulent sea,
> who will now put it to harness? Who
> will harmonize the fierce angry wind?
> You being hidden, what north star
> will pilot the ship to its haven?

In the period immediately prior to the recorded resurrection of Jesus, the Gospel narratives assert that the disciples felt abandoned and alone. Now, long afterward, there are times when that is still the case for many people:

> O cloud, envious
> even of this brief joy, what grieves you?
> Where do you quickly fly?
> How rich you are as you withdraw!
> How poor and how blind, alas, you leave us.

Fray Luis taught sacred theology at the University of Salamanca, where he was denounced to the Inquisition and imprisoned for nearly five years. Upon returning to his classes after

## Thoughts on Creativity, Spirit, and the Ethical Life

being released, he began, "As we were saying ..." This courage and deep understanding are in his poetry.

(Lacking an English source ready to hand, the translation is by the present author.)

The most immediate pleasure rendered by an art experience is its unveiling of the world as seen through another consciousness. Each individual feels the limitations imposed upon her awareness. It is precisely these which are transcended by art.

Nothing intellectual extends beyond the material. Only the subtlest emotional nuances do so. For feelings are prior to thought. And, when accessed with care and honesty, these can be made to provide a sense of what is prior to any structure ascertained by the mind.

There are two kinds of time: subjective and objective. Subjective time does not exhibit a rate. For it is simply indicative of a sequence in mental impressions. Though initially all impressions are simultaneously present to the mind, they are arranged by it into a sequence which expresses individuation and limitation.

It is in light of this that the mind is able to construct a phenomenal world: a realm of space and incremental time. Its principal relations are spatial. The delineation and association of distinct groupings of mental impressions, represented as separate objects, produces a sense of space. Each such association is derived from a close proximity in the sequence of mental impressions. Thus the mind, drawing its impressions from spirit (consciousness), develops its awareness of a material realm, a world of limitations. Prior to this, even the impressions had been distinguished only by their individual character.

But the relations of space are not entirely fixed. For there is change, as the closely united impressions of an association are followed sequentially by another association nearly identical to it, though differing in a few of its constituent impressions. Thus change is rendered within a single object. This is also the manner in which the sequence of mental input becomes a register for objective time. It is in this way that events are introduced into human awareness.

A final arrangement is the distinction between objects in terms of spatial depth—i.e., a third dimension, which provides a sense of distance between objects as well as varied placement with respect to the observer. This accounts for far and near, as does objective time for soon and late, past and future.

In addition to this, there is also a discrimination between that which pertains to the body of the observer and that which does not. For mental impressions regarding an individual body closely accompany the life of the mind that is most closely associated with it and are much less varied than those which do not concern it. Whereas external objects are thought to produce sensations which do not originate within the mind. Consequently, the body is perceived as a locus of awareness.

In light of these considerations, a reason must be adduced to explain the fact that the relations of special and general relativity appear to defy common experience. It is that they are projected in terms of a space-time continuum which is conceived to be independent of subjectivity. Otherwise, they

## Thoughts on Creativity, Spirit, and the Ethical Life

exhibit an unacknowledged theory of the intrinsic workings of the mind.

In any creature, its instincts cannot be conceived as absolute imperatives. Rather, they provide a strong proclivity for certain types of behavior. Of course, if few alternative responses are available, as may be the case with simpler life forms, then the commands of instinct may appear all the more inflexible.

It is recognized that the circumference of a circle and the area of the same are respectively the derivative and integral of one another. This supplies a simple visual representation for illustrating the process of finding a derivative or integral. To obtain the derivative, imagine a circle in which the circumference and center point are drawn. Recalling that a geometric line has no breadth, the problem will be: how many contiguous concentric circumferences, beginning at the center point, must be removed to arrive at the outer circumference of the circle? Clearly, the number of these is indeterminate.

Again, to obtain the integral, the question is: how many contiguous concentric circumferences, proceeding from the outer circumference toward the center point, must be added to fill in the area of the circle? This is also an indeterminate number. The quantity of concentric circumferences remains indeterminate in both cases because a line (thus a circumference) has no breadth. Yet these progressively larger or smaller circumferences must be such as will fully account for the area of a circle. So, whether added or taken away, they are innumerable.

Thus the obvious pleasure of such an illustration. For it renders an abstraction visually concrete to the mind. What is more, all concepts, however abstract or ideal, can be so represented by means of the imagination. For, if this were not the case, the concept would not have existed in the first place.

There is no way that human beings can escape the box of cruelty they have been placed in. It is self-delusion to think anyone can live a life devoid of experiencing unkind acts or of committing them. Yet it is the duty of the enlightened never to do harm where it can be avoided. Nonetheless, such avoidance is not always possible. Though these acts must at times occur, they should not proceed from egoism, whether that egoism is manifested in a reaction to a wounded self-regard or from a will to dominate others.

Cruelty is a fact of life in which there is no beauty, nothing to engage desire, other than a bloated sense of self, which is, in turn, founded upon a perceived personal inadequacy. A psychological compromise of this self, as well as a physical threat of harm to the body, is simply that which must at times be endured. This is so because life is limitation. And limitation begets pain and possible wounds. Therefore, commit no harm which can reasonably be avoided. And where an injury is received, return it only when necessary under a motive of self-defense.

Look upon the love expressed by another as coming from the spirit. For only as such can it endure. A mutual regard of this kind is secured with iron clasps.

## Thoughts on Creativity, Spirit, and the Ethical Life

Because its conceptual faculty is logical, the mind seeks causal explanations. Nor can it accept uncertainties. For this reason, when tangible connections between phenomena are lacking and no alternative presents itself, the mind will attempt to construct a schema of hidden variables. But if the source of causation is in universal consciousness, its nature cannot be known. So neither can a spiritually determinate explanation be deduced.

Causal relations altogether are an illusion brought about by reason. For the close-fitted patterns of the physical realm are less than determinate, however slight the degree of non-determination. All things originate in spirit. It is there that something resembling cause may be referred to. But the nature of spirit cannot be known.

The repetition of a truth may seem redundant. But every alternate way of expressing it differs in some degree, revealing an overlooked insight. Thus it is multiple explanations which round out its fullness.

Human beings alone exhibit evil. For they express malice, which is the desire to discomfit others for the sake of a sense of self-aggrandizement. It is taking pleasure in the demonstrated weakness of perceived adversaries. Their disadvantage augments the perpetrator's personal superiority. Many unpleasant or dark events can be instigated in numerous ways by agents living and inert. But evil belongs strictly to the human.

Ironically, benevolence and good will are not confined to human beings. For example, ravens bringing food and encouragement to a wounded fellow are known to observation. So why should it be that good is more universal than evil? (Note that good and bad are not the contested contraries here.)

Good springs from a manifestation of spirit which is embedded in all things. In living forms, it takes on the character of empathy, which arises from an identification of shared being. But evil slips out of the gap originating in a severance from spirit. It is the result of the human power of abstraction, which allows a person to separate thought from experience. The individual withdraws his physical self from his natural intuitive awareness of the life within and proceeds to act upon an assumption of an independent material character.

Nevertheless, spirit being the ground of any existent thing, every person longs for the universal, indestructible presence he feels within. This contrasts markedly with the outer manifestation of his person and contributes toward his drive for dominance and superiority. Such is the groping of limitation towards its denied illimitable ground. But this alienation from spirit is a severance which cannot be resolved while the denial remains. For its union must originate from within.

Each person is a complete expression of the universal. Thus it is spirit which outlines the general course of one's life. However, as spirit is the inner fullness of self, so is there an outer self which is like dry land arising from that encompassing ocean. It forms the material, or physical, sense of a person. During the course of life, this limited self often gains precedence in the mind, masking the inner life from awareness. As

## Thoughts on Creativity, Spirit, and the Ethical Life

it does so, it strips away the comforting benevolence of the universal.

But if a person should remain disciplined in retaining a regard for her inner self, its influence upon her will be enlarged. In this way greater health, well-being, and even longevity can be attained, though necessarily contoured within the purpose of spirit for that individual case. Yet, whatever its prescribed limitations on an individual life, the beneficent influence of spirit can extend well beyond the confines of what can be derived from an isolated material existence which forgoes acknowledgment of its spiritual origin. For a mind so enervated has needlessly confined itself to a false and wounding view.

Eternity is in a moment. Little is it understood that past and present are mere extensions of the present for the sake of narrative illustration.

The ego is indestructible. It can be employed creatively for benevolent purposes. Or it can snuff out well-being through the desire to dominate and restrict.

The human heart is a fickle instrument. Unless there is tolerance and thoughtful give and take, it will falter. Hence the complexity of moral issues. Though moral precepts are grounded in general principles, the exigencies of the moment are of prime importance. These modify or at least strain principle. So there must always be a governing long view.

People abandon truth because they deem falsehood to be more immediate and real. It is the chief dilemma of the race and is likely to continue indefinitely, so long as it is not deliberately addressed by the entire human community together.

So much of the infirmness of human nature results from an equivocal faith in the presence of good in each person. This good is the foundational self which grounds every personality. Yet an often alienated material identity is built upon it over a lifetime. It stands in opposition to the original and obscures it. So to regain the inner truth, a person must apply diligence and sincerity toward seeking it out. Unfortunately, such perseverance is rare, though it be the genuine mark of a lady or a gentleman.

Scientific theories are models of reality. Now at the level of everyday experience, such views have been incorporated into the ordinary structure of the mind's development. Thus they are behaviorally adapted and are found acceptable to reason. But when investigations probe regions beyond the scope of this mundane model—as in the case of quantum phenomena—their findings can be difficult to assimilate and may be arrogated by the mind in ways which are inappropriate to the "ordinary" structure and seem threatening to reason.

There is but one means to a facile existence. That is to assume the character of an ameba. Yet it is not certain that even this creature has an easy time of it. So what is the reward of a complex mind which reiterates problems interminably? Why nothing at all, save the satisfaction of knowing where one has been.

Voltaire resembled an ascending balloon in that his reputation rose to heights which were attained by the amount of hot air inflating his mind. The balance between emotion and reason was tipped in favor of the former: the heat of emotion. Nevertheless, he was an influential figure in his day and remains so to this time. But for him to dismiss Leibniz by means of *Candide* is something less than an astute exercise of judgment. Its nearest equivalent is Samuel Johnson's refutation of Berkeley by kicking a stone.

An attempted division of any number by zero would yield an infinity. But neither zero nor infinity are finite quantities. Consequently, neither of them are numbers. Hence multiplying the quotient and divisor together does not yield a numerical result.

Plato's philosopher-king is unlikely for two reasons: A politician attains to and holds power by means of cunning, which rests on his ability to discern emotional states in others and anticipate their future actions. Once in power, a ruler must maintain his position by the same means. And a continuing need to exercise this faculty allows little opportunity for extended periods of thoughtful contemplation. For the entire tenure of his rule is a matter of expediency.

Conversely, wisdom is the capacity to gauge human circumstances in broadly conceived terms, irrespective of any manipulative purpose. In light of this, it can be seen that cunning is the contrary of wisdom, their forms of development being diametrically opposed. For, while the exercise of cunning demands a frictional involvement with others, wisdom requires a mind at peace for extended periods. Consequently, a contemplative life is rarely of any concern to a politician, and can at best only be occasionally, or intermittently, indulged.

In a rare case, a Lincoln or Frederick the Great may emerge, but almost never a Plato or a Socrates. Marcus Aurelius is probably the most remarkable exception to this. For he was truly a philosopher. Yet there are those who would accuse even him of too great an indulgence in the matter of his succession, since his son Commodus turned out to be an unsatisfactory emperor, the seeds of which it is assumed he ought to have discerned.

Though it may husband, even nurture, high culture for a time, democracy inevitably results in a lowering of standards in human deportment and aesthetic and moral creativity. It dissolves into the fever of a mob. This is unfortunate. For it was originally instituted to establish and preserve the rights of individuals. These are what underwrite a freedom for self-improvement and innovation.

Unfortunately, self-determination is a characteristic which must originate in each person. It is not a gift from authority, but is only protected by it. In general, most people do not develop independently, even in the most secure circumstances. They drift along at the heels of others, adopting their habits and opinions. This is why democracy is apt to collapse under its own weight over time.

## Thoughts on Creativity, Spirit, and the Ethical Life

The world's social problems can only be solved by a complete and universal change of heart. Though this is possible at any time, it will likely require a worldwide disaster to bring it about. Until then, the familiar cycle of political systems will continue.

The Life Principle. What is this? It is awareness, both individual and general, which is grounded in universal consciousness. Within it are feelings, collations of which are emotions. These are opposed to other sensations. For the elements of emotion are prior to those contributing to a knowledge of space and time, the former being subjective, the latter developed by the maturing mind into an objective physical lattice.

So the Life Principle is consciousness exhibiting emotions prior to any other field of awareness. For these comprise the means and moods of spirit, which guides individual life from within, when it is permitted an influence. But the inner life must be deliberately accessed. For it is not akin to the superficial emotions generated by ego. These act as a screen and are no more than collations of feeling misdirected by a mind convinced of its material limitations.

To infuse one's sense of self within the inner person, as opposed to the outer, is to become grounded in the Life Principle, the source of all things. But, due to a seeming material precedence wrought upon the mind by experience, few are able to break through to this source. Nevertheless, it is possible. For the material illusion can be set aside, freeing an individual to grow in the subtlety of spirit.

### George Lowell Tollefson

Every conception of God ever conceived is a magnification of the self. Every conception of the self is born of the spirit within, even when its origin is misunderstood. So is it not clear that they are the same?

Robert Frost crafted poems that speak simply and remain fresh in the mind. In one example, *Mending Wall*, there is the question of territorial instinct, the need to claim possession of something and exclude others from it. Frost begins the poem, "Something there is that doesn't love a wall." His neighbor retorts, "Good fences make good neighbors," and clings to his viewpoint, until the poet, in a humorous spirit, sees him, "Bringing a stone grasped firmly by the top/ In each hand, like an old-stone savage armed."

    In *Bereft* he writes of someone who has lost a loved one. This person stands on his porch in sorrow, hearing the wind's "deeper roar" and seeing the "somber clouds" massing in the west. He finds himself suddenly alone in his house and in his life, with "no one left but God." Conversely, *The Tuft of Flowers* expresses simple joy in a beautiful thing: "a tall tuft of flowers beside a brook/ A leaping tongue of bloom the scythe had spared/ Beside a reedy brook the scythe had bared." This is "sheer morning gladness at the brim."

    Frost did not experience an easy life. He enjoyed farming but was not good at it, having a habit of sleeping in till noon. He was a first rate but unorthodox teacher. And he suffered many personal losses, including a son who committed suicide. But out of this came a poetry of gentleness and often joy which reminds the reader that the simple things shared by all

## Thoughts on Creativity, Spirit, and the Ethical Life

are full of mystery and beauty. To read this poetry is like taking a walk in the mountains or a forest. They can lighten one's day, because they accept the burden of living and find good in it.

It is important to find one's center of gravity—to discover the inner self and discern the direction in which it would lead. It is in this way that breakthrough insights are achieved and transforming lives of influence are lived. Most people do not do this. They labor at molding the outer, social self to suit what they anticipate others might want. Thus they fail to become acquainted with their true natures.

Of course, discovering this nature and nurturing it is not a guarantee that earthshaking, time-immemorial events will follow. Each individual has her peculiar destiny, large or small. Whatever is the case, it is always a vital gift. And it contributes irrevocably to the progress of the race. But the willy-nilly favor of the crowd leans this way and that, blinded by lack of access to the inner life. So no person on the path of truth should measure herself by the general opinion of others.

Nevertheless, human beings crave favor and pine fretfully for it. Unable to suppress this tendency, which is a product of the isolated ego, they must not be governed by it. They should press forward in the direction of inwardness. For that is the ground of themselves and general being. Within it are the seeds of destiny. There is but one destiny. It is the unseen unity of spirit.

In this world, life unfolds event by event. For time is the material of a perceived world. It is an expression of limitation:

a cornerstone of the physical. In universal spirit there is but the moment. All things are simultaneous therein. Thus the spirit of limited knowledge, which constitutes a person, has every event present to it. But in material existence there must be sequence. So the prior knowledge is hidden within a shadow of unfolding experience. It can be accessed only as an intuition. But neither can this be set forth in the imagery of life. It must be both apprehended and acknowledged without evidence.

Because people of the present share Shakespeare's perspective, it is difficult to imagine a time when he will recede into a viewpoint of the past, as has occurred with Homer. The latter's outlook remains apparent. The means of his genius is manifest. But its hold on modern sensibilities is not what it was for the ancient Greeks. Neither will Shakespeare dominate a future age.

With both relativity and quantum mechanics, physical science is becoming more and more an expression of the mind. This does not mean that it presents any less of a description of material experience. What it indicates is that the world is becoming increasingly recognized as an expression of the mind.

In reference to the work which was produced prior to the lily pond murals, Monet's principal achievement was not as it seems. It was not confined to a capture of fleeting effects of light and atmosphere. Rather, it was a demonstration of the stupendous variety of subtle emotional variations. No two of these paintings are alike in the precise mood expressed. Neither has any other artist exhibited such a range of emotional nuance.

Art is of the province of mind exhibited in terms of heart.

The time will come when human beings will be transformed into the mindset of spirit. But they will not be perfect. Perfection is an idea created in the material mind in compensation for its pervading sense of limitation. As for the transformation, it will simply remove the more egregious elements of an undisciplined ego.

People will come to recognize the importance of behaving in accordance with their own underlying sense of unity. Personality quirks and serious emotional disorders will persist for a period. But in time they will be smoothed over to an extent which is consonant with universal harmony.

Every human being is a pyramid of internalized traits so complex that one wonders how the blocks were set in place with such a unified precision as to form a personality. At the top is the visible portion of personality. But beneath are all the supporting and conflicting elements. It is this complexity of an inner universe in relation to a universe without which is mystifying.

There is as much force of creativity within as without, and without as within. Such phenomena cannot be brought together in the manner of the easy integration of a puzzle. For with the sum of many people there are multiple universes within a universe, multiple infinities within the infinite. It is for this reason that no ethical system, no political plan, ever resolves the dilemma of social integration toward an achievement of human happiness.

Physics is a philosophy. It is a metaphysics. Though confined within the parameters of proportion (mathematics) and experimental verification, however indirect the latter may be, it must be modeled from common experience. Even such an intellectual anomaly as a probability cloud describing an electron in terms of its variable location, is a "cloud."

The science of probability itself presents an illustration of the working of the mind in terms of its various levels of logical certainty. For the imagination must either form its imagery on the basis of concrete reference points of a daily encounter or upon a close adherence to operations of the mind.

That is, the concrete reference points are apprehended in terms of symbols, metaphors, and analogies drawn from common experience. And the operations of the mind limit the manner in which these can be used. So given, as in the former case, the relationship between concepts and supporting imagery, however shadowy in suggestion the imagery may be, a working imagination is needed to ground the most abstruse reflections.

Therefore, upon what ground does a logical positivist stand when she declares that there is no place for metaphysics in philosophy? Would she have it that all speculative matters must be shackled by the mathematical and experimental parameters of physical science? This is a narrow consideration indeed! For it demands that no suppositions beyond those immediately instrumental to science should be entertained. So

## Thoughts on Creativity, Spirit, and the Ethical Life

there can be no thought as to a reason for science itself. Thus it hovers in midair to no purpose.

Does language analysis provide an explanation for the whole of human awareness? Can any form of conceptualization secure a smothering blanket over experience? What then of the profound depths of a Rembrandt self-portrait? Is this not as concrete and meaningful an encounter as any other? Yet no articulation in words has compassed it, though the effort of attempting to do so is always worthwhile.

As regards an earlier statement concerning Voltaire's criticism of Leibniz, it must be conceded that, by taking a subjective outlook (which is the general viewpoint of Voltaire), religion has done a better job of handling the problem of evil than has philosophy. But can every consideration be confined to a subjective approach? What is the truth of such a position?

Spirit (universal consciousness) is receptive to those who approach it with sincerity. As the innermost core of a person, it cannot be denied to him. Would it declare to him, "I disown you"? It would not. But, conversely, a person can, and often does, regard it with indifference. In fact, so much is this the case, and so frequently does an individual cling exclusively to his external, fabricated, social self, that he grows utterly unaware of his inner nature. Subsequently dead, he clings until the termination of his days to a false and meaningless life.

Morality originates with the inner person. If honest with herself, an individual will behave justly toward others. But, should such an intimate purity be forsaken, every other relationship is accordingly polluted.

Religion arises from two sources: intuition and reason. A deep intuition proceeding from spirit presents itself as a series of related feelings. These collectively constitute an emotional state, which is simply recognized and neither explained nor derived from any other source. The conclusions of reason, on the other hand, follow from conceptual precedents which, be they either definitions or axioms, are interminably preceded by other reasons, or explanations. For there is no end to these, as any concept is inevitably preceded by another.

So great religions begin with intuitions, or spiritual insight. These express an irrefutable authority, since they stand out powerfully in emotional experience and are independent of explanation. They have been immediately recognized and accepted by those who have experienced them.

But the followers of an inspired founder come armed only with a rational faculty. Consequently, they must interpret and explain what they frequently do not fully understand. As a result, they belabor the original insights with intellectual discussion and debate, turning them about in the turmoil of an uncomprehending mind, until they are rendered all but meaningless.

Out of such impoverished explanations come doctrines and laws. For these are promulgated by later generations which, deprived of so much as an acquaintance with the original feelings attendant upon the insights, pervert and replace them with formulas of their own making. The aboriginal vision is shunted to a subordinate role, obscured by established prac-

## Thoughts on Creativity, Spirit, and the Ethical Life

tices and rationalizations which are largely the work of unsubstantiated imagination.

Moreover, as a further emotional augmentation, superstitions are allowed to grow. For they are encouraged by the legalistic authority of the faith. In time, these become the soul and principal substance of the new religion, an institution which extinguishes truth and nurtures free works of imagination.

Nothing persists like the unruly imaginations of people. It is against this that the much feebler faculty of reason must stand guard. Even so, reason is only periodically effective in stemming the freewheeling imaginative tide. For ungoverned imagination presents an immense flood eternally engaged in suffocating the majority of humankind. This is the reason there is always a need for a renaissance, or starting over.

The surest means of destruction of a democratic republic is that it should become too democratic. For the general populace is ever a collective of unreflective minds which must ensnare both themselves and others under tyranny.

Reason, the universal gift of humanity, is generally accessed by only a few minds. For memory substitutes as a useful crutch for the majority of people, who prefer to follow the thinking of their predecessors. As this practice informs a good part of the more sophisticated professions, it is what generally passes for original thought and merits the esteem of the uninformed.

There are two kinds of slavery imposed from within. The first is a subjection to the senses, the second a submission to the ego. The former degrades a person to the condition of an unthinking animal. The latter magnifies the effects of the physical impulses. For example, the desire of either sex to physically manipulate or make a "conquest" of another person is sensual craving enhanced to exploitation.

As a rule, neither drive can be fully eliminated. But the bodily impulses should be brought under the guidance of principle, whereas the ego, though utterly unquenchable, ought to be channeled into constructive behavior. Instead of functioning as a goad towards the domination of others, it should be exercised creatively for their sake.

Considering not only the acquisition, but the increased subtlety of language in modern humans, it is not difficult to understand how the high level of development of abstract thought in Homo sapiens sapiens may have come about. But the wonder is that such a thing should ever have occurred. Could it have been a superfluous capacity evolved unwittingly as an offshoot of the refinement of tools? Or did it originate in some other way?

In fact, it is something which is independent of externals like tool making, having been born within the mind without specific, but rather a general, environmental provocation. Emerging from a faculty of unity lying at the heart of human awareness, it has of its own accord thrust the development of the human race in its present unprecedented direction.

## Thoughts on Creativity, Spirit, and the Ethical Life

Considered in terms of itself alone, the consciousness of material experience is nothing more than a loose, ever-shifting conglomerate composed of fragmented units of sensation. But to impose an increased faculty of unity over this largely fragmented character of the mind and thus render it meaningful to spirit, the inner unity of consciousness has engineered a means of encompassing perceived phenomena in such a manner as to withdraw them from their scattered and unrelated condition.

To facilitate the process, concepts came into being to supply an engine for generating complex structures of mental apprehension. Words, serving to signify these concepts, were made for the specific purpose of standing apart from experience. In this way, ideas were born and brought together in interrelated, logical trains of thought. The concepts formed subordinate and parallel relations to one another which, when exactingly established, exhibit an ineffable power of unity.

This power of unity is the source of certainty in logical relations. It is a faculty which lifts a thinking mind out of the context of experience and sets it apart in a realm of its own. It is, of course, expressed entirely in material terms. For it cannot be otherwise, since the imagination will not advance beyond its physical environs, its concept-forming images having been drawn from them. Yet in its increasing sophistication the abstract thinking process yields a journey of spirit into itself, unexpectedly thrusting limited being into what are at least quasi-universal terms.

Any system of thought is open-ended. It can never become a self-enclosed circle of interrelated meanings. For every axiom or definition demands further explanation. And this cannot come from propositions derived from them. Accordingly, the problem of open-endedness is one of the fundamental limitations of reason.

Despite its limitations, the importance of reason cannot be overstated. Though reliant upon imagination for its supporting imagery, reason excels it in the certitude, clear delineation, and close-fittedness of its thought. The mind's need to integrate disparate elements in its broad field of awareness and to believe in what it has assembled and arranged cannot be represented by even the freest products of imagination.

The ignorance, superstition, and self-imprisonment of the race knows no other gate to the liberation of its faculties, no other entrance to wisdom, no other path to self-conquest and mastery of its environment. But human beings must beware of the taint of arrogance which may attach itself to reason. It is the belief that this faculty is omnipotent and therefore infallible.

Reason, as an instrument of thought and knowledge, is riddled with drawbacks and limitations. For it is strictly of this world, a cordoning off of physical experience by a materially restricted mind. But it is also a tool which, when confronted with the fragments of experience, can bring them into a workable and reliable order. It can make physical existence feasible and in some degree comforting.

The problem of evil is best referred to humankind's habitual focus of its increased self-awareness on the demands of its animal nature. It is from this that it must be liberated. It should

## Thoughts on Creativity, Spirit, and the Ethical Life

turn its attention toward its inner spiritual core and hold it there. Having done so, and having effected this difficult feat collectively, no doubt initially with great effort, the race would gradually raise itself to a higher state of being. But the universally acquired discipline that is necessary to accomplish this is no light matter. Yet it will come. For it must.

The foremost principle of life is to trust in the spirit within. For it is the fount of the most honest emotions. Abraham is reputed to have heard a voice. It was more likely something which he felt. Whatever its expression, in comparison to it all philosophy pales into speculation, every institutional doctrine withering on the vine of wrongfully attributed authority.

How do images arise to express an emotion? What is felt is exhibited by the mind as imagery, the images being drawn from material experience. It is not difficult to understand that the imagination is pressed into service by any emotion begetting experience, regardless of whether the experience is material, thus producing a motivated reaction, or whether it is an emotional state directly induced by spirit.

But in either case the process is independent, allowing for an intervention of will. Hence the dilemma: how can this be, when all products of the mind are held to come directly from spirit? It is a matter of perspective. This is the immaterial view. And the former is the representational view. In the immaterial view the entire fabric of experience is a direct expression of spirit. Whereas in the representational approach there is an assumption that physical experience may be treated as independent of the mind.

As a result, the immaterial perspective locates will in the spirit, while the representational approach places it within an interaction between subject and object. It is the difference between what was referred to as "primary" and "secondary" mind in *The Immaterial Structure of Human Experience*. The former is the realm of true origin and full encompassment. The latter constitutes a more limited embrace, which is that of human consciousness. It is here that the experience of time emerges. Within spirit, however, there is only the instantaneous.

Human awareness, which is universal consciousness in a self-induced state of limitation, abides eternally in a timeless domain unrecognized by the material mind. Consequently, this more circumscribed consciousness cannot be extinguished. For, in their emotional origin and execution, an individual person's memories are those of spirit.

But whether or not, in a projected conception of an afterlife, they can be transferred into a quasi-material domain devoid of sorrow cannot be ascertained from this life. Yet, if this prospect is not to be affirmed, neither is there any reason to despair of it. For the query naturally arises: why should it not be the case?

An inspired link between imagination and spirit-infused emotions is quite rare but profound when it is established. It is the phenomenon of spiritual vision and the source of great leaps in human progress in art, literature, religion, philosophy, and science. What is initially only felt as a hunch, insight, or impulse in a particular direction is subsequently more fully embodied in mental imagery. The images are then converted into concepts, the concepts into trains of reason. That is how visions and theories are established, becoming new cities of the mind, yet to be demolished and reconstructed under the impress of subsequent waves of such inspiration.

How greatly this differs from the common imaginations of humankind! For the latter are a mix of borrowings and patchwork replacements originating in the social ego with its shallow and falsely oriented purposes. They are imaginations grounded not in spirit but in the exigencies of the moment.

Here are to be found an influx of flaws into even the genuine products of spirit. For, unfortunately, the emotions of spirit, arising from the deep self, are frequently alloyed with these baser elements born of the social identity of the person. Hence the often observed need to reconstruct what ought to have been a perfect edifice of thought.

Spirit cannot be said to host either good or evil, since everything emanates from it. For how can the author of all things hold punitive council over its own creation? Whatever weakness there is in human nature, including any failings of the will, was originally authored as such without human participation. So, though there should be a cleansing which separates the bad from the good after the living of a life, no enduring punishment can be justly administered.

The spirit lives through and is the life of every individual, as well as being both ground and support of all things. As it is direct, pure in intention, and without guile, it is also trustworthy. Therefore a person should be likewise toward others. This is the indisputable source of morality, which affords an ethic of great simplicity.

But behavior of this caliber cannot be consistently depended upon should it originate in fear. A horror of retribution makes a person weak, not strong. For it generates distrust. It is a sword of Damocles hanging over the head of an offender. What arises from it is an atmosphere of apprehension, sure to soon become an expression of distrust.

Langston Hughes, a black American poet, is probably best known for his poem, "The Negro Speaks of Rivers," which resounds with lines like, "I've known rivers ancient as the world and older than the flow of human blood in human veins," and concludes with, "My soul has grown deep like the rivers." The poem has a rhythm which feels like the slow movement of centuries. It is enduring and beautiful.

But there are other poems of equal merit. One is called, "Mother to Son." And it begins, "Well, son, I'll tell you:/ Life for me ain't been no crystal stair." Using the image of a tenement stairwell, the poem goes on to express the mother's years of hardship with images like "tacks," "splinters," "boards torn up," and "no carpet on the floor—Bare."

The mother assures her son, "But all the time/ I'se been a-climbin' on,/ And reachin' landin's." This has not been easy for her because she has been "goin' in the dark/ Where there ain't been no light." It is a tale of struggle, of a parent's anguish concerning the eternal question: How do I prepare my child for such a world?

It might seem to be an insurmountable problem, given her tribulations. But she concludes by saying, "So boy, don't you

## Thoughts on Creativity, Spirit, and the Ethical Life

turn back./ Don't you set down on the steps/ 'Cause you finds it's kinder hard./ Don't you fall now—/ For I'se still goin', honey,/ I'se still climbin',/ And life for me ain't been no crystal stair."

This is a woman who has not had it easy, in part because of race. But it is a poem that speaks to everyone. One way or another, every person has been there. He has seen it, felt it in himself or in others, because one person's suffering, a single individual's courage in lonely struggle, becomes another individual's enrichment in understanding.

The principle of life is in all things. It is an expression of the unity, or a drawing into unity, of spirit. For example, a seemingly inert object like a stone expresses a static unity. A living organism, such as a plant or animal, exhibits a dynamic unity, which undergoes a continual process of change as it absorbs external elements into itself in order to maintain its physical existence. Higher intelligence sifts and organizes experience into knowledge, so that in the lower animals it may achieve greater physical and psychological freedom and in human beings it may ascend to an understanding of its condition.

Through a use of mental imagery based strictly on material awareness, by means of which it enfolds physical experience into itself, an increase of understanding approaches, without achieving, the transcendent unity of spirit. It is this advanced apprehension of knowledge which is the principal cause of human suffering. For suffering is imaginatively and psychologically magnified as the awareness of limitation increases. But, in fact, there is suffering in all living things, just more of it in the human.

Such is the underlying character of the human mind that it strains within the chains of material bondage toward a liberating union within universal consciousness. But this cannot be fully achieved. So everything which restrains it becomes painful, mournful, sad, a cause of anguish and weeping. Physical and psychological limitations, particularly when increased, are its restraints. Consequently, there is an especial terror of death due to its unperceived and unrecognized agenda. For the physical mind knows not that death is a moment of liberation.

Jesus did not die for the forgiveness of sin. Humanity is already forgiven. But, like Socrates, he gave his life for the truth. His was a transcendent truth which he could neither fully reveal to his followers, nor explain to his tormentors. Nor could he deny it.

It is a fact not well received that human error is an unavoidable condition. In its myriad forms its nonacceptance leads into ever deeper error. For the human ego struggles against limitations which are its very character and definition. Thus it visits anguish upon itself and others, raising the index of suffering beyond what is natural.

Why should human beings suffer? Because it is a struggle against limitation which realizes spirit. It is through strengthening by means of a vigorous application of pressure upon its capacity that an athlete or questing mind seeks to increase its tone and resilience. And there can be no such enhancement without discomfort and sometimes pain. Nor could the spirit

## Thoughts on Creativity, Spirit, and the Ethical Life

realize its rich array of intuitions without a concrete expression which, in turn, must continually strive toward its spiritual origin.

The fundamental mental faculty of unity, which is consciousness, is the source for the principle of life. It is that which in living things can be said to bring complex molecules together in such a way as to conserve high energy levels for an extended period without returning to a lower state. In other words, it is a means by which an incorporation of diverse elements into a unity is achieved. For not only are a number of elements brought together in a greater compound. They are rendered capable of both duration and increase. Living occurs for a span. And metabolic growth may also take place.

As for the mind, this same principle of unity, or life, is again the faculty of consciousness. For it is this alone which enables a recognition of unities among things. By means of this faculty, objects, events, and processes can be identified and further organized. The same consciousness, operating as a unifying faculty, also leads onward toward a steady increase in mental organization, facilitating the human quest for universal understanding. In this manner, the mind rises toward, though never quite attaining to, a completely integrated comprehension of and union with its experience.

Experience can never be fully integrated by the material mind. For there will always be questions. In other words, the mental apprehension of experience does itself generate experience.

Spirit is not matter, but the source of matter. Matter is not spirit. It is an expression of it. Yet something remains in matter that is spirit. But this is easily overlooked. It resembles a voice which utters words that convey sound without a consideration of their meaning. For it is in resemblance to this sound, when it is considered alone without meaning, that the material realm takes on its illusory appearance of independence.

Thus the material realm and the physical character of words may each appear to be self-contained. For it is only subsequent to an initial experience of either that the former is considered to have a source and the latter to have meaning. Nevertheless, the full expression of either is transcendent, since it is spirit which underpins both the workings of matter and the meaning of an utterance.

One of the principal dilemmas of the human race is its ambivalence in sexual morality. The hormonal impulse exhibits a drive toward promiscuity. But for most, though not all, people, there is also an emotional need which is oriented toward the formation of an exclusive and enduring individual attachment dependent upon good faith. Thus so much as a hint of a wayward expression of this physical impulse in one person may lead to a generally futile, and often harmful, response of possessiveness and jealousy in another.

Reason alone could not provide a demonstration of the deepest moral truths were it not for the subtle guidance of an inexplicable upright feeling. This is because common emotions, which are generated by physical experience and subsequently

## Thoughts on Creativity, Spirit, and the Ethical Life

placed within an order of thought, are not of such a character. They are of a strictly practical nature devoid of transcendence.

Moral truths, on the other hand, lie in close association with an individual's innermost self. They are hidden gems which can only be mined as a result of detachment from externals. But once entertained, they will fill the mind with that rightness of proportion which is likewise achieved in the creation of the highest art. This is why such a work must be conceived as profoundly moral, though it should exhibit little concern with rules of conduct.

In magnifying the hormonal effects of the sexual impulse, egoism not only encourages psychological scenarios of sexual conquest, it lends itself to powerful fantasies in which a lover imagines that the love object is the fulfillment of every hope, much of it unrelated to any realistic future happiness. When the relationship fails, a sense of devastation and desperation ensues. This occurs with both sexes and is the source of much anguish.

Reason, however faltering, is the remedy. It must play a leading role from the beginning of the relationship. Perhaps it may be too analytical. Hence the importance of feeling, even to the point of idealism. But such an emotion must not blind a person to real circumstances. And a consultation with one's deepest inner core is the necessary source of sound judgment. This is often referred to as relying upon the spirit, the spirit being simultaneously the innermost nature of a person and universal in character.

The greater part of warfare is an expression of unmitigated national vanity, generally accompanied by protestations of national security, including a desire to maintain it by securing access to outside resources. In addition to this, there are other contributors to the problem, such as a false hysteria or the greed of the business community. But even these are inflated into vanity by politicians and public organs of communication prior to implementation.

A lesser origin of military action does arise from a more legitimate and immediate motive of national self-defense. This is when a nation is under attack or threat of attack. But it too must often be construed as proceeding from communal pride inflated by whatever means in order to engage the emotions of the multitude.

So what if nations as such did not exist? Would mere centers of ethnic identity inevitably exhibit mutual hostility? Or could they not gently meld into one another at their borders? Perhaps they could. But this would require a sense of universal good will and tolerance. And it would depend upon an extraordinary degree of honesty, as difficult to practice as a modest sense of a people's proper place in the intercultural community.

The Greeks introduced the life of reason into a small pocket of their people, but not by any means all of them, as attested to by the death of Socrates. In the present age, the situation has changed little, if at all. Yet a time must come when the rational mind becomes a prized possession for everyone, or at least for the majority.

## Thoughts on Creativity, Spirit, and the Ethical Life

This is not to assert the perfection of the reasoning faculty. There are glaring limitations concerning it. Yet even under such a shaky certitude, it may still be a criterion of choice. Outside of it, there is spiritual transcendence. But this must be exercised with caution and kept out of the hands of manipulators.

Every person should insist upon his direct access to spirit. For each individual is a full expression of the transcendent. For this reason, instruction may be required at an early age to prevent misguided apprehensions. But there can be no need for the continued presence of a mediator in adult life, be that agent strictly personal or broadly institutional.

The Protestant branch of Christianity is right about some things, Catholics about others, and the Eastern Orthodox persuasion concerning still others. Jews, Muslims, Hindus, and Buddhists have their legitimate take on the matter. But the problem is that religions always come to assume that they are incontrovertibly right about everything concerning matters of the transcendent. Yet their final appeal is to historical hearsay, past and present authority, and a generally ossified tradition. Hence the dilemma.

There is no enduring sadness in the world because human beings are direct expressions of spirit. In this life, they just do not know it.

In death, human consciousness is subsumed under the universal awareness of spirit. But this does not indicate that a personality should be entirely lost. No, an individual nature is simply enlarged to the greater sphere, where it continues to subsist without the flaws it once had, such shortcomings having been products of limitations which, having been removed, leave no blemish.

Setting aside developments in science and its supporting technology, the nineteen hundreds can be referred to culturally as the century of fads. It was an era which sought to invent meaning rather than find it. What had been forgotten was that truth lies in the heart of things, where it is gradually revealed by means of honest investigation. It is not to be thrown up upon a production line limited to the crude imaginings of the moment.

What are laws but plugs in the dyke of human misbehavior? There can be no perfection of laws. Patches do not make a whole cloth.

Just as it is difficult to discern whether a statesman governs in his own interest or in that of the people, so is it hard to determine when a churchman represents the character of the transcendent or when it is himself and his colleagues he serves.

A half-frozen human spirit is the norm. It is what makes it so surprising when a fully open heart is encountered.

To exhibit a fully open heart in the present world is to be a turtle without a shell. Hence the greater multitude of hard-shelled spirits.

## Thoughts on Creativity, Spirit, and the Ethical Life

Many would be original. But few are. These are the ones whose interest lies in being true.

A socially constructed personality may lead to failure. The inner spirit of a person is a witness to this tragedy. But it is not harmed by it.

Whatever may be the character of an afterlife, it is evident that there is something within a person which will endure. This is easily felt. But its description cannot be set forth in certain terms.

Many words describe a thing. Only a few are needed to bring it to mind.

It is much easier to recognize a truth than it is to render it in conceptual form. That is why Einstein needed a decade to articulate the general theory, which he already knew.

Is it not strange that an artist or a theorist can conceive the germ of an interrelated set of ideas before embarking upon the long labor of creating its integrated expression? Does not a simple cloud withhold a complex of rain, hail, or snow until the moment of release? Yet what is the cloud but this effusion which it gives forth? It does so and is spent.

    Likewise, an artist or theorist is not only the progenitor of a multifaceted work, but is himself the work created. Human destinies, whatever their future course may become, are lived in preparation for the unfolding of their integrated acts. For these are the ghost of something more enduring than the ephemeral circumstances of a life.

The personal presence of someone is always more impressive than the physical space taken up. For a personality is full of shifting detail and event, not to mention the expansive character of individual expression. That is why an overwhelming absence is felt when she has gone.

Societies inevitably act in betrayal of their ideals. For it is in this very act and its reaction that they work out their true purpose and a meaning for the future is given.

Being and nothingness are the two surfaces of a leaf. It is the life between them which is meant.

The disintegration of age is an unwelcome liberation of the mind. Yet it is the freedom of this departure which puts a seal on the journey.

There is no cause for standing in opposition to science. It has its incontrovertible truths. But there should be a recognition that science is confined to the senses and to the material structures of the mind. Mathematics, a reflection of the bones of that structure, is accordingly a shadow of the architecture of phenomenal awareness.

Yet it is not transcendent. It does not penetrate beyond the physical universe. Nor can it do more than suggest the character of universal awareness. For human sensibility cannot probe

## Thoughts on Creativity, Spirit, and the Ethical Life

beyond its limitations. It only "feels" that there is more. What this feeling is is something other than sensory awareness.

Its origin is deep emotion, the kind of primal feeling which is not a spawn of sensation, imagination, or reason. In its struggle to apprehend this, human awareness gropes for imaginative representation, the elements of which it must retrieve from material experience. From this it constructs the crystalline structures of reason. For concepts are ever dependent upon imagery, whether the images are hidden or manifest.

But the attempt is weak, utterly inadequate, which is well understood. Yet the original source, the feeling and its deep emotional input, remains strong. It cannot be denied. Hence the central dilemma of the human condition. For here is a creature bound by limitation and death, but, when willing to see what it cannot discern, becomes acutely aware of the transcendent.

Every religion is a leap in darkness. But it is also a partial ascension into light.

Van Gogh said that he only felt truly alive when he painted. How many have been so dedicated to one penetrating pursuit or another? Were they wrong? Are they wrong now, deluded? Or have they struck upon a shoreline beyond which lie happy regions of liberated understanding?

Is it conceivable that a simple chemical reaction, and nothing more, could in some way be responsible for consciousness? Can the stone cold death of a material entity explain life? Is not consciousness awareness? And is not awareness a process and thus a response to process as well? It must be that awareness and process together are the key.

There is not only human reason which can apprehend a process, but a more encompassing awareness and its intimate relationship to processes unfolding within it. Could not this offer to some deep, transcendent understanding beyond human vision a means of working out its own recognition of what it has projected into being? In this way, the entire universe would be alive, and much beyond it as well.

What if it should be the case that all the imaginations and subsequent rational constructs of humanity were merely guesswork and did not touch the hidden truth? Would this lend to human effort a pall of futility? Not at all. For the striving is itself an opening to truth.

It has been said that painters think in terms of color and line. Is this non-conceptual? No, because for great painters at least there is always the involvement of a conceptual element in their work. Which is to say that a painter sees ideationally and progressively through the substance of her medium. But perhaps this process does not resemble reason in its usual sense.

There is a type of conceptual thinking which employs imagination and feeling in a direct way. It is something other than the proto-reasoning which can be attributed to higher forms of non-human life, such as chimpanzees, wolves, and ravens. For the latter is not conceptual. But this is. It is language based.

## Thoughts on Creativity, Spirit, and the Ethical Life

There is more than one kind of language. There is a species of thinking which hews so closely to the supporting imagery of concepts that it takes on the direct form of those images, shuttling the guiding conceptual principles behind them, where they form a shadowy but very much present backdrop. It is the reverse of the normal process of images resting behind concepts.

An example of artistic thinking would be the palpable presence of peasant life in Camille Pissarro's work, even when no human figures are depicted. Beautiful as the landscape may be, the sweat and labor of the country peasantry is detected. This is a guiding conceptualization hovering unannounced behind the picture elements. The same can be said for any other prominent artist, such as Berthe Morisot, whose sensual brushwork delineating fabrics in many of her paintings heightens an intended awareness of femininity.

All things in the spirit are instantaneous, immutable, and therefore simultaneous. For this reason, the creativity of spirit is not an unfolding, insofar as spirit itself is concerned. But in the material realm the creativity of spirit is perceived by creatures in terms of an activity, or as a progression.

The character of artistic insight is not philosophical in the abstract sense. It may be more accurately described as the capacity to bring into acute focus a range of experience which has not been previously expressed in such a fresh and penetrating way. But from this comes the impression made upon the viewer, listener, reader, etc. This evokes contemplation and, upon occasion, intensive thought, which supports an enhancement of philosophical understanding.

Human will is grounded in spirit. But in varying degrees it may appear to function in a manner which is independent of that source, due to the widely held illusion that the material ego is the self. For it is a deep inner awareness which is the domain for the true expression of will. Consequently, the path to a harmonious life is to be sought in this inner sanctum with which the intemperate mind must align itself.

As this is done, a person will grow in the knowledge of her fundamental destiny. She will not then easily stray from it. Emotive intuitions forming subtly within will be regarded, thus guiding her away from the false impulses of an egoism based on a purely social sense of personal identity. In keeping with such an intimate accord with spirit, it is not inappropriate to view the relationship as personal.

Though it is true that "person" is a human conception based on material limitation and cannot be used as a classification to encapsulate and define that which is transcendent and unknowable, it is nevertheless useful to express the intimacy. And it is reasonable, since all things emanate from spirit, or universal consciousness, including person. For this reason, spirit may be related to in personal terms without being limited by the concept.

Universal consciousness is wholly expressed within each individual human being and within every other material thing. For this consciousness, or spirit, is an indivisible unity. Yet there is variation and distinction because differentiation between individuals is brought about by the limited content of personal consciousness, not by consciousness itself. To attain to an understanding of this frees a person from a fear of isolation. It thus undermines egoism, which is a product of this fear. Self-respect is not only retained, but enhanced. And it is this which strengthens the determination to adhere to the true self.

Some of the short stories in Edgar Allan Poe's *Tales of the Grotesque and Arabesque* are portrayals of a mind under stress. But Poe does not rely upon clinical psychology. His work is an expression of human frailty. To fully appreciate his atmosphere of terror or horror, a reader should read deeply enough to discover not only fear or the unthinkable, but gallows humor.

Take the story, "The Tell-Tale Heart." Tension grips the reader from the opening sentence: "True!—nervous—very, very dreadfully nervous I had been and am; but why *will* you say that I am mad?" All the twisted passion of an unhinged mind is in this statement of false confidence. But there is something more than strained emotion and dislodged awareness here. There is laughter, Poe's laughter, the reader's sympathetic smile, at such a howl of anguish irrationally, even comically, released from an overburdened heart.

In the same opening paragraph, Poe draws the reader further into a realm of insanity and the hardly believable: "Above all was the sense of hearing acute. I heard all things in the heaven and in the earth. I heard many things in hell." Later in the story, when the murderer spies upon the old man's "vulture eye," he opens the bedroom door so slowly that, "a watch's minute hand moves more quickly than did mine." This fact is supposed to be proof of the killer's "sagacity."

When the victim awakes in terror, the killer imagines he can hear his heartbeat across the room. He is concerned that "the sound would be heard by a neighbor." After the disposal of the body, the police come to investigate. Again the murderer hears the heartbeats. He foams and raves and swears, walks about making "violent gesticulations," and swings his chair against the floorboards where the body is concealed.

Confronted with these exaggerated details, a reader wants to laugh out loud. But she knows how far her laughter is from the emotions in the story. To cause her to sense this difference is Poe's special gift in presenting a deranged mind. What the stories truly represent is the general human psyche rendered upset and thoroughly offset from normality by the sudden realization that it is enclosed in a limiting bubble of the feeble reasonings and imaginative constructs of culture, religion, and science, outside of which lies a looming terror of the unknown. Herein is the underlying concern supplying the creative impulse behind so many of these stories.

Jealousy, envy, competition, anger, and hate all arise from the social self, not the inner spirit. To put these fragmentations of life away and move inward toward an absence of disharmony, greater productivity, and peace is a desirable goal. It was with this in mind that Albert Einstein is reputed to have made a distinction between his political and scientific efforts. He said his efforts toward reform were for the present moment. But equations are for all time.

## Thoughts on Creativity, Spirit, and the Ethical Life

Though it is certainly true that equations are a construct of the material mind, it is also the case that the drive to assimilate knowledge within a greater unity is a matter in accord with the character of spirit. For it is akin to the holistic nature of inner awareness. It is with such a distinction in mind that Einstein made his statement. For he was a man of peace.

The world is as it is. And people are what they are. For nothing productive can be said about the perfection or imperfection of either. But, while this is so, the cultural and spiritual evolution of humanity may yet lead to a gentler regard. Out of this can spring a more peaceful, harmonious, and relieved world.

Unregulated imagination is a major pitfall of the human race. It is proto-reasoning, the means the great majority of people (and perhaps all people at one time or another) choose to represent experience. In the most highly developed mental processes of animal species short of humanity, it is this form of thought which is employed. For it is most closely related to the indicator-response behavior which conditions animals toward the location of food, shelter, and the avoidance of danger.

Proto-reasoning, which involves imaginative free play, also allows animals to engage in sportive activity and a dream life. But the human version is freer yet, providing for the construction of a complex mental map representing material experience and even beyond. All this without the necessity of a careful analysis and the investigation of evidence. But it is much too inexact. For it permits a good many unwarranted excesses.

So to tighten the thought process, in the last two and a half millennia a more regulated form of imagination has been recognized and developed. It is reason, a powerful though by no means infallible instrument. This faculty is as old as Homo sapiens sapiens. But its potential has only more recently been recognized and systematically employed.

In terms of mental accuracy and discipline it is greatly superior to the unregulated form of imaginative thinking. For it is deployed with care and, most importantly, a consciousness of its efficacy. Its uses are many. The most obvious examples are science and philosophy. But it is also helpful, when employed, in bringing a measure of sobriety to political responsiveness.

In addition, it can trim much of the imaginative free play from religion, leaving it more adapted to genuine human needs and the clear evidence of what has been experienced transcendentally within a natural context. This does not preclude consideration of the miraculous or the sensory unknowable. But it does bring any improper motives of spiritual claimants to light. It can be made to answer strictly to the requirements of the human heart, where these are appropriately applicable, and to the material evidence which surrounds exceptional events.

In spite of an increase in investigation and explanation characteristic of the present age, much of human experience retains an element of magic—especially a mystery, not of the process, but of the presence of life. What is to account for living things

## Thoughts on Creativity, Spirit, and the Ethical Life

and, more exceptionally when it is properly understood, a living universe? Can a physical cosmos with its mechanical origin supply a sufficient explanation?

If so, what of that calm state of recognition behind the usual frenzied awareness of life? By this is meant the settled condition of mind which sees events, including the very personal protagonist undergoing those events, as though these things were a passing show. There is an unaccountable and settled presence of spirit in this: a life and an awareness which encompasses material experience and is not a product of it.

The spirit is fully embedded in one person. Not a particle of it is extraneous. But it is also in other persons and all things. This strange suggestion of duality in character can be likened to multiple concentric circles located within a single encompassing circle. None is touching the other. And each is neither greater nor less in importance than its neighbor. Moreover, in examining their respective circumferences a beginning and an end cannot be discovered among them.

There is merely an illusion of limitation provided by their concentric natures, one appearing to reside inside another. But this is to be considered no more than a pattern representing the sequential character of material things. For each is replaced by its neighbor. Yet they take up a role together in the broader scheme of things, where they collectively exhibit an eternal duration in universal awareness, which is their encompassing circle of being.

The foundation of morality is trust, or its progenitor, good faith. Thus a person should neither steal, lie, murder, nor slander another. For it is these things which bespeak ill will and break down trust. The same principle applies to Jesus of Nazareth's statement that one should love God with all his heart, mind, and soul.

The word "God" is a designation for spirit. For it is spirit which is universal awareness, the foundation of experience. Awareness is consciousness. Since it is both unbounded and indivisible, there is but one consciousness. This is fully expressed in each person. It is the inner self. But, as there is also an outer, social self, a distinction must be made. The social self is the sense of individuality which is built up by observing the actions and reactions of others and emulating what one imagines those others think best. Such a practice often reduces a person to an inordinate regard for his ego and consequently a subservience to opinion.

Doting upon the social self can lead to a loss of awareness of the presence of the inner spirit, which is the true self. It is in this way that a person's life is lost among appearances, while to love the spirit with all one's being is to affirm the genuine basis of life. Furthermore, it is to maintain good faith with oneself, which predicates a general trustworthiness in one's dealings with others.

Upon its initial presentation to the mind, the Pythagorean Theorem appears transcendent and, as it were, of an immortal origin. But is it? Let the matter be looked into in terms which are limited to the functioning of a human imagination. So to begin: in ancient times squares were known and easily imagined.

### Thoughts on Creativity, Spirit, and the Ethical Life

These need not have originally been conceived by measure, but merely as a result of a general appearance which could readily be recognized and drawn. Moreover, as they may be visualized in different magnitudes and thus fitted into one another, let various greater squares filled with contiguous smaller unit squares of a uniform size be considered. For this will be applied in a later paragraph.

Now it may well have been that the whole number 3, 4, 5 relations of the three sides of certain right triangles were discovered by means of a rope which was subsequently knotted to hold the relations for future use, as is generally reported to have occurred in either Egypt or Mesopotamia. Furthermore, varieties of this relation, in which each of the sides would be raised to some uniformly higher multiple (such as 9, 12, 15 or 30, 40, 50), could have been produced simply by adding a multiple of the original length of the rope and an equivalent multiple of each of the triangle's sides, which had been previously marked by knots on the rope. The usefulness of this procedure could have been discovered by trial and error.

Other examples exhibiting these kinds of relations, which would satisfy the Pythagorean formula $a^2 + b^2 = c^2$, might have been chanced upon by similar practical means involving the perpendicular bend in a rope at what is now understood to be a right angle. This would have been followed by an acute angle turn in the rope at the other end, the two ends of the rope being subsequently joined together without sacrificing the perpendicular bend. Yet such a method is unlikely to have led to a generalized theorem.

However, a contemplation of the unit squares filling the figures suggested in the second paragraph could have been extended by a further consideration, now quite familiar. Observing the original 3, 4, 5 relation, a figure composed of nine unit squares three on each side might have been constructed. This would have been followed by a four-sided figure utilizing sixteen component units, giving it four units to a side. Finally, a five unit four-sided figure enclosing twenty-five such units (a sum of the units in the first two figures) would have come to mind.

Now all the elements of the 3, 4, 5 relation, squared in the manner of $a^2 + b^2 = c^2$, are represented by quadrilaterals with sides which are perpendicular to one another. Each of the four sides of each individual square encompassing either 9, 16, or 25 unit squares will be of the same length. Thus each of these greater squares will represent one of the squared components of the 3, 4, 5 relation. Yet it was not necessary that these operations should have been carried out by more than crude measure and the relations discovered by anything but trial and error.

Consequently, this much could have been accomplished with drawings, wherein a leisurely perusal of the three figures must inevitably have suggested that the twenty-five unit block precisely contains the total number of units in the nine and sixteen unit blocks. In addition, it may be observed that four of the units from the nine unit block can be evenly fitted up against one side of the sixteen unit block. And the five left over units may be placed in the same manner on an adjacent side of the block in question. The result is a twenty-five unit square.

## Thoughts on Creativity, Spirit, and the Ethical Life

But this does not of itself generate a general insight equivalent to the Pythagorean Theorem. So how might this have come about? Perhaps it would have been derived from the fact that the existing squares are composed of identical units (insofar as this could be visually determined). The units represent whole numbers which, when tallied in terms of one of the sides (3, 4, 5) of each of the squares composed of 9, 16, or 25 of them, can be multiplied with themselves to get the number of these units in each respective square. But this alone does not constitute a proof. For a logical statement like the theorem must be certain of its derivation from consistent principles if it is to represent a universal idea.

What was needed was an unchanging and reliable measure. Here the introduction of a standard rod, or rule, plus a protractor-like device for standardizing right angles, must have been introduced. And so they were. Once these were put to use, a more dependable consistency of results was affirmed, thus confirming the vague outcomes obtained by the use of a rope and drawings.

From this, general conclusions could have been drawn. For exact (or at least near exact) measure alone suggests an earnest search for a conceptual generalization which will stand up to repeated enquiry. As a result, the theorem would have been "discovered." But discovered in the phenomenal realm of common experience, not within some transcendent cloud of eternal ideas.

To assert this limitation for human thought is not to suggest that there is no transcendent realm beyond the phenomenal. It is simply an insistence that the human mind derives its ideas from phenomenal experience. Whatever occurs beyond that can only be a matter of conjecture. That is, with one exception: the nature of consciousness. Yet even this, though it is directly experienced, must be described in terms of what it is not.

Considered as a whole, Spinoza's system of thought is beautiful because it brings the purpose and character of God and humanity into close proximity. But in the details it is devastating. For it limits human potential to the material alone.

All the advances toward social justice which have occurred and are occurring have been and will be of short duration, so long as certain shadows remain in the human heart. What are these? They are vanity and egoism which in multiple subtle forms motivate behavior beneath an apparently calm and unaffected personal demeanor. Many of these remain unknown to the individual, as they are concealed within complexes of emotion.

So is there anything that can be done about them? There is. They can be rooted out, slowly, meticulously, sometimes even painfully, through determination and consistent effort. This cannot be brought about in a day, neither a week, a month, nor a year. For it is gradual in accomplishment. Its goal is not perfection. Perfection is an unrealistic and impractical ideal. But it can be carried out to a remarkable extent. In the process, the elements of emotional deviance will be revealed.

To begin, the most important adjustments are a positioning of the will toward effective change and a willingness to see it through. This involves the suppression of oversensitive and hyperactive responses to what others say and do. It is advisable to move like a sloth through most social interactions, not dully and tardily but in quietude of spirit.

Be willing to demonstrate consideration and kindness where it may be interpreted as weakness. But restrain excessive shows of the same. For every individual has a right of self-protection, of putting up a guard against unwarranted offense. There is a prerogative to be kind to oneself as well as to others. Fairness must be universal. It is rancor and ill will alone which are its foes.

Why fear death? Consciousness is prior to experience. What precedes the material realm must follow it. Though it is true that the introduction, development through maturity, and deterioration of the body occur with an unmitigated persistence and regularity made glaringly present to awareness, the fact remains that these have limits.

For the mind can peer around them to explore another condition. In doing so, it sees with the eyes of expectation and an emotion of sustained awareness rather than with a myopic physical vision. Reason may doubt. But imagination does not fear to penetrate beyond the mundane, though it is obliged to use material imagery in forming its representations.

The feeling of this possible beyond is persistent. It occurs in all departments and conditions of humanity. It is the aforesaid emotion of "sustained awareness." As such, it is not a product of fear, though fear may often play an accompanying role. It is an insistent reaching, which is as natural to human beings as consciousness itself. For it is the insistence of awareness that it alone has no limits, as it is undivided and unbounded.

Thus this innate reaching occurs in spite of material experience. It expresses a hope which, while not dispelling a fear of death entirely, at least mitigates, or nullifies, its all-inclusive power. For it is a truth securely lodged in the heart, in the unseen recesses of the deep mind. And it is far greater in influence than the accumulated impact of accustomed events. For this reason, it has never been eradicated from the race. Nor can it be.

It has often been said that belief in a transcendent power is nothing more than a desire for the kindly assistance of a lordly benefactor and provider. Certainly it may and generally does include such a motive. It can even be labeled wishful thinking. But this does not preclude something more. Gaze upward into the starry night and ask: is it so, or is it not?

Such an attempt at a bald and forceful interpretation of the universe can be forbidding. That is why most people do not venture it. For in the imagined instance of the first possibility there is an uncomfortable coldness, an abandonment of meaningfulness. But in the latter possibility, should one proceed so far, all is restored to a pleasant warmth.

What is this warmth? And why should it be considered? It should be because it is more than a projection of desire. It is a natural response. For the emotion producing it is not found in any outward condition. Rather, it is placed there because it is initially encountered in the innermost sensibility, where it is more deeply adhered to by the conscious seeker than is the material sense of self or the universe. In other words, when discovered, it is immediately and irrevocably recognized as prior to physical experience. That is its incontrovertible truth.

## Thoughts on Creativity, Spirit, and the Ethical Life

It seems to be the conviction of many that Thoreau's two year sojourn in a small cabin beside Walden Pond was an attempt to demonstrate that one should subsist with as few technological amenities as possible. He should choose to live permanently "off the grid," as the saying goes. But living in this manner was not for Thoreau an end in itself. Rather, it was intended as an illustration of the importance of a person's being fully cognizant of the fact that every added material convenience must be paid for, generally in extended terms of labor extracted from many days of a person's life.

This effort is deducted from an individual's time on earth, which could be more profitably devoted to contemplation and thought regarding the world and his own condition within it. Such an adherence to the nature and circumstances of one's existence promotes inward growth and a more profound appreciation of life.

More to the point, much of the quest for material amenities has little to do with personal comfort and convenience and a great deal to do with vanity. Goods are accumulated for show. They are meant to make an impression on others, whose fleeting opinions are of little substantial worth in comparison to the value of understanding oneself and one's circumstances in an intelligent and meaningful way.

Epistemology should be regarded as a science. This is not so strange, if one considers that its entry into the hallowed halls of scientific investigation may be brought about by observation, as is the case with other such endeavors. But for this to be accomplished, the processes of the mind alone must be studied without concern for the evidence of the senses.

This requires a broadening of the concept of empiricism, which at present is narrowly focused upon data derived from sensory awareness. A theory of knowledge based on material evidence is too limited. Moreover, considered in terms of the perennial human quest for self-illumination, or self-understanding, it is deeply unsatisfying.

A few pertinent questions might be ventured. They are: What is the origin of ideas, including mathematical concepts, which play such a vital role in physical science? Are these human inventions or discoveries the proper origin of which transcend the powers of the mind? If the former, as they surely must be, then what is to account for the initial mental reception and subsequent ordering of experience?

What is the nature of consciousness and its possible active relationship to knowledge? How might a perceptive appreciation of the arts be accounted for? And what is the cause of the perennial persistence of religion, which cannot be satisfactorily accounted for by a reference to a universal sense of human weakness and vulnerability?

Any activity which draws people together into a cooperative and mutually sustaining social unit is a reflection of and progression toward an increased awareness of the oneness of spirit. It is not easy to bring this about. Competition and endless wars alone attest to the fact. Nor is its necessity readily understood. But here are both the reasons and the means for its importance:

## Thoughts on Creativity, Spirit, and the Ethical Life

Spirit is universal awareness, which, as universal consciousness, is the source of each limited individual awareness, each personal consciousness. Appended to this simple observation is the question: is not every human activity in some form or another an effort to burst the bonds of felt limitation? Life is an ongoing struggle, which inevitably involves others, laterally in one era and vertically through all eras.

So can it not be seen that each individual awareness is internally pressing outward to extend itself toward universality? Even the many episodes and varieties of vanity are perverted instances of this drive. They are shortcuts to the truth which inevitably fail. Being admired by others, particularly in unproductive ways, does not guarantee an extension of one's personal reach.

Growth toward greater universality is a process which must involve the full human community, understood both in lateral and vertical terms. Human beings are spirit. Their true home is to be achieved collectively in the same. Yet it should not be thought that this would preclude the persistence of a prominent individual awareness. Rather, it is a matter of that awareness being transcended so as to embed itself in all in such a manner as to reflect the all as one.

It should not be thought that, because the inner, spiritual self is the true foundation of the person, the painstakingly constructed social self should be altogether ignored. This would constitute a fatal and impractical view. For the latter is most certainly necessary to an integrated functioning of an individual within the complex relations of society. Without this the individual is left spurned and adrift.

Rather, it is simply to be advised that the spiritual self supplies the proper rudder for guiding one through life, while the social self may be seen as the inevitable armor necessary for survival. In other words, amidst the complexities of daily life, a person should never lose sight of her most dependable guide. Nor should she neglect to present a pleasing practical appearance, so long as it is honest.

Considered as an expression of human needs, every culture is complete within itself. All are equivalent. Yet there are evolutionary differences. For it cannot be denied that the Greek development of reason as a discipline independent from free imagination was a forward step of extraordinary significance. It constituted a break from the entire preceding human condition.

It may be paralleled with the startling rise of paleolithic advanced tool making and art, since this introduced the possibility of a greater understanding concerning both human nature and its circumstances. Viewed in this manner, cultures without such a benefit as the concerted use of reason and its enormous potential cannot be considered equivalent to those with it. For it is as momentous an advance in the character of humanity as language attainments were in paleolithic times.

All people are "sons" of God. They are spirit. But most do not know how to live within their potential, whereas Jesus of Nazareth did. That is the sense in which he was "anointed" with the spirit.

## Thoughts on Creativity, Spirit, and the Ethical Life

The story begins with a simple statement: "There were once five and twenty tin soldiers; they were all brothers, for they had all been born of one old tin spoon." The name of the story is "The Hardy Tin Soldier," or "The Steadfast Tin Soldier." And the translator is H. W. Dulcken. Hans Christian Andersen, the author, goes on to say that "each soldier was exactly like the rest; but one of them had been cast last of all, and there had not been enough tin to finish him."

This handicap is not a problem because "he stood as firmly upon his one leg as the others on their two; and it was this Soldier who became remarkable." What is remarkable is his steadfast love for a paper ballerina in a gauze dress, wearing a "narrow blue ribbon over her shoulders, that looked like a scarf."

He is an earnest young man. And he decides she is for him, partly because they have something in common: she looks like she is missing a leg too. The reason for this is that she is dancing and has lifted one leg, which cannot be seen by the soldier. But no matter. Such a close and important means of identity, once lodged in the human heart, becomes a burning love.

Soon the tin soldier is caught up in unexpected adventures, where he proves his courage by standing at military attention with his musket firmly shouldered. He remains this way through every adversity. These adventures carry him far and wide, while in his heart he holds true to his dancer.

Eventually he returns and is unexplainably thrown into the fireplace where, as he is melting, the ballerina is blown by a gust of air into the fire with him. At last they are united. And they die together. Thus ends a story of struggle, emotional longing, occasional joy, and hope. It is all that is necessary.

There is a simple method of representation for time dilation in the special theory of relativity. It is as follows. Consider a clock moving uniformly as compared to another at a state of rest. In distinction from the clock at rest, the time passage of the one in motion will occur more slowly. This is a result of time dilation within a separate inertial framework which is in a different comparative state of uniform motion. The moving clock, as observed from the position of the stationary clock, appears to be running slower and, in fact, is.

To visualize this effect, without any attempt to definitively define it, imagine a rectangle exhibiting adjacent sides of different length. One pair of parallel sides is long, the other short. Multiplying one long and one short side together yields an area for the rectangle. But rather than area, assume that it yields the fundamental laws of physics within a specific inertial framework.

These must be the same in all inertial frameworks, whether moving uniformly or at rest. Consequently, though the sides of the rectangle may change in length, they will do so in proportion to one another, yielding the same area within the figure, which represents the same set of physical laws. These cannot change.

Now the two adjacent side lengths of the rectangle were originally four and two meters. This is representative of the condition of the clock at rest. But the rectangle representing the clock moving relative to the stationary clock, and doing so in the direction of its side of greatest length, undergoes changes. These changes in the rectangle are only tentatively reflective of what is actually occurring with the moving clock. But they are of illustrative interest.

Let the clock be moving at such a velocity that it is shortened in its direction of motion by half. Thus the measure of the long side of the representative rectangle is also reduced by half from four to two meters. And, in proportion to this, the length of the shorter side must be doubled from two to four meters in order to yield the same area, which, as has been stated, maintains accordingly a consistency of the physical laws associated with it. For these must not change.

So the sides are reversed in measure. What was four meters is two meters. And what was two meters is four meters. The side which was originally long, but now is shortened, crudely represents the physical contraction of the clock in the direction of its movement. The side which was originally short, but now is extended in length, does the same with the phenomenon of time dilation.

In other words, the face of a hypothetical clock (as opposed to the real one's presented here) may, for illustrative purposes, be presumed to have been lengthened in the direction of the progress of, say, its second hand, which does not go round but straight across it. As a result, the clock face is conjectured to be twice as long as it was, requiring the second hand to move double its original distance. This corresponds to the lengthened side of the rectangle.

Consequently, in returning to the original objects of interest, as the uniformly moving clock marks one second, the stationary clock marks two seconds. Hence the apparent slowing of the moving clock. It is, of course, marking time properly. The difference is in the point of view of the stationary observer. But the results are nevertheless real. The moving clock will not regain its lost time with respect to the stationary clock when it becomes stationary itself.

Of course, the time and length relationships of the clocks are more complex than would be indicated by a change of proportion between the sides of a simple rectangle. The example of rectangles which has been adduced for the purpose of illustration, is intended merely to demonstrate in as simple a manner as possible the peculiar effect of time dilation as it occurs in the special theory of relativity.

Accordingly, the illustrative rectangles present neither a physically nor a mathematically exact parallel to the actual behavior and relationship of the clocks. But they do give some idea of the inversion of phenomena reflecting the shortening of an object in relative motion accompanied by a dilation of its time.

Time is change measured in terms of comparative distance. Were this not the case, it could not be known. For change requires motion. And motion involves distance, or displacement from one location to another, however minute the displacement. The displacement can be envisioned as the movement of the hands on a conventional clock. But a digital clock would be no different. Neither could a chemical or physical change occur without displacement. Nor would the regular alterations of an atomic clock do so.

Thus it can be seen that only distances are concerned in the matter. There is distance. And there is change. Nothing else. There are no independent, floating units of time which cannot

## Thoughts on Creativity, Spirit, and the Ethical Life

be clearly understood in physical terms. Consequently, time is change strictly understood in terms of comparisons of distance. It is entirely a matter of distances. Otherwise, people would have no knowledge of it.

It is no violation of good behavior to recognize oneself as strong in body or mind or both and to take pleasure in the fact. It is only wrong to exhibit a false confidence where this is not the case, or to exaggerate where it is. Appropriate self-assessment is not only good but necessary, so long as it does not partake of a desire to denigrate others.

However, a person cannot assert her superiority in any matter without often exciting some degree of envy. For that is surely the general outcome of such matters in a world in which most people do not seek their full potential. They find it easier to deny it in others and to force them into a denial of themselves.

So, to keep the peace, a person of greater attainments is frequently induced to exhibit restraint and, at times, an unmerited display of modesty. But this should never be done to the extent of negating one's true character, as it is unfortunately quite easy to blunt one's personal achievements by too much display of reticence and false modesty.

The propensity of the spiritually illumined resembles emotion but is different. It is that which guides the great artist, scientist, philosopher in discovering new truths, or insights. For it leads to original imaginative representations followed by reasonings, which would not have otherwise occurred. It is not the imaginings alone, since these are dependent for their imagery on material experience. Neither is it the reasonings, which are no more than a tightening, or application of thought discipline, to the imaginations.

Rather, it is an unaccounted for opening of the mind which precedes these articulative events. With an intellectually unanticipated abruptness, new possibilities become available. The mind slips into their welcome suggestion to take up a new direction. For at best they resemble an impulse, something which originates an emotion but is not of its character.

Emotions in their familiar character are responses linked to the phenomenal realm and can be conceived to originate accordingly. But there is no such connection between the above spiritual propensity and the phenomenal environment into which it is projected. It is an unannounced expansion of the mind available only to the few who are appropriately receptive. It is of the nature of genius.

There is an increasing subjectivity in physical science which can be said to have originated with Kepler and Galileo in the seventeenth century. This was when mathematics was rigorously introduced to function as a parameter delimiting conceptual representations concerning empirical investigations.

Mathematics is an exact science in its own right, which is purely of human invention and closely parallels the proportional structures of material experience as they present themselves within the mind. The application of mathematics lends an admirable rigor to the proportions and guides their refinement accordingly. It is in this manner that observation is disciplined by thought.

## Thoughts on Creativity, Spirit, and the Ethical Life

Of a more recent occurrence is relativity, which meticulously adheres to mathematical relations at the expense of common sense observation. For these relations now demand an extraordinary precision of measurement. And the thought process must be altered accordingly. Thus the science has been moved further into the subjective realm of thought. And the precision of its results has become greater than that of the Keplerian and Galilean conceptions.

Consequently, it is all the more distanced from immediate sensory evidence, although it by no means ignores or excludes it. Rather, the theoretical structure is developed to an unprecedented complexity. These methods, though increasingly subjective, are objectively confirmed, rendering an enhanced triumph of mind over sense without violation of the principles of careful observation. The most critical of these principles is causal relation. These too are shifted to a greater depth of imaginative representation. For it cannot be denied that imaginative apperception is intimately involved in material experience. Without it there would be no recognition of such experience.

Concurrent with relativity was the development of quantum mechanics. In this instance, the science has moved so far inward into subjectivity as to raise fundamental philosophical questions. Most of the issues raised have yet to be resolved, though the science is itself quite powerful in its practical applications.

One of its most pressing problems is that of causation. Where statistical methods are presently required to make determinations, concern must exist in matters of close physical relations. Do these rest upon any sort of determinate structure, perhaps hidden from immediate access? Or are the relations not strictly causal? Moreover, how much do such observations depend upon the mind's direct involvement in perception?

This is not to say that the mind is in a position to alter reality. It is simply to assert that perhaps it has discovered its own intimate role in structuring the fundamental relations of the physical realm. By probing ever deeper into the nexus between sensory impressions and the way they may have been initially laid out by the mind, that mind has drawn a circle around itself which it must seek to untangle in order to clearly understand the sophisticated progression of its efforts.

Universal consciousness, or spirit, is the ground of all awareness and the source through which emanate those things that are made present to awareness. For this reason human consciousness, being an expression of the same, is universal awareness self-limited as to its content. The limitation occurs by means of and within universal consciousness, rendering human consciousness in its condition of narrowed awareness.

So a question arises: how does an individual person relate to all-encompassing spirit? Certainly such a finite range of experience and the interaction solely with it of volition, as is characteristic of human awareness, is severely restricted in its options. For both the range of actions and their materially conditioned options are determined by one universal source. It is from this alone that they emanate and are made a compact whole. Thus, it would appear, it is by this as well that they must be regulated without possibility of redress.

There is no sensory window between the physical and its general cause, since the cause cannot be directly known. Yet

## Thoughts on Creativity, Spirit, and the Ethical Life

the experiential realm made material to human sensibility does not present itself simply as a hard factual block. It is not inflexible. Nor is it entirely unresponsive to human desire and intervention.

Rather, it is perceived as a complex and somewhat blinding maze supporting multiple enclosed paths, each leading sequentially into another. Thus a choice between two alternatives having been taken, another set of options inevitably follows. But all such possibilities cannot be seen at once, as one might hope to do on a chessboard.

Due to its apparent narrowness, this is generally referred to as fate, since it is neither broadly free nor utterly bound. Which is to say that such a constricting material presentation of experience functions as a closed receptacle within which one is obliged to operate with room to act but little to dream. There is freedom in little more than a narrow sense of choice.

Moreover, the choices would seem to be largely determined. So an attitude akin to Stoic submission is required. Every person is humbled in this way by life. Yet there is no such thing as an absolute sway. There is maneuver space. For an individual may petition universal spirit for what can be referred to as a reasonable change. This is an alteration in circumstances which does not violate the general character of experience.

Such a request may or may not lead to a satisfactory result. It may be denied, and that without a reassuring voice of explanation. In this case, the prevailing situation must be accepted. But on the other hand, the desired outcome may be granted. Either way, the greatest boon to the petitioner is that such a request can be legitimately put forth, since it demonstrates an intimacy between the individual and the universal.

The intimacy is true, private, and real. For petitioner and petitioned are one, being united in all things save acuteness and range of awareness. Spirit is the inner self. And the whole of destiny is known to it. Though this projected order of events is at best only occasionally felt by a person, while never granted to him as an explicit form of knowledge.

Spinoza's masterwork, the *Ethics*, is both profound and excruciatingly thorough. There is within it a richness of moral observation and understanding of emotion, or recognition of the means by which the mind is moved in one direction or another. But there is also for the reader a major point of contention. It is the absence of will. For how is he to reconcile the many beneficial insights of the work with its governing principle of determinism?

If God and the physical universe are to be conceived as one, and if such a unity is demonstrated to unfold with an inflexible mechanical and logical exactitude, where is an opening for individual choice to be found? How does a morally conscientious individual select an appropriate pathway to what Spinoza refers to as an intellectual love of God: that mode of behavior which brings one joy and peace of mind?

Where all is predetermined, no such choice can be made. Thus Spinoza's entire, and admittedly quite beautiful, ethical system, which he has painstakingly worked out in closely fitted detail, is rendered meaningless. For it is alternative possibility alone which gives purpose to any individual human existence.

# Thoughts on Creativity, Spirit, and the Ethical Life

Art historians, particularly biographers, are apt to expend far too much time and effort on Vincent Van Gogh's emotional problems. Granted that these were intense and that a surcharge of emotion is suffused throughout his art. They are not extraneous. They are endemic and purified into transcendent vision. The swerving lines, swirling vortices, and impasto brushstrokes are redolent of the presence of spirit in all things.

This is Vincent's religious view as worked out through a struggle for sensible meaning, avoiding the ethnocentric bias and conflict between the various religions. It is a faith for all humanity. Everything is an expression of the beauty and activity of spirit. Even the darkest moments in an individual life are found to glow with a penetrating inner truth. Nothing is wasted or lost. This is Van Gogh's gift to the world. It far outweighs any consideration of his troubles.

There are times when the waywardness, fickleness, and inconstancy of human nature are enough to nearly defeat the most stalwart optimist. Can a human ideal, so possible, so easy to imagine, so close to realization, so much present to the human mind, ever be attained? Under this burden of doubt interfused with hope a positive soul must soldier on till the unexpected dawn of victory breaks over him. It will come. But the question remains: how and when?

Socrates is represented as having posited the idea that if a person understood the truth, she would do no wrong. The problem with this observation lies in the concept "to know," or "to understand." A person may be readily conversant with the abstract expression of a moral insight without grasping its full significance.

For example, she may conceptually comprehend that it is wrong to lie. For she sees that it is destructive of a general atmosphere of mutual trust which is beneficial to everyone. But she is also convinced as a fact of experience that many people cannot be trusted. So she will lie to protect or promote her personal interest. She will choose this ideally errant course of action because she can neither envision nor put her faith into a broader moral context, one which, however obvious yet seemingly unattainable, would settle the relations of people for their own good.

The function of life is enjoyment. But an admixture of meaning brings a greater satisfaction into living. Material existence, being burdened with heavy trials (which trials ironically give it focus and direction), it is beneficial to commit oneself to an understanding of the many obstacles to be encountered.

Then the pleasure of existence, though infinitely subtle, will be augmented. It will serve to counterbalance difficulties with an enriched assimilation to understanding of the multiple impediments which cannot be avoided and which, if allowed to do so, may well raise understanding to wisdom.

If a person should attempt to imagine heaven as a condition resembling present life, while devoid of its usual trials and tribulations, it is a vision impossible to sustain. What would an individual do in such a thoroughly eventless realm that presented little or nothing with which to interact purposefully? It is a fearful condition not to be desired. No. Therefore,

## Thoughts on Creativity, Spirit, and the Ethical Life

spiritual life must be entirely different, unimaginable in terms of present experience. Or, if possibly imagined, difficult to assimilate or comprehend.

All things emanate from a universal awareness. And human beings are restricted forms of that awareness, just as a spectrum is separated from white light into specific wavelengths. In either case, there is light by means of which experience is known, either fully or in part.

Responsible religion partakes of the fairy tale. For it is composed of a series of partial or wholly fabricated stories enhanced with piquant maxims, in which both together faithfully image forth underlying emotional truths. Irresponsible religions are unworthy of mention because they fail to do this.

Throughout recent centuries science has been an encroaching religion. It has gained its significant foothold due to an impressive capacity to anticipate nature. But it is utterly remiss in representing emotional needs, especially those nearly invisible urgings which are difficult for the intellect to discern and assimilate. It is therefore inadequate as a means of spiritual support.

It is inappropriate to think it easy to know which emotional needs are best represented by religion. For this requires a pervasive imaginative vision, which is given to few. The emotions upon which religion seeks to base its assumptions are often quite ethereal, as they reveal themselves to the mind independently of human understanding.

The four-dimensional space-time continuum, as initially mathematically contrived by Hermann Minkowski, is a convenient and powerful intellectual tool. But it is not a product of the senses. It is a fabrication of the mind. The three physical dimensions are augmented by a fourth, which is time.

This is feasible because time is measured by means of comparative distances, which are spatial properties. However, the augmentation does not physically transform the continuum into direct sensory experience. For it is representative of change, not an entity. The fact that it produces appropriate experimental results arises from the consistency of measure, which is spatial in character.

The reason the general concept of space-time is functionally successful is that the entire phenomenal array of experience is a product of the mind. This does not mean that human will controls all events and relations. Rather, the mind is the medium through which experience is apprehended. So it participates in what it knows.

Thus, adding time to space and representing the whole in spatial terms is a convenience of the intellect which, due to its predictive power, functions as a major enhancement to scientific investigation. As long as appropriate proportional relations between similar properties are maintained, as is the case where time is measured in terms of comparative distances, a predictable outcome can be derived from such a mental model. But it should not be thought that the material realm is physically four-dimensional.

## Thoughts on Creativity, Spirit, and the Ethical Life

When considered in conventional macroscopic terms, quantum action at a distance is baffling. For it defies causal explanation. But the question is: in spite of appearances, is there any distance separating the observed phenomena? Undoubtedly, there must be insofar as physical measurement is concerned. But this is the product of a peculiar form of illusion.

It should be noted that it is the mind which produces both the measure and the thing measured. That is to say, it is intimately involved in the matter. So much so, in fact, that when experimental results are thought to be simultaneously apprehended in two quite divergent realms, micro and macro, the mind superimposes the former upon the latter in a rather peculiar but consistent manner. In other words, similar experiments will yield similar results.

Why should this occur? It is a result of a disparity between the indefiniteness of the former and the definitive character of the latter. Consequently, it makes an odd and thoroughly baffling distribution of the first within the second. But, so long as it does so consistently throughout experimental experience and the measures retain uniformity, the outcome remains a potent and useful instrument. Nor does it matter for such purposes whether a comprehensible and familiar model of the world is maintained.

In Ernest Hemingway's novel, *The Sun Also Rises*, Jake Barnes is a World War I veteran whose wounds prevent him from having a physical relationship with Lady Brett Ashley. He is an American foreign correspondent living in Paris. And he tells the story of how he and his British and American friends, including Brett, vacation together in Spain.

As in much of Hemingway's work, the novel is full of eating and drinking. It includes a fishing trip and bullfights at the Pamplona Fiesta that include a preliminary "running of the bulls" episode which this book made famous. The novel contains some of the finest impressionistic descriptions of action and countryside in American Literature. Full of color and life, its dialog sparkles with repartee that reflects the fresh air and sunshine quality of the descriptions. The book is almost entirely written in dialog and consequently is a quick read.

All but one of the men is in love with Lady Ashley. And she becomes briefly infatuated with a bullfighter. This leads to quarrels and a fistfight. Because she cannot physically love Jake, she loves randomly and without purpose. These five people are representative of what Gertrude Stein referred to as a "lost generation" which came out of the war with shattered values but a heightened lust for life. Thus it would appear that, when social and moral expectations fail, the physical is intensified.

By means of spare, sensual prose, the reader is made to feel the sun on his back and the cold ache against his teeth of wine chilled in a mountain stream. He witnesses the violence of bulls pitting their great bulk and strength against the calm poise of a matador. There are crowds at the fiesta, exhibiting their hilarity, drunkenness, and friendliness. And there are dancers in the streets along with fireworks. What there is not is anything dull in this sensory-intoxicated presentation of thoughtless abandonment.

### Thoughts on Creativity, Spirit, and the Ethical Life

Emotion lies in the heart of awareness. Which is to say that there is an elemental impulse in awareness which acts as a prodding toward emotion. It is the emotional response to this prodding which is subsequently expressed through mental imagery. That imagery is drawn from within the confines of experience. Much of experience is sensory in character, in particular that portion of it which provides content for imagery. What is meant by sensory is mental input, an input which is prior to material experience and provides the means of its development.

This is not the same for all creatures. For example, some species on earth detect light outside the human range, while others exhibit a broader reach of olfactory experience. In addition, there are those which are cognizant of variations in the earth's magnetic field. So it is necessary to concede that what is generally interpreted as physical sensation varies. It is out of this variance that a host of different forms of imaginative representation arises.

These images being diverse and individually distinct among species, they will yield different concepts in those which are capable of thought. Hence it is the case that reasoning creatures of different origin may find their expressions opaque in relation to one another. Consequently, due to this lack of uniformity in the imaginative basis of conceptual development, it is readily seen that reason cannot be relied upon as an intergalactic form of communication. Nor is it likely to be spiritually relevant. The ground of all being cannot be assumed to think as humans do.

In order to grasp the rather peculiar functioning of the mind in matters concerning action at a distance, it is requisite that the mind's unique capacity for self-bifurcation be acknowledged. This division of awareness is rendered possible by its two principal levels of operation, primary and secondary.

Though primary mind is generally unrecognized by a mature human sensibility, having gone through its early development and cast this original foundation into the background, it is the faculty which provides the mental input responsible for material experience. These are the sensations which both construct and reveal the objects of the world. Secondary mind follows, aiding in the development of objects and their physical dimensions. It is this secondary mind alone which is recognized by every human being.

Consequently, in cases where experimental results at the microscopic level are wont to introduce problems of action at a distance, there is this factor of mental displacement. But the cause of it is hidden. So how does it come about? It occurs because the mind has long since made itself familiar and thoroughly comfortable with the macroscopic structures of its common experience. These are necessary to its sense of orientation in the world. So it cannot readily introduce the microscopic results into such a ready-made environment.

For this reason, it places them willy-nilly where it will. However, it does so in a consistent manner, which is confirmed by the experimental evidence. It is this predictable irregularity which is the source of the problem. What is to be made of it, when the mind is prone to interpret consistency as reality?

Should the causal construction of the macro environment be placed in doubt? Where then is there a secure foundation for science? If general causation is undermined, the inevitably resultant probabilities found to be governing the entirety of physical experience are not an attractive proposition. For they are apt to leave one with a nauseating sense of insecurity.

But the micro experimental results do defy the macro structure, since at the level of common experience there cannot be a distance between simultaneous, coordinated events if causal consistency is to be maintained. A reasonable explanation of this apparent anomaly must be found. It is that there is no distance between these events. They are, in fact, variations of a single occurrence. Thus the false appearance of distance is simply to be understood as a result of the mind's arbitrary positioning of micro results within the macro realm.

What is a symbol? It is similar to a concept in that it is an imaginative image (or set of images) which is detached from its usual flexible character. That is to say, it is more regular in function than an image. For the latter may vary somewhat with every occurrence, whereas the symbol retains a consistency both of character and reference.

It is held to an array of specific, interrelated images which it evokes. And it is this regularity of procedure which endows it with resemblance to a concept. But unlike a concept, it is without definition. Here it is more like an image and therefore cannot be ensconced within a logical matrix. So in relation to the former it is more free and to the latter more stable in function.

Should a person consider Heisenberg's uncertainty principle in the simplest of terms disregarding the experimental complexities of the quantum environment, she would likely discover rough parallels to it in common experience. For example, regarding the motion of a projectile, it is to be readily acknowledged that its velocity and position cannot be considered within the same context.

One or the other must be selected and focused upon, while its alternative is set aside from consideration. If velocity is chosen, position falls out of focus. It cannot be determined. For it is continually in the midst of change. Conversely, if position is emphasized, velocity is rendered meaningless because to assert a fixed location is to deny motion, hence velocity.

A similar situation occurs with regard to wave and particle phenomena. A wave does not exhibit a fixed character within its period of oscillation. This is particularly the case concerning a probability wave. The latter's statistical determinations indicate that its phenomena are of an unfixed character. On the other hand, a particle is fixed as to its character. Its phenomena are collected within a defined point. So it exhibits a precise condition insofar as its particle nature is concerned. It may move about. But its exact moment of determination is gathered into an undistributed unity.

If one were to view the trajectory of a common projectile in this light, its developed flight path would be comprehended as a unified whole. This would be justified by the fact that its individual increments of motion could not be fixed. Consequently, they are indistinguishable from one another. They are a single phenomenon.

For these reasons, it can be seen that the whole of material experience vacillates as to what is to be gathered into a unity

## Thoughts on Creativity, Spirit, and the Ethical Life

and what not. The matter is left up to the organizing and contemplating mind. So it cannot be any wonder that in the enlarged common sphere of rough and gross determinations causality is settled upon, while in the more precise, minute examinations of the quantum realm particle relations should be found to be somewhat indeterminate, leaving the investigating mind to its fallback remedy of probabilistic thinking.

For example, when an instantaneous velocity is computed by means of compressing its motions to an infinitesimal degree, this is a matter of compacting its trajectory to a point. In the compression, there is no longer any motion worthy of consideration. In the compaction, the flight path is ignored, since it is a distance. A distance without measurable increments is rendered meaningless.

This discussion of instantaneous velocity is different from the previous considerations of projectile motion and wave versus particle phenomena. For it represents a narrowing down for the sake of precision, rather than a problem of choice. But it is advisable to remember that the mind is a flexible if somewhat repetitive instrument, not only in its observational approach to phenomena, but in its original participation in constructing them. Thus it must in special circumstances confront alternatives in point of view, as they are necessary to maintain the uniformity of the whole. So in certain situations, a choice must be made, an approach taken at the expense of its inverse complement.

Granted, moreover, that the mind lacks an absolute freedom in its constructive participation in experience. The world is in some sense given. Yet, in spite of this, it cannot be denied that the mind is intimately involved in the process of constructing, augmenting, and revising the character of its experience.

This means its subtle determinations and incidental, but not infrequent, switchbacks in point of view cannot be ignored, both as regards its repetitive behavior in confirming an accustomed pattern of experience and in its willingness to occasionally reformulate what it has already so regularly affirmed on previous occasions.

The life of the mind is sacred. It belongs to no one but the person who possesses it. This should be respected above all things. It is of far graver consequence than any civil right. It is spiritual, eternal, and endemic to the person concerned.

Over time, democracy gradually erodes public intelligence. As manners and tastes decline, so does the habit of thinking. That is why it is essential that a settled aristocratic element be maintained in such a society. It should be flexible and based in some manner on intelligence, so that an entry into and an exit from it are retained. But it should not be abolished or simply melded into the crowd. For the pride and self-respect of the few leavens the whole.

The present writer may be considered to be irreligious while simultaneously God-intoxicated. For what is meant by "God" is spirit, or universal awareness and foundational creativity, not a figment of imagination founded upon an arbitrary aspect of the human genome. Within spirit, all things may be encountered, including the accustomed comforts and responses which are associated with the crude representations. But it is more

## Thoughts on Creativity, Spirit, and the Ethical Life

than sufficient that everything should emanate from this source. Nothing more about it need be known. The many representations of it are at best superfluous and at worst harmful.

Ah, to retrieve the living Jesus from the morass of ambitious fabrications infesting his image! There has been much emendation and modification over time. And some of it followed almost immediately upon his departure. But there remains a core of penetrating and heartfelt observation which is clearly the work of spiritual genius. This is the collection of parables and maxims.

The soul is not to be considered separate from the body. Rather, the body is to be understood as separable from the soul. For it and all of materiality are of a lesser condition.

Spirit, or consciousness, is manifest at every level of physical existence. The only distinction lies in the presence or degree of material responsiveness. Thus the entire fabric of physical reality proceeds from an inanimate state of consciousness, functioning without responsiveness, to a chemical interaction with the environment, as is the case with most plants, to the sensory awareness of some plants and all animals, to emotional expression in higher animals, to the imaginative faculty closely following upon the emotional, and finally to the rational. For each of these conditions consciousness is a ground. Beyond the physical is pure awareness, of which living humanity occasionally enjoys but a glimpse.

Low intelligence is a principal cause of bad laws. Nothing better illustrates the fact that cunning at the expense of wisdom most often informs the practice of politics. Cunning is the general feature of undeveloped minds, which occupy the most numerous portion of a population. People vote for what they are.

Hemingway's acutely sensitive and highly sensory temperament were the principal elements lifting his style into prominence. He no doubt learned various grammatical and compositional techniques which placed these features in bold relief. But attempts by others to imitate him too closely have always resulted in futility because they neglect to consider the personal ground of his talent.

It is inconceivable to think that spirit, or universal consciousness, should offer any systematic judgment upon humankind. It is humanity itself which determines its fate. For example, according to the prophets, Northern Israel and the kingdom of Judah both became internally corrupt and divided before they were overrun by foreign powers. They disdained the poor, neglected the disabled, widows and orphans, and displayed little general regard for one another. Clearly their fate lay in their behavior. The judgment upon them was their own.

Again, when the future King David hid from Saul in a cave and cut off a piece of Saul's cloak without killing him, he was using good sense. To usurp the throne by violence would only lead to further usurpations, possibly affecting himself when he became king. So his own judgment was clearly involved in his actions—i.e., waiting upon the timing of the spirit. Consequently, the result was of his own making as much as it was that of the spirit. Of course, it is reasonable to note that he was himself a direct expression of spirit.

The life of the mind is of far greater import than that of the body. In this light, it has been suggested by the philosopher Hegel that the universe might be evolving toward a higher state of intelligence. However, his notion of its termination in a condition resembling that of the Prussian state is repugnant. Better an evolution towards greater individual responsibility resulting in a freedom of mutual cooperation.

Egoism lies at the heart of human ambition and a will toward dominance. The problem raised by this inclination is a matter of direction. If it results in an effort to influence others in a freely rational, productive, and peaceful manner, it is well employed. But if its purpose is to suppress and distort their judgment in its own personal interest, then it is harmful.

In either case, such a desire in any person gains its impetus from a suffocating sense of impotence discovered in the face of a universally limiting world. People are made aware by the unlimited character of their conscious faculty that there is a condition without such impediments. This, of course, refers to consciousness without regard to its content.

Yet every human being lives in a tightly fitting, restrictive world frequently exhibiting unpleasant alternatives of action. Understandably, they long to transcend it. But they cannot. Hence the ambition, however frustratingly limited its reach.

For an immortality achieved in the minds of others is to be preferred over seemingly nothing but isolation and death.

The reason mathematics exhibits such a power for revealing, or drawing into sharp focus, the intricacies of the physical world is that both are in great measure a product of the human mind. This is not to say they are a result of fancy or imagination. Such a case would be solipsism. For much is received through the mind which is independent of its will and remains unknown in its origins to the mind in its maturity. It is this latter condition which sets an inviolable pattern within which what remains to the human intellect must be created by it in a manner largely conformable to predetermined circumstances.

The consideration of most importance here is that the working of the mind, with all its strengths and limitations, flows through both mathematics and physical awareness, the former being consciously invented following the latter's partial but definitive structuring by similar means.

The body is of no enduring value, except as a housing for the mind. It is simply part of a set of circumstances promulgated for the purpose of the mind's activity. For this reason, the idea of God, when properly understood, should not reflect a character of anthropomorphism. Not even reason can be exalted to this level. For no limiting attribute expressing the human condition can encompass the ineffable essence of spirit. This can only be known as the innermost core of the mind, revealing nothing of itself but its immaterial origin.

## Thoughts on Creativity, Spirit, and the Ethical Life

Monet's extraordinary contribution to art is the subtlety and breadth of his emotional expression. The observation that no two of his paintings are alike in regard to the treatment of the fleeting effects of light and atmosphere is merely an external observation. What are of greater interest are the emotions elicited.

Like its handling of subject matter, each of his paintings arouses a different response. These are constitutive of quite subtle variations: moods which are similar but never identical. Over the whole extent of Monet's oeuvre an unlimited range of emotional states is engendered. For great is the variety of possible moods.

The symbol arose from the image, the latter being a free representation as opposed to a faithful reflection of an object understood to be external to the mind, whereas the former may or may not be so. The symbol is flexible like the free representation. But it is more specific in reference. The concept, on the other hand, evolved from free representation as a result of a precisely delimiting definition having been applied to it. It is this logical stabilization of the imagination which rendered rational thought possible.

Subsequent to this development, inductive responses were disciplined by deduction, giving a clearer focus to human and physical behavior and, in general, rendering science possible. This reasoning faculty, insofar as can be ascertained, is peculiar to humankind and is thus specifically characteristic of it. So, in this way, the moment of the concept's origin became a point of emergence for the enriched variety of human culture.

There is a Chinese legend of a philosopher known affectionately as "the old fellow," or Lao-tzu. His recorded observations, set down in the *Tao Te Ching*, are generally dated to six centuries before the birth of Jesus. According to the story, Lao-tzu concludes that he has struggled long enough teaching his philosophy. So he decides to leave home never to return. On the way he passes a frontier outpost, where the guard begs him to leave a record of his ideas. That record is the book.

Taoism, the philosophy contained within it, expresses reverence for an all-pervading, regulating force which flows through the universe. To live in harmony with it is to take no action contrary to it, yet leave nothing undone. It is a way of least resistance. It resembles water: "The supreme good is like water, which nourishes all things without trying to. It is content with the low places that people disdain. Thus it is like the Tao."

Water works gently without creating a fuss or drawing attention to itself: "Nothing in the world is as soft and yielding as water. Yet for dissolving the hard and inflexible, nothing can surpass it. The soft overcomes the hard; the gentle overcomes the rigid. Everyone knows this is true, but few can put it into practice."

Not rushing into action, but awaiting the right moment, is not easy: "Do you have the patience to wait till your mud settles and the water is clear? Can you remain unmoving till the right action arises by itself?" This again is the way of least resistance, an economizing effectiveness of action that flows harmoniously through all circumstances with the energy of the Tao.

## Thoughts on Creativity, Spirit, and the Ethical Life

It is not impatience and egoism: "He who stands on tiptoe doesn't stand firm. He who rushes ahead doesn't go far. He who tries to shine dims his own light." It is the way of humility with confidence and strength. It is a reverence for nature and the spiritual source, ebb, and flow of the natural order.

This is a philosophy which says that a person can be either strong or yielding according to the conditions encountered. She does not have to make noise to be heard. She does not have to be heard to be effective. To have understood this at the beginning of one's years would have been invaluable. Now old habits make it insurmountably difficult.

(The translator of the quotes is Steven Mitchell.)

The idea of determinism, or inflexible causation, is nonsense. The phenomenal realm is rather a set of close-knit patterns, whose predictable and tightly fitted character renders it almost indistinguishable from a rigid structure. But it is definitely not absolute. What is to be understood by this is not a matter of free will seeping in at the corners of logic. Rather, it is a recognition that will is prior to matter.

Viewed from a strictly immaterialist perspective, will is introduced to experience as a formative agent. This is not a centrally located impulse directing from a single vantage point all that occurs. The motivation for a good part, but not all, of material change is worked out among multiple simultaneous and instantaneous manifestations of individual determinations, which are initially realized prior to what takes place in the world. It is in this manner that spirit is expressed through each living entity and every inanimate thing, inanimate things alone being centrally regulated by it, except where influenced by human, animal, plant, or other such living agency.

Unlike inanimate things, persons and other forms of life may appear to be autonomous. And so they are. But they are the activity of one spirit within which they are rendered individually unique. Consequently, at times human beings with their rational faculty may contradict their transcendent nature and act contrary to it. But their general yearning is toward the unity of consciousness, so that in the end the character of spirit is realized.

Spirit is awareness. It is universal consciousness. It is not reason. Neither in its universal self is it volition. These latter elements require some form of limitation in order to be exercised. Reason is the manner in which the phenomenal mind negotiates the structures of the material experience it is intimately involved in. Will, understood within a material context, is that which inclines toward either of a pair of alternatives which are expressive of limitation.

It is for these reasons that it is fruitless to refer to universal spirit as conceiving a plan for the world, if by a plan what is implied is spirit reasoning beforehand about a creation. An equally impotent statement indicates that spirit wills conditions for the world. For the material does not emanate from it for the sake of any satisfaction or fulfillment.

Universal spirit does not will in relation to itself, since it encounters no limitations within itself. But it can be petitioned within a material context because the petitioner is spirit under a self-imposed limitation. Within a material context there are such limitations. Thus decisions are to be made, limitation being the author of choice. However, though petitions can be rendered to spirit, the latter responds according to the harmony of the whole, which may or may not permit a positive action in an individual case. Hence the inscrutability of the transcendent in such matters.

As for miracles, these are not to be understood in terms of a violation of the course of nature. Such apparent exceptions to accepted rule, as related according to tradition, are exaggerations. Yet they do often reflect what has occurred more subtly and beneficially than can be understood or explained. Consequently, they are generally given an unnecessary facelift of picturesque magnification in compensation for a darkness of comprehension and also out of a desire to attract and hold adherents to a religious persuasion.

Much of religious belief originates in wishful thinking. Such desire is subsequently manipulated by a growing power structure which appears in the midst of increasing numbers of votaries. This is not to say that the manipulation is entirely deliberate or harmful. For it is a response to the need for order. However, it does follow the egoism inherent in human nature. This tendency inclines to draw things in a tight circle around it, the center of the circle being the organizers.

Nor is it to be thought that the wishful thinking of the many should imply that there is no truthful foundation to the religion. But the foundation is deep, deeper than most can comprehend, which is why the element of truth falls off precipitously upon the departure of the original seer and founder. Those who follow as disciples are of ordinary capacity.

Consequently, they are apt to misunderstand much of what they have received.

For example, the Hebrew idea of God contains much that is profound, a great portion of it recognized as unfathomable. This is readily acknowledged in their scriptures and teachings. But there is also much within their tradition which is blatantly barbaric, having been lifted from the surrounding cultures of the time when their religious understanding was being developed. An example is the ritual of sacrifice, altered and further magnified in significance in the ideas it has spawned in Christianity.

The Hindu vision of the universe exhibits similar problems. This religion displays great depth and penetration of insight. But in the interest both of speculation and control the articulation and practice of Karma has resulted in the unnecessary suffering of many who have been consigned to struggle at various levels beneath the benefits of the few.

The human struggle consistently displays such irregularities in which there is an alternation between the demands of animal and spirit, between material limitations and their projected needs and that which transcends them. Nevertheless, there is spiritual progress, in spite of many reversals and downward trends of a temporary nature. For, once securely grasped by the human imagination and intellect, an insight toward greater clarity in the ongoing human effort to achieve inward and outward harmony is never quite forgotten, though it should sleep a thousand years in Byzantine or barbarian incomprehension.

## Thoughts on Creativity, Spirit, and the Ethical Life

Silence introduces a person to her thoughts, if she has the courage to meet them.

Spirit is impartial, is in all things, and needs neither to receive praise nor project love. But if loved by someone who embeds his person in it, it will shower love upon him in return. For the love given is the love received, all being one spirit.

The sense of mystery seems to increase with knowledge. There are unfathomably deep levels for understanding and undiscovered valleys between any high mountains of understanding which have been raised up. So why should such possibilities be thought to have limits? Neither is it the case with the mind nor the world. Are not both ensconced within the breast of awareness? Consciousness is the universe.

It is not a solipsism to assert that the mind encompasses the material universe. For the mind is a facet of universal awareness. The intellect, for all its limitations, probes outward in undaunted discovery. The possibilities of awareness are unlimited. Consequently, though the mind feels the slow advance of its frontiers, it will not remit its determination.

Imagination is limited in its resources to material experience. But it is unlimited in its recombination and variant restructuring of these.

In his essay *On Liberty* John Stuart Mill pointed out that centralized power tends to increase. Why is this? Why do human beings unceasingly seek to dominate one another in multifarious ways? For that is the reason any powerful entity inclines toward its own aggrandizement. It desires dominance.

This behavior is not strictly human. Mammals, birds, fish, even insects do the same. Of course, they do not institute social structures of a political nature. But some of the higher life forms do develop hierarchies of dominance. And where lesser or more isolated beings do not, they still insist on maintaining their appropriate space in relation to other members of their or some other community. In one form or another, they will fight, if necessary, for the individuality of their person.

Thus they struggle incessantly against one another for food, territory, or, as often concerns mammals, birds, and some fish, a position within a group. And this behavior is not simply attuned to matters of physical survival, such as the availability of alimentary resources or access to a mate. The more sophisticated life forms often jostle for influence and the ineffable pleasure of being socially on top.

Any such sense of self might be difficult to accept in the case of insects, which appear to be entirely governed by instinct. But there is something of its kind even here. For no sentient creature is uniformly programmed out of all evidence of an individual mentality. If it were, it could not meet unexpected contingencies. There is always at least a tiny bit of freedom, or of what must be interpreted as choice. And within it nothing animate escapes the urge to assert the significance of its unique self.

Why otherwise would it be willing to fight and perhaps die in its own interest? Why not let circumstances decide every issue encountered? Survival? Why should it matter? In other words, what gave the first consciously responsive creature the *will* to defend and protect its own condition as opposed to that of its enemies or its fellows, or even as opposed to a physical obstacle?

What is will? Within a material context, will is derived from the pressure of an individual consciousness in opposition to its limitations. Due to the narrow functioning of mental focus, these limitations are necessarily encountered in pairs. Here a choice is made. Subsequently, perhaps, another choice is exercised between the outcome of the first choice and a further alternative. For an inherent sense of person (an individual consciousness) engaged in organizing the mind and even to some degree its circumstances, pushes through a related series of decisions, which are presumably entertained in its interest.

So what is this impulse? It is an expansive sense of unlimited consciousness acting in the midst of a realm of material impediments. The process continues throughout life and is experienced as will. This ought to be inoffensive in character insofar as one's own species is concerned. But if, as is generally the case, the sense of self is inclined to understand that it is being deprived of inward growth, then, in its beleaguered and narrow perspective, it seeks control and dominance over its circumstances. As humanity is social in nature, this results in egoism, which can seek to define itself in social and sometimes political terms.

The drive toward social control is almost invariably destructive, although it does occasionally shed benefits. For the most part, it is harmful. The alternative is a channeling of the ego into a desire to influence others for their benefit. Artists, philosophers, scientists, et cetera (at least those whose work is of an enduring high stature) do this.

But they are generally under some degree of control by others with cunning interests, be these political, industrial, or purely economic. In spite of this, their creative influence is nonetheless gradually infused into the minds of the thinking populace and suffused more slowly throughout the community.

Why does so small a minority of people have such an effect? It is because they alone imbibe lingering counsel from the inner self. They focus on their inner being and pay attention to its intimations. Deliberatively or otherwise, they recognize their inner self as their true nature, differing from the false outer mannequin nearly all people, including them, must in varying degree suffer themselves to invent. This social effigy is designed to satisfy the perceived expectations of others. It values what they think, rather than the improvement of its own understanding. That is why they transcend it to reach what is deeper within them.

International warfare is a product of egoism, primarily of those who seek or hold power. It is often supported by a general vanity worked up in the populace. Such a malign influence as is needed to affect the people in this way is not strictly political, though it is ultimately exercised by such means. For it arises in diverse quarters. News sources, business interests, and factional elements may be the initial instigators.

Internecine conflicts can be the result of ambition on the part of popular demagogues. But it is also frequently a reaction to mounting oppression from the top. For there is never enough power to satisfy an insatiate desire for control. So, in this latter instance, people are forced to rebel to alleviate grievous pressures. In either case, the problem is self-promotion at the expense of others, rather than a positive effort being exercised in their interest.

The inner self is true because it is directly grounded in spirit, which is universal consciousness, or universal awareness. Though the greater reach of that awareness is shadowed from individual view in earthly life, the inner self is yet free of the constraints and limitations of the material mind, whereas the social self is a product of them.

The intellect is essentially imaginative, even in its subtlest forms of reasoning. Hence language itself is an opaque instrument, capturing at best only a part of the whole. That is why clarity of expression is of the utmost importance.

Every number is encapsulated within the boundaries of nothingness, which is what keeps it from being another number. For example, it cannot be said that 1 is limited in the number line by a 2 on one side and a -1 on the other. It is limited by 0, the numerical symbol of limitation. This is made clear by the fact that a 0 has been placed in the number line between 1 and -1. For here it must be positioned for clarification, though its presence is understood to form the boundaries of all numbers. Stating it between 1 and -1 is convenient. But stating it between all numbers would cause undesirable redundancy, hence confusion.

Nevertheless, it is always present. Accordingly, the operation 2 × 1 can be clearly understood because the limits of 2 and 1 are thus sharply delineated. Likewise, in moving from 1 to 2 in the number line, there is a point at which the 1 is no more and a 2 takes up its existence. This in spite of 1.999... grading ever so subtly into 2.

For it must be assumed to have a finite limit, however small. That limit is nothingness, a zero. It can be ignored in mathematical operations, and often is, because the quantitative discrepancy between the two numbers (one of them being extended indeterminately in diminishing increments beyond a decimal) is assumed to be negligible.

It is this same limitation by zero which makes the individual quantities in an indeterminate string of natural numbers finite and thus comprehensible. And it is also why the entire string of such numbers is finite, though it is indeterminate in extension. Every finite number, however closely bounded by another finite number, say the last two digits of a trillion integers beyond the decimal of pi, must each in itself be presumed to be bounded by nothingness, the nothingness (zero) of its individual limitations.

It occurs to this writer that the principle of inertia may not hold when considered in terms of the fully extended material universe. Its proofs are indirect. And though the unvarying states of undisturbed motion or rest are repeatedly affirmed at a close and familiar range relative to the vastness of interstellar space, it cannot be demonstrated that a body would retain this character indefinitely at a very great distance.

## Thoughts on Creativity, Spirit, and the Ethical Life

If this conjecture should prove to be valid at some future time, it would undoubtedly be so because human thought (and therefore science) bends experience toward subjective comprehension. The most objective principles are subjectively oriented because the mind combines and fits the facts of experience to its limitations. Thus, in its attempts to engineer human understanding, it produces, as it were, a necessary fishbowl effect.

The bulk of the human race behaves in the manner of a colony of termites, blindly moving about in tunnels of manufactured experience. For such people, received opinion is superior to original insight.

The mystery genre is relatively new in literature. Within it, there is a greater emphasis on deduction. Its parallel is the development of science, which signals a decisive shift away from habits of vague, though occasionally deep, emotional intuition. Here is the struggling emergence of an increasingly recognized utility of organized and disciplined thought.

The Western novel supplies the American fairy tale. It represents an understanding that laws are inevitably perverted by evil to the detriment of good. Hence the protagonist skilled in the use of a six-shooter or repeating rifle. He reverts matters to their proper order.

Philosophy is a medicine which salves every ailment with the exception of the one it creates. That one is to take thought to its extreme limit in a particular direction, beyond which it cannot reach. The solitary cure for such a dilemma is to reorient the entire thought process. Hence the small but growing crowd of competing philosophies. Yet collectively there is a link between them. For their general movement proceeds toward an enlarged comprehension and insight regarding the human condition. In spite of conflicts, it is the surest path to wisdom.

Wisdom exhibits a power beyond knowledge. It gives direction to it. As this pertains to an understanding and management of human experience, there is a question of outlook, which changes with the maturation of wisdom. Yet the more such insight arises from within in disregard of any external influence, the greater its capacity to organize knowledge and the deeper its grasp of it. For the bedrock of experience is the inner self, which is that from which experience proceeds. Whereas the outer social self, when employed without guidance from within, is apt to lead astray, confuse direction, and clot the arteries of thought.

Shakespeare stands beside Homer. His mirror held up to the modern world is as fine tuned as Homer's was of the ancient. The Greek bard continues to be admired. But he is no longer representative. So it will be with Shakespeare.

Aristotle reoriented Platonic thought and brought it down to earth. But he was unsuccessful in clipping its wings. This may be just. For materiality and transcendence are equally necessary points of view. Humanity must adapt to the physical

### Thoughts on Creativity, Spirit, and the Ethical Life

world without losing sight of what can be experienced but not expressed.

Leo Tolstoy's novel, *War and Peace*, exhibits the familiar passion generally found in nineteenth century Russian fiction. Its portrayal of life is rich and varied, causing the reader to feel as if he is being carried along in its living stream. It is such that the present writer has the unforgettable remembrance of getting up from reading it to get a cup of coffee. Upon returning to look at the open book, he was startled to discover black marks on a white page. The reality conveyed by Tolstoy's imagination is quite intense. And that is a principal reason why the book is generally considered to be one of the three greatest novels ever written.

In chapter one of book nine, Tolstoy digresses from his story to relate the substance of his view of history. This view is a theme which underlies the structure of the novel and lends dramatic power to its story. He argues that great men, like Napoleon, do not determine the outcome of historical events. Rather, those events determine what great men do.

Taking an example from nature, he says,

> When an apple has ripened and falls, why does it fall? Because of its attraction to the earth, because its stalk withers, because it is dried by the sun, because it grows heavier, because the wind shakes it, or because the boy standing below wants to eat it? Nothing is the cause. All this is only the coincidence of conditions in

which all vital organic and elemental events occur.

He continues,

> In historic events, the so-called great men are labels giving names to events…. Every act of theirs, which appears to them an act of their own will, is in an historical sense involuntary and is related to the whole course of history….

Of course, there is more than a theory here. Reading the story involves such an intimate participation in it, as if the reader were himself a part of its history, that it is experienced as a fish senses the currents in a stream and as that fish is unconsciously aware of the coordinated movements of the school it belongs to. Within the story are the passionate emotions of individual lives caught up in Napoleon's 1812 invasion of Russia. These enter the heart and worry the mind. And what reader who has encountered the young, foolish, idealistic, and headstrong Natasha has not felt as if he knew her?

*The reason mathematics works:* If a person should cling to the commonly held empiricist view of physical existence, as opposed to the transcendent, she will discover that the mind is nonetheless intimately involved in structuring what it perceives. For, though regarding the material world as external, it must form a template, a map of experience. This for her is the world's structure.

### Thoughts on Creativity, Spirit, and the Ethical Life

In withdrawing the faculty responsible for constructing the template and employing it independently, mathematics is formed. Moreover, it chooses to reckon with quantitative matters alone. Yet these relations are also to be found within the more complex physical realm. So when mathematics is applied to experience, it engages exclusively with the quantitative character of what it finds there. In this way, a simple, exact, and practical representation arises. Thus is revealed the iron skeleton of modern science. Yet it too is a product solely of the mind. There is nothing in it which is not purely human.

Though the development and advance of culture should proceed on the basis of reason, it is not this alone which is gradually raising humanity out of the swamp of animal impulses. Rather, the ongoing elemental struggle between consciousness and materiality has brought it about.

The conviction that any two adjacent sides of a triangle must be greater than the third is not intuitive. Rather, it is the product of an idealized concept, which, as a concept, is itself a work of the imagination brought within the restricting parameters of a definition. Consider two adjacent sides of a triangle as drawn out into a single straight line. The remaining side must then be shorter than the combined pair and conterminous with them. For all vertices have been removed. Thus, as there are no vertices, there is no enclosed area.

Now bend the first two lines at an obtuse angle which is greater than the previous angle and is minimally divergent from the original straight line. It thus forms a very wide vertex. Consequently, the two vertices adjoining the third line will be quite acute. Consequently, that side will be longer than the one which preceded it. Nevertheless, it will fall short of the combined length of the other two.

In addition, a narrow area will be opened between the three lines. There are, as a result, three sides and three vertices forming a triangle. The delimiting definition of this figure is that a triangle must have three sides and three vertices which enclose an area. Underlying this definition is a work of imagination, though idealized to be sure. For exact measures are not empirically feasible.

Reason is fueled by imagination when imagination is disciplined into concepts and then the concepts are arranged into logical relationships. Furthermore, when the whole has been tempered by experience, humanity is in its proper element. It is scientific. Moreover, it is simply thinking in a manner appropriate to its potential.

But how little this applies in some cases. When focused upon mundane and practical concerns, and even at times when exercised within a more rigorous discipline, the mind is often enveloped in a swath of opinions and fancies in matters which lie outside the subject of immediate concern. This leads to errors in judgment. For people are easily swayed by impulse and will, doing what they would not have done had they been more circumspect.

Kant's *Critique of Pure Reason* is indeed impressive. One wonders how it grew to such well thought out proportions. However, it enthrones reason at much too high a level. Any instrument of thought is a human faculty whose products are not an imperishable expression of eternal transcendence.

Reason is fitted to human use. Moreover, it can point to that which lies outside its own powers. For it is capable of responding to human need. But what it cannot do is discern the inner workings of what lies beyond its reach. Neither can it assert its privileged position as being quartered within a mystery.

There is an access, an unlit tunnel of subtle impulses, which can lead a person toward what cannot be understood. Experience has demonstrated for many that this faculty is unerring when properly followed, the demands of will having been quietly laid aside, while an inner certainty pervades in their stead.

This is followed by a human warmth of emotion which arises when strife is cooled to stasis. For will is the author of division and opposition. It is walled in by narrow choices. And it struggles accordingly. But in an approach to universal awareness, there is no division without unity, no enclosure without transparency and transcendence. This is felt but not seen. For though there is an opening to spirit, there is a limited understanding of its nature.

Art gives people access to themselves. Its insights break down the inflorescence of commonly held false opinions. As these are removed, a person sees more clearly into himself. But the effect is fleeting, since shallow-mindedness is easy and comforting to the ego. So art must do its work for each generation, following upon the eternal path of emotional deviance.

Kant's *a priori* representation of time is unacceptable. The explanation is too general and vague. Intuitions must be accounted for, not simply posited. Rather, it is the case that increments of subjective time are the result of limitation in the material mind's sequential presentation of mental impressions. This is initially prior to the recognition of any object.

As concerns objective time, changes observed among limited objects are the cause of its recognition and incrementation. For its measure is a result of that change, just as the origin of subjective time arises from the sequencing of mental impressions. Similar observations can be offered concerning the character of space. In either case, concepts follow experience and imagination.

Inasmuch as Hemingway was a naturalist, he was a romantic realist like Zola. They developed realistic characters and situations within an exotic atmosphere of heightened sensory awareness and emotion.

Hugo's *Les Misérables* and *The Hunchback of Notre-Dame* are of a value not always conceded by critics since the advent of realism in the novel. The fundamental framework of Hugo's stories echos deep within the human psyche, awakening transcultural recognitions which extend beyond time and place. And they are exceptionally well told.

Faith in oneself, when true, is spiritual guidance. But it must be uncompromisingly honest. Each individual person is spirit (or universal awareness) in its fullness, yet in a self-limiting state which diminishes her personal experience and understanding. Nevertheless, as direct emanations from spirit, all things are expressions of the same. So how is it that many people err and fall into confusion? Are they not manifestations of the whole?

Imagine a stream encountering an obstruction so great as to break it entirely into rivulets. Each of these then runs an independent course, encountering obstacles and responding to them under the influence of a gravitational pull. Yet all will be true to their destination: the sea. So it is with people, who are individual in the shape of each encounter and in the exercise of self-will, while their total career is inexorably gathered into the unity and destiny of all. However, in each case it is clear that the way to that unity and mutual outcome may be varied.

It is of great moment to follow the truth. But this is not to say any advantage connected with such a practice accrues to spirit. Spirit is neither in need, vain, nor proud. A recognition of the truth is rather of benefit to the person. For to attain to an inner harmony and adhere to it without deviation is to find rest in quiet self-assurance. Here a subtle peace substitutes for the raucous wanderings and conflicts of others. Though it is certain that the whole remains undaunted in purpose regardless of internal fragmentation, it is the uncertain individual who feels a loss.

Unlike science, philosophy takes many forms. But it is never lost in confusion. Either its practice is without guile, or it is not philosophy. Its multiple avenues to insight may lead it in what appear to be conflicting directions. But this is simply the limiting work of reason, which must pursue a narrow path of logic. Such are the restrictions of thought which necessarily crimp vision. But every sincere effort drives through language to the heart of its matter. In this way, wisdom progresses.

A crowd of metaphors clouds the mind. But scattered too thinly, they fail to nourish it.

Though imagination is more important than reason, reason *is* imagination subjected to a close scrutiny and binding restraint. For imagination without these conditions is wavering, hesitant or extravagant, and decidedly uncertain. The two together are what give thought its fullness and flexibility.

Religions are said to be picture philosophies. And the best of these are like Leonardo da Vinci's *Mona Lisa*—charged with mystery and inscrutable power. One must search beneath their surface for what is grounded in the human condition.

Words both reveal and obscure. In the act of lighting the mind, they shed darkness. For they define. And to do so is to limit. To limit is to obscure. Thus language is ever layering meaning upon itself, supplying extended explanations in its attempt to achieve clarity.

The communism of Lenin was not that of Marx and Engels. It was a cunningly skewed and flawed interpretation. Thus the effect of the former construct has been to conceal the humanity of the latter.

### Thoughts on Creativity, Spirit, and the Ethical Life

What is individualism? When Rembrandt ceased painting the dramatic works which brought him high fortune and turned to producing penetrating portraits and self-portraits that delivered him to penury, this was individualism. When Spinoza sat in his garret, rejected and ostracized by his community, dying from lung disease while supporting himself as a lens grinder and writing his *Ethics*, this too was individualism. Anything short of these is redolent of a kind of social promenade.

America has yet to master a balance between individual freedom and social responsibility. Allowing freedom to fragment society is anarchy, an invitation to tyranny, suggesting the populace be put in chains. But what alternative is there when every individual is a tyrant? One among them must inevitably arise in suppression of the rest.

Literature is concerned with the human condition. Regardless of its mode of expression, which should always be a means and not an end, it is immersed in experience. Style affects tone. And often it is productive in bringing the subject matter into sharper relief. But the emphasis on subject remains. This is the case even if the work is highly imaginative, as in a fairy tale. Style, though important, is subordinate to topic.

*Tristram Shandy* might appear to be an exception, until it is understood that sentiment and mental focus (as elements of human experience) are the true subjects of the work, making it as much a poetic and philosophical essay as a story. The style is translucently experiential, the superficial expression and symbolism representing recognizable emotional and psychological responses.

The visual arts differ markedly from this. For they are inherently self-referential. A visual artist is occupied with seeing. And this seeing, though psychological and emotional like any literary work, is also physical in a way in which literature is not. This reflects the fact that what is viewed initially is the painting or sculpture as an object, the matter with its emotional and psychological depths being subsequently added thereto in the mind of the viewer.

Hence, for example, in painting the techniques of impasto, sfumato, chiaroscuro, and tenebrism contribute an immediate visceral effect which is as important as the subject matter and is yet an integral part of it. So here the style emerges in equal emphasis with the subject, whereas in literature it remains subordinate.

No one has been able to fully penetrate the heart and mind of another person. This is why people love stories. Stories do penetrate, but not fully. So for this reason there are uncountable numbers of them, creating the illusion of an exhausting coverage which is never realized. The work of exploration is always free to continue. And, when original in presentation and outstanding in insight, it endures.

The acceptance of light as an absolute standard of measure in physical science—finding it a constant in possession of a supreme velocity—is not a surprising development. For the visual is apt to have been chosen to predominate because it is the most acute of the human senses. It is critically involved in every experiment.

## Thoughts on Creativity, Spirit, and the Ethical Life

What this suggests is that scientific development is increasingly becoming a matter for epistemological consideration. Human beings, in fashioning their theories, are of course adapting their concepts to the evidence of their senses. But they are also shaping them to the subtle workings of their minds.

Nothing can be properly and consistently observed which exceeds the proximate evidence of sight. Sight is closer to thought than is generally understood. Nor can the fundamental rules of association as exhibited in logic be contravened. Hence, in this latter instance, the apparent remarkable precision and necessary use of mathematics as a tool.

But do these considerations alone embrace the unapproachable limits of experience? And does the universe, given its most farsighted prospectus imaginable, present human curiosity with as full a nature as speculation desires? Or is it, even at its greatest extremes of interpretation, little more than an impressive extension of the myopic vision of humanity?

It may well be the case that far beyond anyone's imaginative and rational reach lie unfathomed truths which contradict not only present thought, but possible modes of thought. For example, at the quantum level reason has been put through a series of philosophically exasperating trials.

May it not as likely be the case that the cosmos should unfold unconformably in contradiction of complacent expectation? There are perhaps startling and at present undesirable limits which shall confront the mind's effort to know all. It is not unlike what happened when the American nation crowded up against the Pacific shore and was thrust back upon itself.

The future of physical science and exploratory ambition may yet suffer such a fate, if it has not begun to already.

An unquestioning embrace of materialism may seem quite solid and replete with good sense. But such a view terminates in emptiness and despair. For it shuts out the inner life and snuffs its possibilities.

Religion, well organized, evolves into an increasingly deep materialism. Outward practices which incrementally replace inner awareness contain no sustaining elements. The spirit burns out. And the self falls away into ash.

Each person's single act, and thus cumulatively his life, springs from a moral and emotional complexity which cannot be penetrated by reason alone. That is why it is inadvisable to be careless or dismissive in passing judgment. But if judgments should be limited, it is nonetheless prudent to recognize that practical concerns do demand them. For an individual must discern motive, however tentative his understanding of the inner workings of another mind, in order to decide whom to associate with and trust and whom not.

It is equally necessary for a society to be able to divine what behavior is to be tolerated and what not. In this manner the artificial edifice of social mores and relations is erected. It is a must. But it should not be forgotten that such a structure is fundamentally unsound. For in its inaccuracy it continually fosters the hurt, anger, protest, and revolution which inevitably accompany social life in all but the most severely oppressed peoples.

# Thoughts on Creativity, Spirit, and the Ethical Life

Why is it that most people place matter before spirit, when the only way that anything can be known about the physical world is through the mind? The word "matter" is nothing more than a sign remarking a stubborn human predilection toward the external. Why this preference? Could it be the intensity of personal encounters with pleasure and pain? These are certainly convincing in their way of an independent opposition to a person's interest. This may be so. But there is something more.

The human mind is the author of much of what is understood about the world. For it is imagination which both enters into and reflects experience. And it is reason that builds the structures which humanity prefers to attribute to an external realm. This is to say, it builds a map by means of which to negotiate the varieties of sensation. Granted that much concerning that realm is independent of human will. But it is not independent of awareness. That remains internal.

But again, what is to be made of the fact that other minds experience worlds that are somewhat independent of one another in many particulars, while remaining integrated and strangely consistent in fundamental structures? Does this not make such a realm independent of the mind? What, in fact, is the mind? Should it be confined to the feeble workings of imagination and reason, not to mention a blind fretwork of sensation? Surely all of this is remarkably limited and individually distinct.

However, what is of interest is that there is something more to be encountered, something lying behind the whole, viewing the panorama of life with mild amusement and occasional indifference. It is this, however hidden or obscured in most people, which is of the greatest moment. For it is awareness in its purest bare presence.

Simpler, more elemental than imagination, and more encompassing than reason, it is entirely naked of definition. Awareness it is, unadorned with any explanation, but a ground supporting every particular of sensation and mind. And there is nothing to refute it, nothing from which it may be thought to have been extracted. It does not emanate. But everything is enclosed within it. It cannot be described in positive terms. For it is a consciousness which is complete within itself and unlimited, independent of its material content and therefore undivided and without empirical delineation.

A common sense view is an opinion which has not been thought through. This state of mind is nearly universal. For the greater part of any people share an unwillingness to exercise reason with care, particularly when it involves personal matters. They prefer the ready adoption of slogans which have been repeated enough times to appear true. Having absorbed and expressed them, they give no further consideration to the matter, being nonetheless vehement in defense of their position.

*The antinomies of behavior in Kant:* Imagine living next door to Anne Frank and her family and knowing that they are hidden in an attic. A member of the Gestapo arrives and enquires as to whether there are any Jews in the neighborhood. There are two possible courses of action: reveal the truth or choose not to do so.

## Thoughts on Creativity, Spirit, and the Ethical Life

If the chosen alternative is to lie in order to protect Anne and her family, then the practical categorical imperative is violated. This is the specific convention that to tell any lie is to determine according to the dictates of reason that all people should be free to lie when they think it necessary.

This is, of course, undesirable. For it opens a pathway to every form of deceit and mutual distrust. But at the same time, this behavior does satisfy the universal categorical imperative, which demands that no person should be treated as a means to an end, but only as an end in itself. Anne and her family are protected by the lie, rather than betrayed for the sake of the liar's personal safety and convenience. However, if the chosen course of action is to tell the truth and reveal Anne's presence, then the practical imperative is observed and the universal imperative is violated. Anne and her family's hidden status is betrayed.

This conflict between imperatives demonstrates the rigidness of Kant's deontological approach to ethical matters. A person cannot behave dutifully according to the strict dictates of reason. For reason is conceptual. Concepts have definitions to give them precise meanings. And it is the nature of a definition to isolate meaning. So, where one meaning leaves off and another begins, concepts must inevitably exhibit gaps between them.

Deontology leads to contradictions because these gaps are indicative of unique circumstances and subtle motivations which are far more refined in expression than can be encompassed by a single concept or even a coalition of concepts. Emotional in character, stridently individual, and welded to a specific situation, every moral decision demands an insightful grasp of multiple intertwined subtleties. Such a situation cannot be compassed by reason alone. For it demands empathetic sensitivity and a purely imaginative intelligence.

To understand what this implies, it is helpful to envision the arts. Here there are a myriad of delineations of subject matter, often representing the same motif. How many ways does Matisse express his general attitude of joy? Every painting is different. Or he would fail as an artist. Yet the whole of his work is closely interwoven in theme and unmistakable in similarity of mood.

Again, an example from visual portraiture will make this clear. Velasquez's portrayal of Athene in *The Spinners (Las Hilanderas)* reveals the determination, authority, and concealed anger of the goddess. One need only study the expression in her face to find such clues combined in a single image, though she is clothed simply as a peasant participating in a contest with the young woman Arachne.

The moral issue concerning Arachne's evident hubris, which is the occasion for the painting, is complex and untenable if approached in rational terms alone. What is required is an understanding of both the overweening and unnatural pride of Arachne and the imperative importance of person and authority it offends.

There are multiple ways in which the situation might have been resolved. But a proper choice among them requires an acute discernment of the entangled fretwork of emotions and expectations involved. As it turned out, according to the story, and as shown in the background of the painting, Athene eventually revealed herself in all her splendor. And Arachne was transformed into a spider, a creature entangled in its web of conceits. It must be assumed that this was the necessary outcome, though full insight into the balance of details is unattainable. So it is with most ethical situations.

Kant's rigid emphasis upon reason in his ethics and in his epistemology reveals a tendency toward intellectual absolutism. Absolutism, though it may be complexly developed in its theoretical conceptions, is simplistic in application. Hence this general attitude, which was further developed in the work of Hegel, is what so greatly offended Kierkegaard. It was also less than to the liking of Schopenhauer, though in him, fine writer and thinker though he was, there is yet again an unpleasant hint of the absolute in his almost overwhelming pessimism.

Facing death is something people do unconsciously every day. It is part of the business of living. But most people are inclined not to think about it. War changes that. It brings home the miracle of existence. In Eugene B. Sledge's memoir, *With the Old Breed*, one can obtain a glimpse into this. The book describes a Marine assault on the beaches of Peleliu in the Second World War:

> One of our NCOs signaled us to move to our right, out of the shallow defilade. I was glad, because the Japanese probably would pour mortar fire into it to prevent it being used for a shelter. At the moment, however, the gunners seemed to be concentrating on the beach and the incoming waves of Marines.

I ran over to where one of our veterans stood looking to our front and flopped down at his feet. "You'd better get down," I yelled as bullets snapped and cracked all around.

"Them slugs are high, they're hittin' in the leaves, Sledgehammer," he said nonchalantly without looking at me.

"Leaves, hell! Where are the trees?" I yelled back at him.

Startled, he looked right and left. Down the beach, barely visible, was a shattered palm. Nothing near us stood over knee high. He hit the deck.

The amount of enemy fire being used to thwart the landing was intense:

> The heavy mortar barrage went on without slacking. I thought it would never stop. I was terrified by the big shells arching down all around us. One was bound to fall directly into my hole, I thought. If any orders were passed along, or if anyone yelled for a corpsman, I never heard it in all the noise. It was as though I was out there on the battlefield all by myself, utterly forlorn and helpless in a tempest of violent explosions. All any man could do was sweat it out and pray for survival. It would have been sure suicide to stand up in that fire storm.

# Thoughts on Creativity, Spirit, and the Ethical Life

Many of these Americans, most of them young and inexperienced, made it up that beach. But later it was decided that perhaps the island had not been strategically important.

Absolutism in thought is a logic which accounts for everything, but is itself unaccounted for. It is an illness suffered upon occasion by philosophy, mathematics, and science.

Life is light, color, sensuousness. When filtered through an intellect, it is spiritual vision. Otherwise, it is nothing more than animal existence.

The fundamental impulse of animal existence is physical expression. The principal drive of human awareness is the assertion, maintenance, and possible enlargement of the range of individual consciousness. It is here that the conflict between appetite and values originates. The physical hungers seek simple gratification without impediment. The demands of consciousness as ego are constraint and control of the self or others. Most often it is others without regard to the self, the self being permitted to function as a spring of appetite.

A ready example of such a contest is found in marriage. This bond, at least in contemporary times, is generally initiated by sexual desire. The relationship is commonly held under the constraint of a limitation of this need to two people. For the union is predicated upon a trust which applies directly to the physical impulse.

There should be no further expression of that appetite than the union. Otherwise, the confident assertion of the self-esteem of one or the other person will be violated. That is, the importance of the social placement of an individual awareness is negated. The person feels herself to have no dignified bearing among others.

The conflict between appetite and ego takes a different turn at a social level. This is where ego often develops into an appetite. The possible enlargement of individual consciousness becomes not only a goal, but a need of unlimited proportions. Political power, material wealth, and, on a smaller scale, simple bullying arise as instruments of the expansion of the sense of a public self. These personal enhancements must come at the expense of the diminution of others, where many attain smaller stature in the enlarged presence of the one.

Consequently, the only just mode of self-aggrandizement is through creative expression. There are many forms that this behavior can assume. One need not be an artist, a breakthrough scientist, etc. A good moral character alone is perhaps the finest and most universally acceptable attainment a person can achieve.

Everyone exhibits some type of ego. It cannot be avoided. The importance of social presence is undeniable. Individual persons recognize that they are part of a greater whole. But it is the undisciplined exercise of this faculty which wounds by belittling others. When implemented in such a manner, it elicits anger and a resentful response. However, if the ego is committed to creative expression and its influence rendered benign through gentle persuasion, rather than by means of an aggressive domination and coercion, the harmonious coexistence of the multitude can be promoted.

## Thoughts on Creativity, Spirit, and the Ethical Life

There is a special magic in language when a good writer can make one see and feel. How does this miracle take place? Certainly, it is indicative of the power of one mind to realize experience in another. A refined and subtle blend of emotion and reason are involved. If deep enough, insightful in an original way, and intellectually astute, it produces something enduring. For readers repeatedly seek it out in widely different temporal settings.

But this gift also raises a conundrum. Some questions to be asked are: Just how much does the mind contribute to experience, even at the personal level of the writer? And where shall a line be firmly drawn between mind and experience? For it would seem that the individual experience which one mind would convey to another is in some measure a product of itself and in equal measure not. So how does the writer know what is true or common enough for general consumption without incurring the sin of exceeding strangeness on the one hand and banality on the other?

Imagination is the wealth of mind. Reason is its strength.

Imagination is independent of language. Reason is not.

When people universally decide that the development of moral character is more important than material advantage one over the other, this will be the time when individual freedom will take on its proper meaning.

"Akrasia" is a Greek concept indicating nothing more than a failure to trust in the universal efficacy of a moral principle. It signifies an indecisiveness grounded in the perceived general waywardness of human behavior. A person exhibiting such a trait fears being cheated or slighted by others as a result of their guile, if he behaves the way he believes he should. So he misbehaves himself. Or he believes the problem is so distant in effect that he need not be concerned with it. But this latter case is fundamentally associated with the former. For he thinks many would do the same. And he would miss out on something if he did not follow their course.

There is no evidence in human experience to support the concept of perfection. Nevertheless, moral imperfections can be minimized as a person's measurement of self in accordance with the behavior of others approaches zero.

The idea of perfection is a product of the functioning of the human intellect. It is a result of pure thought divorced from objective experience, as in the mathematical concepts of a perfect circle or an isosceles triangle. It is entirely subject to the will of an individual, which objective experience is not.

Objective experience follows close-knit patterns, never absolutely exact, but which are understood as causal relations. Whereas pure intellectual thought can be exact. It is from this mental freedom that the determined relations of logic arise. They are the outcome of pure thought combined with will. For it is will in association with the regular occurrence of such rarefied thought which contributes the element of necessity to logic.

# Thoughts on Creativity, Spirit, and the Ethical Life

To assert that spirit is prior to matter, that the body departs from the soul, rather than the soul leaving the body, is to maintain that all things emanate from spirit. Everything has its home in the transcendent. Yet, though the mind is involved in giving form to the material, rendering it familiar to itself, mind is not spirit. For it is also a construct of the latter in the latter's self-limiting mode.

Acknowledging these things is the beginning of an understanding of the center and origin of life. Life at its core is not a subject of beginnings, progressions, or endings. It is expression. Spirit delineates itself within the restricted contours of the material. But neither can it be encompassed by these. Nor is any single mode of its expression alone. For there can be multiple manifestations of spirit. And it is not to be assumed that one part of a total system of expression cannot be transferred to another system of expression, such as might be the case concerning an afterlife.

Multiplicity as well as any specific delineation, such as many things in the former case and a single physical object or person in the latter, are alike types of spiritual articulation. The specific entities, including a personal body, are the unique experiences of the limited mind which is given to human beings. In other words, what a person hears may be assumed to have been uttered. It is as real as it is limited for that individual. But what remains unuttered is unlimited. It is a matter for spirit.

The special attribute of sonship attributed to Jesus belongs to all humankind. All are incarnations of spirit. They are full, not partial, embodiments of the same. For there is but one indivisible spirit, one universal consciousness. But though they are spirit, they are so in its self-limiting form. For they have not the mind of spirit, whatever may be the nature of it. Few people have approached anywhere near to the character of spirit in their understanding. Those who have are inevitably given a special designation by those who have not.

Throughout the more than two and a half millennial development of Western philosophy, its practitioners have largely been in the habit of confounding reason with consciousness. But these are not the same. Reason rains out of consciousness as an instrument of the human mind. It is generally referred to as intellect. Accompanying it is the far more inclusive faculty of imagination. But neither of these is without the prior existence of a less easily recognized instrument of transference from spirit to mind.

    This faculty, also emanating from consciousness, prefigures reason and imagination. Its building blocks are simply limitation and the unity of consciousness. These, acting together as well as in opposition to one another, produce the elemental lineaments of human experience, which constitute the structures providing a sense of space and time. Such structuring elements are objects fashioned from associated mental impressions, which latter are generally referred to as sensations. Objects come about by means of an application of limitation and unity to these associations of the mental impressions.

Pissarro's paintings provide one with a sense of being present in the midst of his work. An ineffable permission is granted to

## Thoughts on Creativity, Spirit, and the Ethical Life

the viewer, allowing her to enter in. And it is largely provided by means of a quiet handling of light and a subtle application and gradation of color values. The viewer finds herself in the depicted countryside, sharing the simple, unpretentious lives of its people. This is a humanitarianism in its gentlest and most profound character. It pervades the artist's entire work.

To state that causal relations do not exist in a precise manner in the physical world, but rather are expressed in close-knit patterns which originate in spirit, is not to determine that they take the form of causation in spirit. For this cannot be known. However, they do appear to be so from a human perspective. Spirit originates. And what results are close-knit patterns which appear to be causal at the macro-physical level.

The two principal maxims for developing a moral demeanor and refining its character in any society are: to be trustworthy and to suppress the ubiquitous desire to dominate others, as opposed to influencing them. In this way, one will be a threat to no one and a help and comfort to many.

In its initial character, mathematics was a creation of the imagination. The logic followed after the concepts had been idealized and accordingly made subordinate to a rigorous consistency in form.

Genius is a product of temperament. Though this is universally the case, it is particularly notable in art, where it consists of talent given an extra vitality through the refined application of intellect. Neither talent nor genius can be learned. But they can and must be developed and augmented. A purely intellectual form of genius would be represented by a Spinoza or an Einstein.

In the arts, there are many more instances of talent than there are of genius. But a couple of examples of talent raised to genius would be a Cervantes or a Hemingway, the former more notably than the latter. Neither can be imitated by another person with complete success. This is due to the unique blend of idealism, irony, and insight into intimate personal relations evinced by Cervantes. Whereas in Hemingway, it arises sensually from his physical makeup, where it is enhanced by an acute critical awareness both in terms of heightened physical detail and cunning repartee in dialog.

A free market is a necessary keystone in support of individual freedom and its offspring: a vigorous development of innovation. But a laissez-faire capitalist economy grounded upon the twin vices of greed and selfishness, as well as a raw, unregulated competition where the slogan "let the buyer beware" is viewed in a favorable light, is an utterly execrable system. In the interest of humane living, it cannot be tolerated. For there must be moral governance in the marketplace.

Should it be remarked that personal behavior cannot be legislated, it may be noted in response that never was a law made that was not morally regulative. It is the nature of such to bind the animal passions under some form of code. But do not allow these observations to be construed as a blanket condemnation of Adam Smith's *Wealth of Nations*. For no fault lies in him. His effort was intended to inform human understanding of the true nature of economic relations and to

## Thoughts on Creativity, Spirit, and the Ethical Life

encourage enlightenment accordingly. It was not meant to be interpreted in the extreme in the interests of a few and a general corruption of manners.

A society without ethics in financial matters soon becomes a seedbed of immorality everywhere. Commerce, like it or not, is the soul of the practical life of any people. To secure one's own and one's dependent's needs demands a daily attendance to these affairs. There is a frequent engagement of buying and selling. And where there is little or no possibility of trust in this endeavor, it will not be found elsewhere. For bad manners in any quarter, particularly one of such regular and absorbing attendance, spreads to and leavens the whole.

To equate consciousness with reason in the manner of Hegel and a good many other philosophers is to consign all nonhuman sentient life to a state of unconsciousness. Anyone who has forged a close relationship with an animal—such as a dog, cat, horse, or parrot—knows this cannot be true. Though these creatures do not reason in the human manner, they are apt to exercise a form of imaginative thinking which resembles it in an elemental way.

Imaginative images passed through the mind and drawn from memory in a repeatedly consecutive manner, allowing for a recognition of indicator-response relationships as a base of action, are a foundation for, if not representing the conceptual essence of, rational thinking. Reason itself is embedded in language. And this faculty, insofar as is presently known, no other earthly creature is sufficiently in possession of. But it should not mean that they are therefore, by a mistaken idealist standard, unaware of anything.

The nearest things to the work of Maurice Utrillo are the still lifes of the eighteenth century French painter, Jean-Siméon Chardin. Just as the former causes a viewer to feel the worn masonry of old buildings, giving them a peculiar vitality, so the latter does something similar for ceramic vessels and copper pans. It is riveting to observe the manner in which a talented artist can infuse a soul into an inanimate substance. The Dutch artist, Jan Vermeer, does this as well with light. It becomes a living presence in his work, investing walls, textures, even persons with an individual purpose.

The playwright Eugene O'Neill's characters represent isolated emotions working in a void though surrounded by people. So much is this a common feature of humanity that there is an awakening to a sense of inward nakedness in these plays. One thinks, "Do others see this in me?"

The source of unity, trust, and good will is spirit, or universal awareness. Find it first here within yourself, then seek it in others.

The distinction between good and bad is not clouded by the fact that well meaning people sometimes err and the ill intentioned occasionally follow the right. If this were so, recognition of the one as opposed to the other would be a matter of gauging percentages. Rather, any demarcation is to be made along the line of general motives.

    The good continue to believe in the right when it is almost impossible to encounter undeniable examples of it in the

## Thoughts on Creativity, Spirit, and the Ethical Life

world. Consequently, their wrong actions are generally self-defensive. Whereas the bad have lost faith in the same and submit themselves wholly to their private conception of a preservation of their interests.

The difference between what is simply bad and what is malice is that the former are acts, when committed, which spring from weakness or ignorance. Whereas the various commissions and omissions of the latter are carried out for the sake of entertainment. Their perpetrators know exactly what it is that they are doing.

A person is never alone, because all things reside within spirit. Thus an individual, being spirit, is deeply embedded in his source. But such a simple truth is not readily known in this life.

In the case of an individual person, there are acts which derive their origin directly from spirit and those which do not. As the occasional will is moved by physical causes, the former circumstance is opposed to it, being moved by spirit. For there is a deeper will that is concealed within spirit. Its purposes can only be engaged when a person draws closer to her inner self, which is the locus of her spiritual nature.

It is in this manner that a person can arrive at a peaceful accord with her destiny. She achieves a knowledge of herself which is unavailable in material terms. As a product of this accession, which may be referred to as a transcendental understanding, she seeks only those acts that are necessary to her purpose, which she discerns by means of her inner self.

For it is by such an intuition that she is able to determine what such a purpose is.

It is also within this frame of reference that what she asks for by petition to the spirit she generally receives. Thus her understanding is clearly shown not to be a matter of intellectual judgment alone. Accordingly, it is not confined to reason. Rather, it involves the subtlest and most elusive of emotional impressions, which are developed in her mind as a response to nearly undetectable impulses received from spirit. These are what signal the orientation of the inner self.

When thus aligned with her inner self, which is spirit, her mind is in right accord with itself. It no longer experiences conflicts in its understanding of nature and its impressions. Hence it discards from her materially actuated will all that is unnecessary, desiring only what is a product of inner vision. It is in this manner that her petitions to spirit may bring results.

Spirit is universal awareness. Every individual has access to it in her consciousness, though she cannot easily recognize its active role. She is rather inclined to see consciousness as an inert backdrop to the dazzle of material sensation. And she is led to view herself as in a tangled and confused maze of momentary impressions through which she must fight to rectify herself and her interests.

But consciousness is, in fact, a pure, singular, indefinable envelope of immateriality from which all things emanate and, accordingly, out of which all events must either directly or indirectly proceed. So to be in harmony with this viable presence is to be well removed from the struggles of life, even though one is yet in the midst of their pressing concerns.

## Thoughts on Creativity, Spirit, and the Ethical Life

Although human beings cannot readily determine why they have been thrust into a condition beset by harms, fears, and limitations, they long either deliberatively or without discernment to overcome or disengage themselves from it. But how should a person find an exit from such troubles without simultaneously incurring death?

To sever herself from purely material pursuits, once their misleading promises are acknowledged, she turns to the invisible realm of spirit, which she fears may not exist. But what is spirit? It is herself. It is the broader limit of what she can know. And she can only acquire knowledge of it through an engagement with her inner person.

Probability is at times a matter of an incomplete knowledge of causes. But at other times it is not. It is rather the expression of a pattern, where the human mind can determine no means of dictating relations beyond that of the pattern. These relations are only statistically predictable. Thus their outcome is never certain.

A recognition of cause and effect renders decisive action possible. This, or something close to it, is what is necessary to the maintenance of physical life. But it would be a truism worthy of contempt, were the paltry human will—a product of the confines of circumstance—able to dictate the character of the whole of material existence. There must be room for possibility.

The deepest untruth is the final affirmation of a truth. Where material circumstances are concerned, there is always opportunity for discovery. And such discovery often negates its predecessor, leaving ample room for a reconfiguration of understanding.

The fact that so much which is a product of fancy attends every religion cannot conceal the fundamental truths upon which the imagined elements are founded. Yet there is an immense difficulty in reducing such accretions to reveal the original spiritual supports.

The crux of fascination in Greek mathematics is its close proximity to the primal workings of the mind. Here the mental source is rendered naked before a penetrating gaze. And much wonder lies in such a purity of conception and its complexity of development therefrom. Viewing the process of this creation in reverse, going back to its source, is to look with wonder and devotion into the mystery of imagination and its increasingly exacting confinement within the requirements of reason.

In offering criticism of one another, it should be recalled that all are wounded animals. Thus the injunction: judge not lest you be judged. For it is not the spirit as universal awareness which judges. It is the limited form of a person, who, suffering the pains of life, ought to remind both himself and his equally supercilious brother of the severe constraints which are binding upon both and render them vulnerable together.

Observe a set of phenomena by means of the senses, fit it to a mathematical formula, which is itself an integral part of a more inclusive network of mathematical relations (a theory), and, if it works at a practical level, it is assumed that a truth has been uncovered. This assumption is indeed valid within its limits.

But it remains worthy of note that the science of mathematics is a creation of the mind. The former mirrors the operations of the latter. Thus its science is most true to its subjective source. Moreover, its reflections upon nature are secondary, though no less true, owing to the mind's pervasive involvement in perceptual awareness.

Here is revealed a deeper realm which lies behind the mind's operations. Spiritual and largely incomprehensible within itself, it can nevertheless be understood in its contributions to understanding. To penetrate this, however tentatively, is to arrive at a more secure sense of the nature of things.

The concupiscent tendencies of human nature have led it on a dizzying spree throughout history. There has hardly been time for reflection or contemplation, these being left to an occasional reticent few, often considered foolish or out of touch with the world, if only momentarily. Nevertheless, such random pleasures have consistently contributed to disappointment, regret, and pain. Whereas a sober intellect, however uncommon, considers the whole and looks with wonder at the general insistence upon such repeated follies.

But the will is weak against the demands of impulse. Falling back into familiar ways, it allows harmful acts to pass unchecked, then rebounds against them in a spirit of condemnation. Better that the condemnation had come first, though it rarely does. Had it done so, the wheel of misfortune could have been stopped. Yet few believe this or wish to, since tomorrow's suffering does not impede the enjoyment of today.

Science builds a mighty edifice. But the solid crust it stands upon is undergirded by a molten, fluid core. This can be ignored, as it generally is. But at what cost? That of knowing the world without understanding it.

To be successfully manipulative in financial matters, political affairs, or military strategy does not require an advanced intellectual capacity, though in rare cases such may be the case. In fact, it might well be said that a greater effect is generally achieved by a more muted sensitivity. For too keen an awareness often interferes with decisive action.

What is required in abundant measure is cunning. This is an animal trait which employs rough imagination adroitly imposed with a modicum of thought. But what is endemic to both cunning and a well-tuned intellect is intense mental focus. It is for this reason that only a few succeed in either department. The majority lack the discipline.

It is not necessary to behave morally out of a fear of igniting the anger of some monstrous egoistic deity. Universal spirit, as opposed to the character of an individual person, does not judge and is never kindled to anger. Yet it is this same spirit, when limited to and expressed within a person, which does judge. For judgment is discernment in response to limitation. In other words, a person must negotiate her surroundings intelligently with shortened vision. So she evaluates curtly and displays a resultant anger.

**Thoughts on Creativity, Spirit, and the Ethical Life**

In light of these considerations, it may be seen that it is the judgment of oneself and that of one's fellow beings which a person must stand in dread of. These arise from a restricted awareness and are set to action by means of circumstances in which a person may be inclined to impose harsh measures either upon herself or another.

Thus, if an individual does what she deems within herself to be wrong, it will return to her as a burden upon her conscience. Accordingly, she will either suffer remorse or convert it into further enormities of behavior, which will more deeply embed her in wrongdoing. It is this limited judgment arising within human nature that a person should fear as proceeding from both herself and from others.

Jesus was not crucified by the Jews as a race. He was put to death by a haughty priesthood and a mob, which were and remain common representatives of the human race. Humankind has not improved since. If Jesus were to reappear in this time and be perceived to stand in the way of ossified views as to his nature and purpose, he would be just as certainly removed. If not killed, he would be ostracized, which is a contemporary form of execution.

The essential goal of any living thing is to encompass, or internalize, its environment. Hence the evolutionary climb toward higher forms which exhibit a more inclusive capacity. As the spirit expressed within any creature is a unity, the creature is impelled toward realizing, and thus enlarging, the unity of itself.

Consequently, an occasional devolution into an environmental niche cannot belie the general forward movement, since the entire biosphere can be understood as a single organism in need of all its functioning parts. Each part is also a complete organism. This resembles a hand which is organized to serve the brain, and a brain the hand.

These materially inspired observations are an expression of the representational philosophical view. But, if the facts of nature have been provided to the human mind in this manner by spirit, or universal consciousness, then a more inclusive view which the intellect may endeavor to achieve is that of immaterialism. The material realm is thus understood as an expression of spirit, which manifests itself in physical terms. This is brought about through the mind at an unseen level. Thus the increase in mental domain of living things is a process which leads back into spirit.

Laissez-faire capitalism, overwhelmingly demonstrated to be a system based on greed and selfishness, need not be so. A free market economy governed fairly by moral laws can be instituted and maintained. Such laws are inevitably controversial, due to ever-changing and evolving cultural differences. But there can be no disagreement about the fundamentals of fairness.

There must be fair dealing amongst all people, be they buyers or sellers. Good will should be established as an admirable principle and enforced by public opinion. For what takes place in the daily transactions of business affects society at large. Should honest and transparent means of exchange be practiced, they will extend into personal relations outside the interactions of domestic commerce. Otherwise the people are sure to be corrupted.

Following the close of the second world war, America became a superpower more or less by default. For the civilized world had been leveled both physically and spiritually. No nation of any material consequence was left standing but the United States. Within itself it was soon to discover the immense potential of a consumer economy, which served to increase its economic and military clout.

Increasing wealth fueling military strength encouraged national ambition. A desire arose among its officials to convert the entire world to its way of life, or at least that portion of it which was considered free and self-determining. Breathing the heady atmosphere of national preeminence, the general populace supported the inclination of its leaders.

Thus the country paid no heed to the long-standing traditions and historical, religious, and ethnic circumstances of other peoples. It forged ahead with a project of nation-building, attempting to bring others in line with its institutions and flattering itself that they would feel themselves privileged to be so.

Having seen what had been achieved in its efforts to aid in the rebuilding of Western Europe and in its having created an environment of peace, order, and demilitarization in Japan, which allowed them to focus on their own economic recovery, it did not understand that this was not nation-building. It was allowing and assisting existing internal factors to take their course.

What was forgotten or not understood was how its own ideals had previously crossed the Atlantic Ocean as a careful reflection upon the works of European thinkers. These with some home contributions had built its institutions. This had made it great when the moment was ripe and unforeseen circumstances lent their aid.

But nearly eighty years later the world economy has fully recovered and more. Seemingly backward nations have stepped forward, staking a claim to and creating a strain on the world's increasingly scant resources. India and China, with their massive populations, have come of age. They have grown unexpectedly in influence and power, drawing heavily on the world market, as the United States, Europe, and Japan have already done. The result is greater competition and a contraction of American dominance and influence.

So what can America do? What will it do? Will it, like the Roman Republic, sacrifice its original ideals in order to enhance its grip on power? Let all things go for the sake of its maintenance of hegemony? It is a tempting and fatal moment of decision. Should the nation choose to maintain dominance, it will cease to know itself. And the world will lose the worthy example of its much vaunted freedoms.

Emerson was not a philosopher in the generally received manner. For he did not support his precepts with closely reasoned arguments. Rather, he employed a species of poetic rhetoric to great effect. Hence his reputation as the Sage of Concord. Subsequent thinkers have not been taught by him. They have been inspired. That is perhaps his most far-reaching contribution.

## Thoughts on Creativity, Spirit, and the Ethical Life

The mystical element in all religions is the same. It lies at their core and is the true fount of their success. Whereas the degree in which they depart from one another reflects the peculiar and individual role of imagination and a subservience to personal inclination.

Philosophy cannot be limited to an expression of curiosity or an exercise of intellectual penetration. It is these and more: a way of life. Thus it was in ancient times. And so it is in the modern era. For example, such thinkers as Descartes, Locke, Berkeley, Hume, Spinoza, Leibniz, Kant, and Hegel each sought to lay out a path toward greater human fulfillment and enlightenment. Such an intention was ethical in nature, regardless of other designs the thinker may have had.

Descartes attempted to clarify thought, thus establishing a reliable method of acquiring knowledge as a means of improving understanding. Locke secured the operations of the mind in the realm of experience and suggested a political program for developing individual freedom. Berkeley countered what he saw as an increasing worship of materialism.

Hume promulgated similar views concerning the unfounded use of imagination in science and religion. Spinoza established the supremacy of the enlightened individual, while Leibniz proclaimed the integrity of reason within each person. Kant sought to buttress science, while leaving room for transcendence in faith. And Hegel made a god of reason by rendering it equivalent to spirit.

All these had their strengths and their faults. None were merely curious or practitioners of mental athletics for their own sake. They were driven by a deeper purpose, as philosophy has always been. They sought to broaden the human spirit in its understanding of itself and, in so doing, to enlarge its potential. For them, philosophy was a way of life, positive and affirming. This is what makes philosophy, however abstruse, an ethical science.

Focus is of greater importance than intelligence. Yet focus without intelligence carries few benefits and is often harmful. Worse than this, intelligence without focus is a form of onanism.

The Vietnam war is for America an example of a series of bungling errors to which the democratic process, with its inconsistencies and indecision, often leads. Unfortunately, the discovery of the mistake comes when matters have become too deep for convenient extraction. Politicians who are afraid to look weak and lose an election, and government and military officials anxious merely to prove themselves, abet and further the problem, while, most importantly, a national fantasy of cultural supremacy, when added to these, can readily founder a republic with otherwise good intentions.

It is an opinion held by a few scholars and critics that Jane Austen's novels are thematically too simple. They are considered limited in conception, naive in execution. Thus they are labeled novels of manners, as if Austen saw no further than externals. This is an utterly preposterous view. Austen's novels have a depth of insight into human motivation and a purity of

### Thoughts on Creativity, Spirit, and the Ethical Life

control in emotional expression which reflects favorably upon the great Athenian dramatists.

Henry James' obliqueness of style can be maddening to a reader of straightforward sensibility and a desire for accessibility and clarity. But his elegance of expression and certitude of detail are unquestionably impressive. Here is "sophistication" lent to American culture as a means of its elevation above a more mundane and earthy appetite.

Balzac lacks the forceful realism of Tolstoy, the complex and penetrating intellect of Dostoevsky. But he exhibits an unanticipated energy of life which quickens the narrated events in such a manner that he becomes no less indelibly lodged in a reader's memory.

In pedagogical practice, the best universities seek to attain a high level of what must be referred to in terms of their enforced limitation, mediocrity. For they cannot surpass this popular average laboriously attained due to a scarcity of insight in most students. Such intellectual penetration is a gift which cannot be taught.

Thus the formal institutions of learning are obliged to impart ready formulas, established protocols, and set procedures which, having once themselves been a product of insight, are alone capable of offering beneficial results. But this careworn methodology, however productive, is not originality.

Cunning applies a fine-tuned emotional responsiveness to those who are willing to be exploited. It manipulates people. Whereas wisdom is focused upon the use of reason and its appeal to a settled state of mind. It treats people as though they ought to be respected. For these reasons, it is certainly notable that, in the short run, cunning often outmaneuvers wisdom.

The explanation for it lies in the fact that a manipulative, or cunning, temperament exercises a kind of spontaneity which resembles an instinct. Consequently, it demands little thought and results in quick and decisive action. Thus it is perpetually enabled to short-circuit the social economy.

It is because of this that Plato's philosopher-king has turned out to be little more than an impractical fantasy. Nearly all political operatives and heads of state are of the manipulative kind. For the most cunning are the ones best able to navigate among others of their type. And these are what make up the great majority of any political community.

As is the case with Balzac, no single one of Jane Austen's novels can be held in comparison to *War and Peace*, *The Brothers Karamazov*, or *Don Quixote*. But, when considered collectively, her works do occupy a high place in literature, as do Balzac's. It is her intelligent sensitivity and Balzac's imaginative energy which make it so.

Elizabeth Gaskell's *Wives and Daughters* is one of England's finest novels, due to its vivid and accurate painting of emotions and Gaskell's special talent for portraying characters, even minor ones, fully in the round. Her humanitarian sensibility is unsurpassed in English literature.

## Thoughts on Creativity, Spirit, and the Ethical Life

Let it be imagined that, for whatever reason, a person is "losing consciousness." As his world darkens, his thoughts become confused and less distinct. This is followed by nothing at all. So what has occurred? Has his faculty of awareness failed? Or is it what he is aware of which has withdrawn from him? If the latter, as it would certainly appear to be, then it is not the faculty of awareness which is diminished. It is its content.

But what of that gap which is generally referred to as "unconsciousness"? The response to this question must be: who is it that observes this period of unconsciousness? It is clearly not the unconscious person. True, he may experience dreams, which are generally not associated with conscious awareness. But it is someone or something else which takes note of the duration of his immobile, unresponsive, unknowing state, including those portions of it presumably not visited by dream imagery. It may be a person or a clock which performs this function.

But, given that the supposedly unconscious person cannot experience a completely unknowing state, could it not be the case that there is no such state? In fact, might it not be understood that there is never an unconscious condition? The appearance of unconsciousness is rather an expression of material awareness. It is, in an important sense, an illusion.

And this illusion, if it may be so called, figures necessarily into the structure of material experience, where it serves the important function of giving a plausible character to the whole. Creatures are physical, need replenishment and repair, and so must rest, even to the point of a demobilized sleep. So they are represented to themselves and others in this manner.

The material realm is made comprehensible in this way to the limited minds which inhabit it. For the physical is a limited world which is presented as a mechanism, the individual components of which are in continual need of maintenance. But such a vision is not therefore a final instance of Being.

It is what the mind has been informed of within its confined state of understanding. For true being is simple awareness alone, unfettered, eternally unaltered, a never failing light which cannot be put out. Material experience, on the other hand, is subordinate, a projection, or emanation, which arises from the faculty of awareness, and nothing more.

The central problem of the human race is that human beings are animals with a greatly enlarged capacity for knowledge. This comes with an accompanying sense of vulnerability which, as a result, subsists in a much anticipated presence of pain, suffering, and loss. Thus the human psyche is bequeathed an air of isolation and desperation which, even in the midst of a multitude of its own kind, allows for little or no solace.

Perhaps philosophy will never arrive at a final truth. But as over time, by means of a more refined explication of the human condition, it approaches closer to a coordinated field of knowledge (however crude in the final analysis) and an increased understanding of it, people will mature in meaningful self-awareness. This knowledge includes the ineffably transcendent as well as matters of the mundane. It is a condi-

# Thoughts on Creativity, Spirit, and the Ethical Life

tioning of the individual to his experience, not the world to him. Thus it is not science.

To understand Spinoza, it is imperative for one to read his *Ethics*. But deeper than the argument set forth in this work lies the subtly revealed truth that the spirit of this thinker is more important than his philosophy. As his system achieves clarity in the mind, one is brought to a position of seeing through to its universal meaning, which is that both human purpose and its justification are to be found within the sanctified individual, rather than in any external circumstances.

Hegel's spiritualization of reason may be deemed excessive. But it is not for this reason to be ignored. If spirit is not reason, reason is certainly its instrument. So an importance lies in removing the quality of absoluteness from his thought, while retaining the inspiration and insight. Ah, the absolutism of German thinkers! Yet, can it be said that they are not brilliant?

Nietzsche's quest for the spiritual in humanity is without the imaginative embellishments of religion. Perhaps it is too earthbound. But if it is, it is nonetheless transcendent.

A problem to be encountered in the Stoics is that their god resides in a far off region of the firmament. It is of no use to say that there is a piece of him in each person, like the dividing of a wafer. For this material limitation inserted into their thought alienates the needful heart of the seeker.

A human animal, like any other, craves security and pines for some form of universal acceptance. But, unlike the animal, a person knows her weakness. Can this be ignored? Why should it? It is true that one's fate must be accepted, stoically if possible. But when it is bitter, why not a petition to mitigate it, whether granted or not?

Michael Gambon was among the greatest actors of his time. There is a richness, subtlety, and depth of characterization in his work which is notably evident in such roles as Mr. Woodhouse in Austen's *Emma* and the squire in Gaskell's *Wives and Daughters*. But his accomplishment is more extensive than this. In fact, the only name which comes to mind as a contemporary comparison is that of Ben Kingsley.

Nietzsche's concept of an "eternal return," implying the absolute, imperishable significance of each individual life when considered outside the falsely diminishing context of earthly events, can be likened to the idea of every individual human consciousness residing within a greater sphere of universal awareness, or spirit, where time has no meaning.

Creativity is the exercise and expansion of the capacity of human consciousness.

Truth to a human being is rightness of position within a context. Thus, as circumstances are ever-changing, the quest continues.

# Thoughts on Creativity, Spirit, and the Ethical Life

**Key to the Philosophy of Immaterialism:** There are **three purposes** for which this philosophy was developed. The **first** is that there is reason to believe that the universe might be composed of mind stuff. This is suggested by research in particle physics, where human awareness and experimental results appear to be interrelated.

No attempt will be made to go into this, as particle physics is a highly specialized field which lies outside the domain of this philosophy. It is sufficient to note that such a view places the old mechanistic interpretation of reality in doubt. The mechanistic perspective is not by any means obsolete. Rather it may be described as incomplete.

The **second** motive behind the development of this philosophy is that there is much in ordinary life which does not fall under a strictly material explanation. **Consciousness** is the single most important of the nonmaterial factors in human awareness. Can it be said that consciousness is merely an epiphenomenon of physiological events? Aside from this, do causal relations truly originate at the level of material perception? Answers to these questions cannot be strictly mechanistic in explanation.

The **third** motive arises from the nature of **value judgments**. What is their role in the development of human knowledge? In other words, can a strictly material explanation of reality account for the development of human understanding? What about the role of emotion in determining expressions of human yearning and motivation?

These guide the reasoning process. For in any such process the question may be asked, why is one logical train of thought pursued rather than another? Thus emotionally based value judgments are critical in the formation of rational structures. And, if emotions are critical in the formation of rational structures, can reason then be strictly relied upon to explain one sequence of emotions as opposed to another?

**Science**, particularly physical science, is empirical in character. Which is to say that it is phenomenally based. It relies upon a close observation of experimental results and an increasingly mathematical theoretical development. The latter satisfies **reason**. And the former references what is generally understood to be **sensory perception**.

But neither of them engages the heart, which is the domain of human yearning, valuation, and motivation. Thus, though science is of deep interest to any contemporary, educated person, scientism is repugnant to many. **Scientism** is the elevation of science into a religion. In so doing, it enters a domain of human experience for which it was never intended.

These considerations have led the present writer to a train of thought which, over a number of years, has culminated in a spiritual and therefore non-materialistic, or **immaterialist philosophy**. Such a philosophy may appear strange, as it did when the seventeenth century philosopher George Berkeley proposed something similar. But it has seemed necessary to fulfill the conditions listed above.

Not since the work of **Descartes** has it been possible to reach a satisfactory compromise between **mind** and **body**, **spirit** and **matter**. Though both have their proper domain of explanation, and may therefore be considered exclusive of one another, in either domain considerations of one or the other must predominate.

## Thoughts on Creativity, Spirit, and the Ethical Life

Accordingly, if both are to be considered together in the more comprehensive domain of philosophical thought, where such exclusiveness demands resolution, it is spirit which has been found to demonstrate the more inclusive view. So this is the perspective which dominates the following remarks.

**Materialism** is a closely related collection of beliefs which includes an objective existence of things that subsist independently of the person encountering such experience. This is the commonly accepted form of human experience. For people are inclined to believe that there is a physical world which is independent of their minds.

A **material viewpoint** entertains the perspective that there is an objective realm of things-in-themselves located in physical space and incremental time. Two of the most important characteristics of an objective material world are that material things exist in and of themselves, and that they are present when not observed by anyone. They also independently undergo a form of change which can be incrementally measured in terms of time.

A **thing-in-itself** is something which exists apart from human consciousness. In immaterialist philosophy there is no such thing. Apart from the mental experience of objects and events in an objective world, there should be something independent of human awareness or any other form of consciousness which supports their objective existence. Immaterialist philosophy does not accept this independent support. These objects and events only exist in consciousness.

**Immaterialism** is the philosophy that all experience occurs in the mind. Thus there is no objective thing-in-itself independent of the mind. This position undermines any argument for causal determinism. Causation must ultimately reside in some form of mind, or consciousness. Free will is therefore preserved, at least insofar as material experience is concerned.

In light of the view that all experience occurs in the mind and does not have a separate existence, it can be said that the universe is essentially consciousness, or mind. This consciousness is a condition for any kind of awareness, since consciousness is awareness. So any idea of an awareness which is greater, or more inclusive, than human consciousness is itself a form of consciousness.

**Spirit** is universal consciousness. There is but one universal spirit. Thus there is only one consciousness. Unlike material experience, pure consciousness, omitting any consideration of its content, is neither bounded nor divisible. It is not finite. It is therefore infinite, or "not finite," as just stated, the prefix "in" meaning "not." Thus there can only be one consciousness: universal consciousness, or spirit. Hence all other forms of consciousness are individual expressions of the **self-limitation** of this one consciousness.

The limitations of a human consciousness are an expression of its content. Such content is determined by universal consciousness and uniquely experienced by each individual consciousness. Since there is only one consciousness, the uniqueness of each individual consciousness arises from the self-limitation of that one consciousness.

**Primary mind** is universal spirit, which in turn is universal consciousness, or universal awareness. Primary mind is universal because it encompasses all other forms of mind, or consciousness. Only a portion of what is known to primary mind is known to a more limited mind. **Secondary mind** is primary mind, or universal spirit, functioning in such a manner as to self-limit itself in order to present the human mind with a limited awareness. It does this by means of **focus**. Focus is the instrument of limitation. Any finite object is an object of limited focus. By employing focus through secondary mind, which is self-limited primary mind, primary mind is enabled to present the human mind with a limited awareness.

**Human awareness** is the content of the consciousness of an adult human being, exclusive of the subjective manner in which mental impressions are initially delivered to that awareness. A mature human awareness recognizes an objective realm. But it does not recognize the subjective origin of that objective realm.

Something which is **finite** is that which is bounded, or limited, in all of its characteristics. A **physical object**, or the **object of a thought**, is limited in both spatial dimension and time. There is nothing about it which is unlimited, or infinite. On the other hand, something which is **infinite** is in-finite, or not finite. Thus it is not bounded, or limited, in any of its characteristics. This does not include the indeterminately large or the indeterminately small. For these are finite entities which are indeterminate in some portion of their finitude.

For example: A number line is mistakenly said to be infinite. This is because a new number can be repeatedly added to it without end. But at any point at which the count is stopped, the length of the number line, and each of its components, is found to be finite. Thus the number line is indeterminate, rather than infinite. For infinite means not finite. If it was infinite, it would not be finite in any way.

**Focus** is the means by which universal spirit self-limits itself in order to produce a material consciousness. A material consciousness results from the limitation of its content. So it is for this purpose that focus becomes the source of the intuitions of **simple unity**, **plurality**, and **totality**. These intuitions render the human mind capable of recognizing and assimilating material experience.

The **intuition of simple unity** is the first of the three intuitions. It is the means by which a finite mind recognizes a unity. An example is one marble recognized as a distinct entity. Here focus limits conscious attention to those impressions on the mind which are the marble.

The **intuition of plurality** is the second of the three intuitions. It is the means by which the finite mind recognizes limitation, finitude, and plurality. An example involves a recognition of more than one marble in which each is observed in individual distinction from another. To recognize more than one marble is to recognize the limits of one in relation to the other. Hence the recognition of finitude and plurality.

The **intuition of totality** is the third of the three intuitions. A combination of the first two intuitions, it is the means by which the finite mind recognizes a unity of pluralities. An example would be a collection of five marbles recognized as a single collection. In this case, the second intuition is employed to recognize limitation and plurality. The first intuition then focuses attention on the collective plurality of individually limited entities by recognizing them together as a single group.

A **percept** is a mental impression. This constitutes the most basic element among the perceptual content of consciousness.

## Thoughts on Creativity, Spirit, and the Ethical Life

Percepts form the whole of material awareness. To state that impressions on the mind are percepts does not imply the agency of the senses in rendering those impressions. Percepts are impressions directly perceived by the mind.

The **noumenal precipitate** is the means by which mental impressions (percepts) are registered in human consciousness. Due to focus, these percepts do not appear all at once. They appear in lineal sequence in the mind, as focus projects one after the other upon a human consciousness. Some percepts may be associated with others in the sequence, due to a repetition in proximity of appearance. The repetition of the same pattern enhances awareness of their associated appearance in the mind. There is no other organization among them.

The **phenomenal precipitate** results from an instantaneous transformation of the associated percepts of the noumenal precipitate into the extensions (objects) of mental and physical experience. These extensions may be objects of thought or physical objects. Insofar as they are understood to constitute physical objects, the percepts are **qualities** of the object.

Thus the human mind, undergoing an immediate experience of material impressions upon it, organizes the noumenally associated percepts into extensions. If the extensions are recognized as external perceptions, the mind further organizes them into physical space. As a result, these extensions become physical objects.

And the percepts composing those extensions become the qualities of physical objects. Otherwise, the mental objects are recognized as images, or extensions in the mind. These mental objects of thought resemble the physical inasmuch as they also are composed of percepts. But they are extended only in thought, rather than in physical space.

**Subjective reality**, in the most fundamental sense (which is that of the noumenal precipitate), is the awareness of percepts, generally but not always, in association with one another. It consists of impressions on the mind. Subjective reality may also be described as the realm of thought, feeling, and emotion, as opposed to the realm of physical objects and events.

So there are two forms of subjectivity. The first is the noumenal precipitate, which generally becomes obscured to the adult mind as a result of the latter's complex workings at a practical level. The second is the subjectivity of thought, feeling, and emotion as opposed to physical objects and events. The second form of subjectivity, with its objective complement, is what has developed in a maturing mind at the expense of a continued recognition of the first form.

**Objective reality** is that portion of human experience in which objects and events appear in a physical context to have an existence independent of the will of the perceiver. This is due to the fact that objective things and events occur in an order which is independent of human action in varying degrees. In other words, the human mind is involved in constructing that world and in manipulating certain aspects of it. But the human will does not determine the behavior of all its elements or events.

**Perception** is the faculty involved in a recognition of material experience. One can be said to perceive a thought, a physical object, a physical event, or feelings. The term is generally used more narrowly to designate awareness of physical objects and events. Feelings, thoughts, objects, and events involve percepts, or impressions on the mind. Feelings and thoughts are considered subjective. Physical objects and events are considered objective.

All perceptions occur as impressions on the mind. If they are independent perceptions, they represent feelings. But many are associated together as extensions. These extensions form images in the mind, which either represent objects of thought or physical objects. Feelings, emotions (which are composed of feelings), and thoughts are subjective forms of mental life.

But when extensions are considered to be physical objects, their percepts are understood to be their qualities. For they are recognized as perceptions external to and independent of the mind. Thus the objects are experienced as existing in physical space. It is these objects, and the events which occur among them, that constitute physical experience.

So a **physical object** is understood to be an object of perception, rather than an object of thought (which is also perceived, but not as a physical object). A physical object is a physical extension which is experienced as existing in a contiguous relationship with other such extensions. The contiguity constitutes **physical space**.

In other words, a physical object is recognized as three dimensional. Two dimensions give it height and breadth. A third dimension gives it depth, or objective distance. And since it is understood to exist concurrently with other physical objects, they are three-dimensionally contiguous. This is what forms **space**. It is in this way that physical space becomes a greater extension which is a multiple of lesser extensions, or objects.

An explanation of the problem of an **empty space**, insofar as such a thing can be said to exist, is that an allowance is made by the mind for the imperfect fitting together of physical objects. For the **figure** (or shape) of physical objects is in part determined by internal properties. Thus contiguous physical extensions create a greater extension, which is physical space. But the extensions, or objects, are irregular in figure. So the gaps which occur between them are empty space.

A **mental extension** is a thought. There are two types of thoughts: **images** and **concepts**. A thought is extended in the mind because its object is an image which either represents a physical object, multiple objects, or something like these. For example, not only do the images and concepts "a man" and "men" refer to physical objects. The more abstract, general, and inclusive concept "mankind" must also, in final analysis, reference something physical, namely human beings.

Images are the essence of thought. For **concepts** are founded on **images**. They are a combination of images stabilized by a **definition** which specifies applicable properties. Even the word "abstract" can, when deliberatively accessed, supply the supporting imagery which constitutes its conceptual character. There is a sense of removing an idea from its concrete meaning. And that sense is represented by a pulling away or a lifting above. These are spatial extensions. Such images are always vaguely present, however disguised by the verbal expression.

A **mental object**, as an object of thought, represents the perceptual characteristics of a physical object, regardless of whether or not it is understood to exist as a physical object. Thus every thought involves an image, or set of images, however vaguely represented in the mind. For its properties may be hidden in a concept. Whereas they are clearly in view in imaginative expression.

But a thought is not understood to exist outside the mind in physical space. The difference between a mental and physical object lies in the attribution of subjectivity or objectivity. When a thought has an object taking the form of an image, the image is an extension. In this it resembles a physical object, which is also an extension.

But, whereas the physical extension (physical object) is experienced as existing in a contiguous relationship with other physical extensions, the mental object does not. It occupies **mental space**, where only one thought can appear in the mind at once. So thoughts are limited by sequence, but not by contiguity, since their objects do not exist in physical space. They are therefore subjective.

**Non-incremental time** is time as it is expressed in the noumenal precipitate. This time is generally only consciously experienced in infancy or very early childhood, prior to a mature formation of the phenomenal precipitate. It arises as a consequence of the sequence in which mental focus introduces percept impressions to the mind. Because percepts are introduced sequentially in the noumenal precipitate, and because they do not individually exhibit dimensions, which are expressions of distance, this time cannot be measured. It is therefore not incremental.

**Incremental time**, on the other hand, is time as recognized in the phenomenal precipitate. It is the form of time experienced by a mature human awareness. It is determined incrementally by means of changes in a distance relationship between two extensions, one of which is undergoing change in relation to the other.

Such a changing distance relationship between two extensions is compared to another similar relationship, the first being held as a standard for demarking the other. It is a comparative measure of motion. Thus the movement of a hand, or change in digits (which latter also involves change in distance) on a stopwatch is used to time the performance of a sprinter. Incremental time can also be expressed in terms of a change within an extension, or object. This can be a chemical or physical change. It too involves motion, but within the object. So the same relations apply, but in a much subtler manner.

Incremental time is subjective only in the sense that it is objective time as measured by the subjective person. This person may note occurrences within his or herself in reference to objective events. However, true subjective time would be non-incremental. But in the mature mental life of a human being, this is obscured by the phenomenal precipitate.

**Change** is a condition which concerns an object whose relationship to other objects in physical space is altered. Or the qualities and, if it is a major change, the properties within it change. In either case, the change is a result of motion. For there is either external or internal movement. External motion occurs between one object and others. Internal motion involves a relation of parts within an object, however small that part may be which registers the change. Any motion involves a comparative change in distance.

**Energy** is the quantitative recognition and measure of change. Kinetic energy is the quantification of change in relation to stasis or to other changes. Potential energy is a quantified potential for change. These characteristics may be understood, and therefore observed, to occur in proportions which are consistently recognized. Thus the change and the relations of change, recognized in quantitative terms, are what is held to be energy.

A **representational viewpoint** is that viewpoint which considers the mind as producing an image or images within itself of whatever it is assumed to have perceived. In immaterialist philosophy, the thing perceived does not exist independently of the perceiver, but has its origin as an image in the mind. Thus it does not exist apart from its mental representation. It is that mental representation. Nonetheless, there can be a representation of the representation, as when a mental image is formed of what is assumed to have already been perceived.

The representational view treats physical objects and events as being objective. The **immaterial view** recognizes that all things and events occur as images in the mind (i.e., secondary mind, as opposed to common human awareness). However, this perspective blurs the distinction between subjectivity and an objective realm.

So the representational view alone is convenient for certain forms of discussion. It may even treat the external realm as entirely distinct from the internal. Though, in its acknowledged relation to immaterialist philosophy, it does not truly believe in this perspective because the immaterial view is more inclusive and takes philosophical precedence over it.

As stated previously, an association of percepts is a compact sequence of impressions in the noumenal mind. To be recognized as an association, the sequence must be closely repeated. When the percepts are transformed into an extension in the phenomenal mind, they become the representative characteristics of an object. When a specific type of percept, like the color red, is assumed to exist in a physical object, it is a quality. Combined qualities become **properties**.

An **image** is an association of mental impressions (percepts) which exhibits the qualities and properties of an object. It can be a mental representation interpreted as a perception. Or it can be recognized as independent of perception. Thus it may be a thought about a perception. But in some cases it may not represent any known physical object.

Whatever may be their circumstances, all mental images, perceptual and imaginative, employ percepts (mental impressions) which are understood to function as the qualities of objects, be they physical or merely mental objects. Accordingly, though an image can be formed which is not found in physical experience, its percepts can always be located in that experience. It is in this way that, while a unicorn is not known to physically exist, its properties do. Other objects may be entirely abstract and ideal, as in mathematics.

**Imagination** is the image-forming faculty of the mind. Imagination underlies all processes of thought. For **concepts** are a unification of properties by means of a definition. These **properties** are represented by images. Now, imagination is a representational term. In the immaterialist perspective, images are directly inserted into human awareness by secondary mind. They are the associations of percepts.

**Imaginative experience** involves imaginative images which appear in the mind. All images appear only in the mind.

## Thoughts on Creativity, Spirit, and the Ethical Life

But some are recognized as perceptions. These are not imaginative images in the commonly received sense of the term. But others are accepted as replicas of perceptions, while yet others are recognized as completely free associations of percepts. These latter kinds of image are both imaginative.

A **property** is a classificatory characteristic of a concept. Properties are composed of percepts, which are qualities in physical objects. They are registered in the mind as imagery representing an object of perception or an object of thought. Usually properties are associated in the plural, where they are what a definition organizes into the concept of an object.

A **definition** brings certain properties together within a concept, which is limited to them alone. The images within the concept can neither expand nor contract, leaving the concept rigidly defined. Whereas the properties of freely imagined objects of thought may expand or contract at will.

So a **concept** brings properties together and limits them by means of a definition. For concepts involve images, which represent the properties. Thus either images or other concepts which are supported by images constitute the properties. Nevertheless, it may seem as if a concept is distanced from its imagery. But this is not so. It is always supported by images.

A **classification** is an organization of properties into a concept by means of a definition. So a classification is a concept. Due to its specification of distinct properties, it has a nesting characteristic, which allows it to fully or partially include or exclude another classification.

**Reason** is a discipline of the mind by means of which concepts are brought together through a continuing transferral of meaning. That transferral of meaning is made possible by the nesting characteristic of concepts. To be sound reasoning, the transferral of meaning must follow the rules of logic. These are ultimately rules of imaginative association, which are limited by the inflexible character of the specific properties of the concepts involved.

In other words, underlying both the concepts employed and the rules of logic which bring them together in a transferral of meaning is the work of imagination. This work is limited by the inflexibility of the fixed properties of concepts. So it may be referred to as the work of disciplined imagination. Specifically, concepts are composed of images, which have been rendered inflexible by a definition. But underlying the logical relations between concepts are certain possible associative relationships between the images supporting them.

A **theoretical system** is a development of thought in which concepts are brought together in statements and statements are brought together in a system. Euclid's Elements is one such system. Darwin's argument for natural selection in *The Origin of Species* is another. Logical statements can be understood as single concepts. Entire systems can also be briefly stated as concepts. Thus concepts, logical statements, and systems are all classifications.

Concepts are incorporated within **logical statements**. For example, the subject and predicate of a proposition are brought together in a logical statement. Then logical statements are incorporated in a system by means of the rules of logic. Euclid's system depends upon proofs derived from axioms and theorems. Darwin's system depends upon a few broadly operative principles observed over a broad range of phenomena.

## Thoughts on Creativity, Spirit, and the Ethical Life

**Intellectual experience** involves concepts, statements, and theoretical systems. The statements and theoretical systems are formed from definitionally associated images representing properties within concepts. To state this in greater detail, it can be said that the human mind experiences images recognized as physical objects. From these object images, and from other imaginatively constructed images whose properties are drawn from the object images and recombined in new forms, the mind builds its intellectual view of reality.

As noted, it does this through associations which are made between the properties of the concepts. However, these associations are not as free as they would be in the unrestrained exercise of imagination. Rather, they are developed in accordance with logical rules. The rules require that the associative relations between properties should be carried out in view of the restrictions imposed by definitional limits upon the concepts.

It is in this way that logical thinking results in statements and the theoretical systems constructed from these statements. It is thinking disciplined by logical procedure. But, to be creative, it must also involve imaginative input. Hence the role of the imaginatively constructed images whose properties are drawn from object images and recombined into new concepts, which are then associatively incorporated in the system by means of logical procedure.

A **feeling** is a percept (mental impression) which is not associated with other percepts. Because it does not form an association, or extension, a feeling is not a physical object. Nor is it an object of thought. It is strictly subjective and does not form an image in the mind.

An **emotion** is a coalescence of percepts of feeling. There is more than one kind of feeling involved in an emotion. A coalescence of percepts is not an association of percepts. Thus the percepts of feeling are recognized individually. Together they form an emotion composed of clearly articulated individual feelings of different kinds.

A **coalescence of percepts** is a series of impressions on the mind (i.e., percepts) which are not recognized as associated with one another, but in which a close sequential occurrence of impressions is recognized. An emotion is composed of an alternately repeated sequence of different feelings.

**Memory** is experienced as a mental record of past experience. However, in immaterialist philosophy no such record exists physically. Rather, impressions of past experience are repeated in the mind at times which are appropriate for the functioning of memory. Whereas, in materialism memory is associated with brain function, in immaterialist philosophy this bodily reference must be considered a correspondence of representations in the mind. For example, a memory might appear to be recalled by a present physical or mental stimulus. But these do not recall it. They coincide with it. It is in this way that the representations of memory occur in association with events.